DYING, DEATH AND BEREAVEMENT
IN
A BRITISH HINDU COMMUNITY

NEW RELIGIOUS IDENTITIES IN THE WESTERN WORLD

1

Dying, Death and Bereavement in a British Hindu Community

by

Shirley FIRTH

PEETERS
1997

New Religious Identities in the Western World focuses on the mutual challenge between minority religions and the socio-juridical structure of the societies at large, especially with regard to the main world religions (i.e. Islam, Hinduism and Buddhism) within the Western context. Special attention is paid both to the influence of social, juridical and cultural contexts upon the institutionalization of these new religious identities, and to the ability of their adherents to maintain or transform their specific traditions.

The editorial board: W.A.R. Shadid,
P.S. van Koningsveld,
G.A. Wiegers (secretary)
The advisory board: M. Abumalham, R. Barot, R. Leveau,
Å. Sander

ISBN 90-6831-976-0
D. 1997/0602/85

© 1997, Uitgeverij Peeters, Bondgenotenlaan 153, B-3000 Leuven

Contents

Table of contents v
Abbreviations viii
Notes on informants ix
Notes on transliteration ix
Notes on translations ix
Acknowledgments ix
Preface xii

PART I: Setting the Context 1

1. Introduction 1
1.1. Death and bereavement studies in a cross-cultural perspective 6
1.2 Bereavement 9

2. Hindus in Britain 13
2.1. The meaning of Hinduism 13
2.2. British Hinduism 18
2.2.1. Settlement in Britain 19
2.2.2. The community in Westmouth 23
2.2.3. The role of the pandits 26

3. Beliefs about death and the afterlife 29
3.1. Historical perspectives 30
3.2. Contemporary concepts of life after death 35
3.2.1. Departure of the *ātman* 36
3.2.2. The ghost in the liminal period 38
3.2.3. Heaven and *mokṣa* 40
3.2.4. Hell 44
3.2.5. Rebirth 45
3.3. Attitudes to *karma* and suffering 48

Part II. Hindu death rituals 53

4. Good and bad deaths 53
Chart 55
4.1. The good death 56

4.2. The bad death 60
4.3. Stage I: Preparation for death 62
4.3.1. Stage I: Preparation for death in Britain 63
4.4. Stage II: The moment of death 64
4.4.1. Stage II: The moment of death in Britain 68

5. The funeral 71
5.1. Stage III: Preparation of the body in India 71
5.2. Stage IV: *Piṇḍadāna* and the procession to the cremation ground in India 74
5.3. Stage V: The cremation in India 76
5.4. Stage III: Preparation of the body in Britain 80
5.5. Stage IV-V: The funeral in Britain: the domestic ritual 81
5.6. Stage IV: The procession to the crematorium 87
5.7. Stage V: The cremation in Britain 87
5.8. Stage VI: *Asthisañcayaṇa*: disposal of bones and ashes in India and Britain 90

6. Stages VII-IX: *Śrāddha*: offerings to the *preta* (ghost) and *pitṛs* (ancestors) 93
6.1. Stages VII-VIII. *Śrāddhas* in India 94
6.2. Stage VII: *Śrāddha* rituals in Britain 99
6.2.1. *Sapiṇḍīkaraṇa* in Britain 102
6.3. Stage IX: The annual *śrāddha* 106

Part III. Social and psychological dimensions of death. 113

7. The British context of Hindu deaths 113
7.1. Caring for the dying 113
7.1.1. Case Study 1. Ramesh 121
7.1.2. Case study 2. Maya and Nalini 123
7.2. After death 129
7.3. Professionalisation 130

8. The mourning period in Britain 133
8.1. The importance of the mourning period 133
8.2. *Sūtaka* and *śoka* 135

8.2.1. Food restrictions 139
8.3. Community support and the expression of grief 140
8.3.1. Weeping and wailing 143
8.4. Hindu widows: Indian perspectives 146
8.5. Hindu widows in Britain 149

9. Loss, grief and adjustment 155
9.1. Grief in a cross-cultural perspective 155
9.2. The three stages of the mourning process. 160
9.2.1. Stage 1: Immediate loss 160
9.2.2. Stage 2: Facing the reality of the loss 163
9.2.3. Stage 3: Reorganisation and recovery 169
9.3. Case Study 3: Leila, Surya and Susheela 172
9.4 The loss of children 175
9.5. Finding meaning 181

10. Good deaths? Prospects for the future 192
10.1. Death in Britain 192
10.2. Practical implications for the future 198
10.3. Concluding remarks 203

Appendix 207
Glossary of key terms 212
Bibliography 217
Index 231

Abbreviations

AV	*Atharvaveda Saṃhitā*
AP	*Agni Purāṇa*
AGS	*ĀśvalāyanaGṛhyasūtra*
AS	Arya Samaj (ĀryaSamāj)
Ban	Banaras, Varanasi
BG	*Bhagavad Gītā*
Bih	Bihar
Br	Brahmin
Bṛ.Up.	*Bṛhad-Āraṇyaka Upaniṣad*
BP	*Brahma Purāṇa*
Ch.	Chapter
Ch.Up.	*Chandogya Upaniṣad*
CM	Chief Mourner
D	Darji
F	Female
Gj	Gujarati
GP	*Garuḍa Purāṇa*
Gr.	Griffiths
H	Hindi
HP	Himachal Pradesh
ISKCON	The International Society for Kṛṣṇa Consciousness
K	Kumhar
Kh	Khattri
Kan	Kannada
Kat.Up.	*Kaṭha Upanisad*
Kauś	*Kauśika Sūtra*
Kauṣ.Up.	*Kauṣītaki Upaniṣad*
L	Lohana
LP	*Liṅga Purāṇa*
M	Male
Mah	Maharashtrian
Mhb	*Mahābhārata*
M	Mistry
Mun.Up.	*Muṇḍaka Upaniṣad*
O'Fl.	O'Flaherty
P	Purohita
Pj	Panjabi
Pl	Patel
Pt	Pandit
ṚV	*Ṛgveda*
S	Soni
Sar	*Sāroddhāra Garuḍa Purāṇa*
ŚB	*Śathapatha Brāhmaṇa*
Skt	Sanskrit
Sn	Swaminarayan
Svet.Up.	*Śvetāśvatara Upaniṣad*
TA	*Taittirīya Āraṇyaka*
TB	*Taittirīya Brāhmaṇa*
TS	*Taittrīya Samhita*
UP	Uttar Pradesh
Up.	*Upaniṣad*
Utt.K.	*Uttarakhaṇḍa Garuḍa Purāṇa*
V	Vaniya
VS	*Vājasaneyi Saṃhitā*

Notes on informants

When referring to informants, details as to caste, region, sex and age will be indicated as in the following manner, e.g. Panjabi Brahmin Male aged 35: PjBrM35; Gujarati Darji Female aged 70: GjDjF70. Fictitious names are given to informants in Part III, without caste, age and regional identifiers to protect identity. Direct quotations based on tape recordings, are edited for clarity.

Note on transliteration

Words used commonly in Britain, such as 'pandit', caste appellations, such as Darji, place names, sect names, and individual or family names have not been italicised or given diacritical marks. Names of gods and goddesses have been given diacritical marks, but not italicised, and all other Hindi, Gujarati, Panjabi or Sanskrit terms are italicised and given diacritical marks. For Sanskrit and Hindi I have followed the standard systems.

Note on translations

The following English translations were used in quotations: *The Bhagavad Gita*, translated by Radhakrishnan; *Garuda Purana* II. (1979), III. (1980); translated by a board of scholars, Motilal Banarsidas; *The Rig Veda*, translated by O'Flaherty, 1982; *Śatapatha-Brahmana*, translated by Eggeling; *The Thirteen Principal Upanisads*, translated by Hume. Ram Krishan translated *Amṛta Varṣa* for this work.

Acknowledgements

My first thanks must go to the Hindus in Westmouth who gave so generously of their time and experience. It is only to honour my promises of confidentiality that I cannot name those who trusted me with valuable information.

Among the pandits from different parts of Britain my thanks go to Pandits Vishnu Narayan, Aba Panchikar, Madan Lal Sharma, Pathak; and Acharya Tanaji and Dr. Bharadwaj of the Arya Samaj temple. Mathoor Krishnamurthi, at the Bharatiya Vidhya Bhavan, helped throughout, allowing me to watch a family *śrāddha*; Pandit Ramesh Mehta invited me to stay with his family frequently and allowed me to watch a number of rituals, painstakingly going over the details afterwards, and Shastri N.G. Shukla, discussed the rituals and allowed me to observe his own family *śrāddhas*. Hemant Kanitkar and Ram Krishan Prashar advised me on many details of rituals and translations and gave systematic support. Sheila Laxman translated the *piṇḍa* ritual. Ram Krishan Prashar also translated selections from *Amṛta Varṣa*.

In India I must thank Om Prakash Sharma in Banares, Riddish Pandya in Baroda, Dr. Parul Dave, Dr. Amita Varma and Dr. Jyoti Parekh at MS University, Vadodara (Baroda), Dr. Desai and Dr. Madhuben Desai in Ahmedabad, Dattatray Thakore and Pravin Sakaria in Rajcot, and K. N. Malhotra, Dr. Meenakshi Gopinath and Professor Sudhir Kakar in Delhi.

Particular thanks for this book must go to Dermot Killingley, who has been an encouraging guide throughout, reading and correcting the proofs meticulously and assisting with translations. I am also greatly indebted to Werner Menski, my supervisor, who shepherded me patiently through years of research. My early supervisors, Audrey Cantlie and Kate Lowenthal, were constructive and helpful. Eleanor Nesbitt, Richard and Sanjukta Gombrich encouraged me and read portions of my work. Gillian Evison allowed me to copy her thesis before it was submitted. Mallory Nye read my thesis and made helpful comments. Jonathan Parry made valuable suggestions over many years. Frances Sheldon for read the draft of the book and made constructive suggestions. Elisabeth Prickett, Richard and Margaret Peterson kindly proof read. Any mistakes remaining are my own responsibility

All Saints Foundation gave me a grant for 1982-1984. The Central Research Fund of London University provided a grant for travel in Britain, tapes and photocopying for 1984, 1985 and 1987. The Spalding Trust gave me a grant which covered my air fare to India in 1986.

I would not have been able to do the research without the help, patience and encouragement of my husband David. Jonathan and Kate made valuable suggestions. My father, Dr. John Rolles, gave unstinting support in spite of my mother's illness. He set me on the road to this work by educating me in India and encouraging me to take an interest in Hinduism as well as in matters medical and psychological. My mother also appreciated this work prior to her strokes. My father died a few hours after learning that I had received my doctorate, having told me he had waited for the news. My mother followed him a few weeks later. In many ways they had 'good deaths', and this work is dedicated to them both.

Preface

This book is an exploration of the religious beliefs, attitudes, traditions and rituals of a British Hindu community, called Westmouth (a pseudonym), with respect to dying, death and bereavement. My observations from this community are compared with material obtained during three months of fieldwork in India and ethnographic sources.

The purpose of the study is to provide a contribution to an understanding of Hindu communities in Britain as well as to the new and rapidly developing area of death studies. It may be of interest to those concerned with the ways in which ethnic minorities adapt to and seek for their own religious and cultural identity in an alien milieu. There is a growing demand for information on the way Hindus and other minority religious and ethnic groups approach and cope with death and bereavement, reflecting changes in the our understanding of dying patients and bereaved people in general. To be more aware of other cultures will not only help those patients and their families, but can lead to greater insights into one's own. In particular, it is important to understand the ways in which religious beliefs and practices provide a framework for explanation and for finding meaning in death and suffering.[1]

The recording of Hindu beliefs and practices, both generally and with particular reference to death and bereavement, has been said by a number of my informants to be important for their own community, particularly the young, in order to help them maintain a sense of their own identity as Hindus.

The book is organised into three parts. Part I sets the context of the study. Chapter 1 introduces the issues confronting Hindus facing death and bereavement in Britain, with a discussion of theoretical questions arising from a multicultural study. The second chapter discusses Hinduism in Britain, the particular community being studied and the changing role of the pandits. In the third chapter Hindu beliefs about life after death are explored, to provide a background for an understanding of the rituals in Part II, and the ways in which people find meaning (Chapter 9) .

In Part II the Hindu concept of the good death is discussed and ritual practices in Britain and India around death are explored and compared, using a model of nine stages from preparation for death, death and cremation, to the final post-mortem and annual ancestral rituals. Readers with a particular interest in the practical and psychosocial aspects of death and dying may wish to skim over the

---

[1] cf. Berger et al. 1989:xii

ritual aspects of Part II, especially Chapters 5 and 6; the discussion of the good death in Chapter 4 is important for an understanding of the later chapters.

Part III contains four further chapters on the social and psychological dimensions of death, grief and mourning. Chapter 7 examines aspects of death in hospital and the professional and bureaucratic issues which affect Hindu deaths in Britain, using two Case Studies of Hindus who died in hospital. Chapter 8 explores social aspects of mourning, with reference to pollution, the role of the family and community, young people and widows. Chapter 9 is concerned with the psychological dimension of grief, infant deaths and questions of meaning and includes further Case Studies. The conclusion reviews the changes confronting Hindus facing death and bereavement in Britain and looks at ways those involved in the caring professions can both help and learn from them.

This book is based on interrupted periods of research for a doctoral thesis undertaken between 1982 and 1994, first for the Religious Studies department at Kings College, London, and later at the School of Oriental and African Studies. The interdisciplinary approach draws on anthropology, sociology and psychology as well as religious studies. Training in social work and bereavement counselling have added further perspectives.

The primary focus of this study is on individual Hindus, seen in the context of their family and community, on their beliefs, experiences and perceptions about death, and their reactions to the changes that are taking place. Death rituals, in which these individuals take part, both influence and are influenced by the beliefs of the community. An important part of the research, therefore, has been focussed on the rituals, and the role of the pandits.

I intended to interview a representative proportion of each community, with a wide spread of regional backgrounds, castes, sects, and ages. I attended temple services and gradually built up a network of contacts on a snowballing system, attending *satsaṅgs* (hymn-singing sessions), and a weekly *havan*, the Vedic fire ritual, following which discussion was invited. Obviously, it was impossible to know how many people would die during the research period. I went to three Gujarati, five Panjabi Hindu and four Sikh funerals. The latter provided useful comparative data, especially as several informants were married to Sikhs, and one elderly Panjabi Brahmin woman had both a Hindu and a Sikh funeral. I attended the mourning rituals in various castes at various stages in the mourning calendar.

Because of the great sensitivity of the subject I decided at the outset not to use formal questionnaires or a quantitative approach, but to use participant observation regarding communal activities and death ceremonies, and semi-structured interviews. I used a small tape recorder where possible, with a check list of questions for my own use which had to be constantly revised in the light of new material which emerged. Informants were assured that material would be treated confidentially, and permission was asked for use of case studies.

While I was initially reluctant to intrude on the funerals and other rituals, it soon became clear that it is customary for friends, neighbours, professional associates and the wider community to attend. Paying respects to the deceased and the family is a social obligation, and one's presence is greatly appreciated. I taped several services at the crematorium and also videoed the *śrāddha* (post-funeral) rituals for the wife of one of the pandits, performed as it would have been done in India, with the son, also a pandit, as chief mourner.

I interviewed seventy-five informants in Britain, several repeatedly over a number of years, especially after a death. These included Gujarati Brahmins, Lohanas, Patels, Darjis and Kumhars. The Panjabis were Brahmins, Sonis and Khattris, and Mochis,. Other informants came from UP, Bengal, Bombay, Madras and Fiji; one couple originated from Sind. In a number of instances the whole family co-operated, so it was possible to talk to both husband and wife and to their children, or to several generations.

The ages of informants ranged from ten to over eighty. These will be indicated (if only approximately) in the text. There was a wide range of educational backgrounds, ranging from elderly women who knew no English to professionals with degrees. Five Hindu and two Sikh medical doctors were interviewed in Britain, but to protect them no identifying details will be given.

There were ten pandits whom I was able to interview, and in most cases, observe conducting funerals or *śrāddha,* as well as auspicious rituals like weddings. Two were Maharashtrian, one each from UP, Bihar and Karnataka, two from Gujarat and three from the Panjab. Pandit Rameshbhai Mehta in Leicester invited me to stay with his family on several occasions and took me along to observe the rituals, painstakingly going over them afterwards. Shri Mathoor Krishnamurthi at the Bharatya Vidya Bhavan also went over a great deal of detail with me, allowing me to observe the *śrāddha* for his father.

In 1986 I spent three months in India, to get into touch with the background of my informants, and to try to obtain some information about death rituals, beliefs and attitudes of families related to them. In Gujarat I interviewed and stayed with representatives of a wide range of caste groups related to (or similar to) my British informants in Baroda, Ahmedabad, Chandod, and Rajkot, and tried to familiarise myself with their various sectarian backgrounds, especially Pushtimarg and Swaminarayan. In Varanasi Om Prakash Sharma, an expert on funeral rituals, invited me to stay with his family and spent a week showing me the cremation grounds, a home for the dying, and the various temples where people go to remove the troublesome ghosts of their ancestors. Here and in Baroda it was possible to observe several cremations. I also interviewed a number of pandits in Gujarat and Varanasi, including several *mahābrāhmaṇas* (funeral priests), temple pandits and family *purohitas.* It was not possible to obtain a visa for Panjab at that time, but I stayed with and interviewed relatives of Panjabi Brahmin and Khattri informants in Delhi, as well as Khattri informants from Uttar Pradesh. Several doctors in Baroda, Pune, Ahmedebad and Bombay gave me valuable material.

When discussing the rituals, to avoid the clumsy 'his or her' I shall go against feminist principles and refer to 'him' for the simple reason that most of the rituals are specifically for male performers, although they may be done on behalf of women, or with their assistance. Where there are specific differences they will be stated.

It is hoped that this research will provide insights into the religious and cultural identity of the Hindu community in Britain, but also have a practical application for those engaged in the caring professions. An exploration of the multicultural dimensions of death and bereavement has a contribution to make to holistic models of care, especially with reference to questions of religion and spirituality in finding meaning in death.

Part I
Setting the Context

Chapter 1: Introduction

An elderly Hindu in a British hospital was found lying on the floor, so, thinking that he had fallen out of bed, the nurses placed him back. Shortly afterwards he was found on the floor again. He could not speak English to explain that he thought he was dying and wanted to die on the floor where he would be near Mother Earth, so that his soul could leave more freely than in a bed. Like many Hindus, he had a clear model of how he should die, yet he died alone, before his family could be summoned to perform the final rituals.

Ideally, the Hindu model of a good death is one which is prepared for and anticipated, with spiritual disciplines and religious practices, settling family affairs, and saying goodbye. It occurs at the right time (in old age, at the right astrological time) and place (at home, on the floor, if not by the River Ganges), in the presence of the family. The opposite of the good death is a premature or bad death, one which is untimely and out of control, which is usually understood and explained in terms of the person's *karma* (2.1, 3.3, 9.5). The family wash and dress the body themselves, and carry it to the cremation ground immediately or within twenty-four hours. Apart from specialist funeral priests in some areas, the only professionals are the cremation ground attendants in large centres; in rural areas the family and community make the pyre. Because of the emphasis on dying at home, many hospitals in India send patients home to die. There are rituals to be performed before, at and after death, by the eldest son and other members of the family, often with the help of the family priest; these are crucial to the departing soul and the future well-being of the survivors. The funeral rites and mourning traditions shape and reinforce belief, provide support for the mourners, and help to give meaning to the event.

In Britain most deaths occur in hospitals,[1] where it is difficult to follow traditional practices during the last moments of life. Relatives may not be allowed to be present if a patient is in intensive care, and there may be restrictions on the number of visitors. The changes may be particularly acute for those from rural areas who may not have previously experienced sophisticated

---

[1] According to the mortality statistics from the Office of Population Census and Surveys 1991, 54% of total deaths were in hospital, 23% in the home and 17% elsewhere. There was no ethnic break-down in these tables (Field and James 1993:9-11).

medical care in modern urban hospitals in India or East Africa.

Medical staff in Britain are often unaware of the religious and cultural needs of Hindu patients, such as the example given above, or their families. Doctors may not grasp the importance of telling patients or their relatives that death is imminent so that they can make preparations. The problems of interaction may be exacerbated if there are language and communication difficulties, since interpreters are not always readily available in the hospitals and children may have to interpret for their parents. Lack of understanding can lead to discrimination which, even if unwitting, is often seen as racism.

Both before and after death professionals take charge. Arrangements for the care of the body and the funeral are in the hands of paid funeral directors rather than the family, leading to the loss of a sense of control. In Britain funerals can rarely take place within the customary twenty-four hours because of post mortems or lack of space in the crematorium, but the delay may be more than a week. The process of cremation is different from one on an open pyre. Even if there is familiarity with electric crematoria, in Britain time is rationed, and coffins are required by law.

Further delays occur if relatives have to be summoned from all over the country and overseas. Immigration law may prevent relatives from arriving in time, if at all, causing great distress.

At a more explicitly religious level there are numerous changes. The difficulty, particularly in the early days of settlement, of finding a suitably qualified Brahmin priest to perform the funeral ritual has meant that at times no priest has been available to conduct a funeral, and lay people have had to do the best they could. Where a priest is available, he may be a family *purohita* (priest) or a temple pandit unaccustomed to conducting funeral rituals. New rituals based on Sanskrit and Purāṇic texts are being evolved, sometimes in an apparently *ad hoc* way. Much of the ritual, which would have taken place at the cremation ground in India, takes place in the family home in Britain. The priest, who in India would not normally enter a house containing a corpse, conducts a ceremony beside the coffin at home and again at the crematorium. If there is no learned priest available, important rituals, such as the *śrāddha* (post-funeral rites) may be performed by proxy in India or by the mourners if they are able to take the ashes back themselves (Ch.5 and 6).

Changes in family structure also affect the way in which individuals and communities deal with death and bereavement. Older immigrants may still live in a tightly knit 'village' community of people from the same caste or area. With greater social mobility, particularly among the young who have been educated in Britain, many families are splitting up geographically, so that where the extended family exists, it tends to consist of three vertical generations in one house, with other siblings living nearby. Since many families in Britain form nuclear households, and since in some families men have been imported as husbands, the old patterns of patrilineal ties may be shifting, although the patriarchal authority structures are still strong. Brothers or sons may be working abroad or some distance away so that they are unable to provide adequate practical support, although financial support may be generous.

Since many of the practices associated with death are *laukika*, based on family, caste and local traditions, bereaved families tend to turn to experienced older members who can give advice and guidance. Where the family is divided and individuals do not know what to do, or who to ask for advice, this can cause much concern, guilt and anxiety. All this has many implications for patterns of marital and familial bonding and in turn for grief and mourning patterns. On the other hand, the existence of the wider family and caste group provides a high level of continuity within the constraints mentioned above, and a strong support system.[2]

Even if Hindus, anxious to preserve their traditions and identity, try to minimise contact with the 'white' majority, as Pocock found nearly twenty years ago, this would only be possible in the short term.[3] Working individuals may have daily contact with non-Hindus, and younger family members are exposed to the British educational system and the cultural values of their peers and the media. They will be influenced by them in such a way that, as some researchers have suggested, they may be significantly different from their parents' generation.[4] They may also feel dissociated from their culture, which can lead to uncertainty and confusion.

Such processes of adaptation and change are also at work in India.[5] There are manifold links and connections between the different parts of the world that are now home to Hindus, and the nature of the changes which take place and the extent to which each community retains the umbilical link to India will inevitably

---

[2] Barot 1980:8ff.; Knott 1986b:33ff.; 1987:156ff.; Burghart 1987:1ff. and 224ff..

[3] Pocock 1976:345-6, 359.

[4] Poulter 1986:3-4; Jackson 1985; Jackson and Nesbitt 1986; Nesbitt 1991.

[5] Michaelson 1987; Knott 1987; Killingley 1991; Menski 1987, 1991.

be related to the history of that area.[6] Hindus themselves are divided by language, caste and settlement history, with a wide range of beliefs, sectarian allegiances, ritual practices and local traditions. British Hindus live in a society in which there are what Knott describes as "concepts of religious pluralism and institutional diversification in which Hinduism becomes one religion among many, and a religion vying with other social institutions for control over the lives of its adherents".[7] This has implications for Hindus' concepts of their own identity, whether they view themselves as primarily Hindu compared with non-Hindus, or, for example, as Gujarati Patels or Punjabi Brahmins. To what extent developments may be given their own, particularly British, forms by aspects of life in this country remains to be seen. Menski shows with reference to marriage, second and third generations of Hindus create their own traditions and rituals.[8]

Arguably, nowhere is the question of identity raised more acutely than in the face of death. As we explore the impact of death on a particular community, we need to be aware of the kinds of psychological, social and religious strategies and mechanisms by which human beings cope and come to terms with it. According to Berger death is a threat to society because it presents it

> with a formidable problem not only because of its obvious threat to the continuity of human relationships; but because it threatens the basic assumptions of order on which society rests. Death radically puts in question the taken-for-granted, 'business-as-usual' attitude in which one exists in everyday life ... Insofar as knowledge of death cannot be avoided in any society, legitimations of the reality of the social world *in the face of death* are decisive requirements in any society. The importance of religion in such legitimations is obvious.[9]

The legitimation of death, and its integration into social existence, is an important function of the 'symbolic universes' which people create in each culture to give meaning to life and to death.[10] According to Berger and Luckman, the task of such legitimations is to "enable the individual to go on living in society after the death of significant others and to anticipate his own death" with sufficient freedom from fear to be able to function normally in everyday life, and

---

[6] Bharati 1972, 1976; Michaelson 1983, 1987; Barot 1980, 1987; Burghart 1987; Clarke, Peach and Vertovec 1990; Nye 1992b:15ff..

[7] Knott 1986b:10.

[8] Menski 1987:180 ff.; 1991.

[9] Berger 1969:23; cf. pp.43-44.

[10] Berger and Luckman 1966:119.

ultimately to die a 'correct death'.

If, for Hindus, the "basic assumptions of order" which existed in their communities of origin are being challenged, both by the changes that are occurring within the community and through interaction with the host community, then death is potentially all the more threatening. The new community may create what Reynolds and Waugh call a new 'language' to cope with the situation:

> Where on the one hand accepted and conventional activities offer the support of society's forms in the face of death, on the other their very regularity and inflexibility may contribute to a collapse under the absurdity of death's presence. The immediate result of this explosive new element in life is the birth in effect of a new 'language'. Though not necessarily verbal it is a genuine attempt to cope with and give expression to a violent new challenge. ... The way is opened for articulating emerging experiences in consort with other moods and attitudes, and individuals wander down many paths trying to make sense of the conjunction of themselves and that peculiar occurrence at that particular time.[11]

The question here is to what extent the 'language' of the Hindu tradition is appropriate to transplanted Hindu culture, enabling the dying and bereaved to make sense of their experience, and how far it has become, or is perceived to be, anachronistic or inappropriate. There may be discrepancies between what people think should be done at the time of death and what is actually done. The changes in ritual which occur as a result of living in Britain may both reflect and influence changes in belief; the encounter with British society at different levels is a further factor in the development of new religious structures, especially with regard to death and bereavement. The 'language' which evolves will need to serve the new generation of British Hindus as well as their parents. It should enable them to find some sort of meaning and sense of identity at the time of death which is emotionally and cognitively satisfying for both the dying and the bereaved.

This is particularly important at a time when the principles of holistic care are being examined and questions asked about the meaning and importance of religion and spirituality in hospice and palliative care. These issues are not clear in Western secularised society, or what Walter calls "the secularised church".[12] A world view which sees death as a process in a continuum between life and the

---

[11] Reynolds and Waugh 1973:1.

[12] Walter 1993:128; see also 1996, 1997a, 1997b.

next life and demonstrably helps the dying and bereaved to make sense of death, has a valuable contribution to make to the discussion.

While there is a good deal of current research into Hindu society in Britain exploring some of the above-mentioned issues of adaptation and change from social and religious perspectives,[13] there has been very little in relation to death and bereavement.[14] In the ethnographic and religious studies on death and mourning traditions in India, which are important for an understanding of the background of British Hindus,[15] there are few references to the psychological dimension of this experience. There is also little work anywhere examining bereavement from cross-cultural perspectives, which is essential in this context. This chapter concludes with a brief overview of anthropological and psychological studies which throw some light on our understanding of death and bereavement in a multi-cultural setting; these issues are discussed more fully in the relevant chapters.

1.1. Death and bereavement studies in a cross-cultural perspective

There are many studies of death in other cultures[16] and an increasing number on death in Western Europe and America.[17] Hertz and Van Gennep both throw light on the social processes by which both individuals and a community come to terms with death. Hertz is concerned to show the relationship between the beliefs and emotions of the mourners, the ritual processes following a death and the readjustment of the social group. Such emotions as are aroused by death are social facts and can be studied. As Bloch and Parry, referring to Hertz, comment, death rituals "organise and orchestrate private emotions".[18] But Hertz recognises that there are differences between Western societies which accept that "death occurs in one instant", and others in which the process of death is drawn out over a period of time, so even if they are social facts, they are not universally identical social facts, or at least not presented in the same form. He classifies the ideas and

---

[13] Cf. Knott 1986b ; Burghart 1987; Menski 1984.

[14] Laungani 1996, 1997.

[15] Padfield 1908; Stevenson 1920; Parry 1981, 1982, 1985, 1989, 1991, Quayle 1980; Raheja 1988; Evison 1989; Gold 1990.

[16] Hertz 1960; Van Gennep 1960; Turner 1967; Huntington and Metcalf 1979; Bloch and Parry 1982; Reynolds and Waugh 1977; Badham and Badham 1987; Berger *et al.* 1989.

[17] Feifel 1965; Ariès 1974, 1981; Dickenson and Johnson 1991; Jupp and Howerth 1996; Walter 1994; plus books on bereavement, and sociological perspectives. Buddhist approaches include Levine 1986, 1987; and Sogyal Rimpoche 1992.

[18] Bloch and Parry 1982:3.

practices associated with death under three headings "according to whether they concern the body of the deceased, his soul, or the survivors", and sees the death rituals as being a process of transition between exclusion (death), and "integration, i.e. a rebirth".[19] Like birth and initiation, such transitions and changes of status take time for adjustment. During this period many cultures believe the deceased is in an intermediate state between death and resurrection, to be purified from sin or pollution prior to his acceptance by the ancestors or his rebirth, and during which time the survivors also have an opportunity to adjust.[20] Van Gennep develops the two-stage concept into three stages of rites, those of separation, transition or a liminal period, and reincorporation. According to Huntington and Metcalf, Van Gennep removes some of "the fear and arrogance of ethnocentrism from transcultural study", transforming "ritual symbols and behaviour ... into that which is simple, logical and universal".[21] Turner expands this theory, seeing the liminal stage as one of transition, "the inhabitants of which are 'betwixt and between' normal social roles, and close to some transcendent and sacred core of social and moral value".[22]

As will be seen in Part II, Hindu rituals in India fit into this type of model, with complex rites of separation at death, followed by a twelve day transitional period during which the mourners are in a state of impurity and separated from society at large, and during which the ghost is perceived to be dangerous. Finally the rites of reincorporation send the deceased to his new life in which he may alternatively be an ancestor, reborn, dwell in heaven or hell, or be absorbed into Brahman. During this period the mourners are engaged in constant activity to ensure the nourishment and well-being of the deceased, thus guaranteeing their own safety. They are then reintegrated into society in their new roles.

In Britain, however, this model is disrupted because of bureaucracy and delays in the disposal of the body, so that the rites of separation cannot take place until the transitional or liminal period is well under way instead of preceding it (Ch.8). The question then arises: if Hindus in the diaspora cannot follow this model, can they 'invent' an equally useful and helpful one?

Hertz recognises the psychological processes the bereaved go through, and the importance, by implication, of representations of death which have room for a concept of rebirth or resurrection. He recognises the psychological value of

---

[19] Hertz 1960:28-29; cf. Walter 1990:92.

[20] Hertz 1960:35; 78 ff..

[21] Huntington and Metcalf 1979:11; Van Gennep 1960:11ff.

[22] Turner 1967:94.

adequate rites of separation and reincorporation. It is the very lack of such rites and social representations in Western society, particularly in its Protestant manifestations, that is seen by some writers as creating further problems for dying and bereaved people in coming to terms with death.[23] As Hertz also pointed out, death in Western society is dealt with very quickly, and people are expected to get on with their lives once the funeral is over.[24] Funerals themselves have often become cursory,[25] seen more as a farewell than a means of ensuring the well-being of the deceased.

Rosenblatt *et al.* see the prolonging of grief in American society as a consequence of there being no transitional period, or a final ceremony which provides a legitimised time limit to mourning.[26] One historical reason for the loss of the transitional period in Western society is the Protestant belief that the fate of the soul is determined at the point of death, so that the living and dead are separated from the moment of death. There is no longer a belief in purgatory in which the progress of the souls of the newly deceased depend upon the prayers of their survivors,[27] and for many hell has also disappeared.[28] Gorer argues that mourning rituals disappeared after World War I and suggests that the failure to handle bereavement with adequate rituals not only creates psychological problems for individuals, but also causes society to become obsessed with "the pornography of death" in the form of horror films and disasters.[29]

In Britain few people, outside minority religious groups, celebrate the anniversary of a death. Although some Anglican churches mention 'Year's Mind' on the anniversary at the request of individual mourners, this is probably more in the way of a commemoration than praying for the deceased.

It is only comparatively recently that an interest has been shown in the psychology of the dying pioneered by Elisabeth Kübler-Ross and Cecily Saunders, founders of the hospice movement in America and Britain respectively. Kübler-Ross showed that the dying who know of their impending death, go through similar processes of loss and grief as the bereaved. In many hospitals until recently, patients were not told of their prognosis or allowed to discuss their anxieties or fears. They ran the risk of dying alone, or of having unwanted

[23] Gorer 1965:8; Walter 1990:32, 48, 102; Katz, Peberdy and Siddell 1993:29-33; 50ff..
[24] Hertz 1960:28.
[25] Walter 1990:9ff..
[26] Rosenblatt *et al.* 1976:96-97.
[27] Katz, Peberdy and Siddell 1993:24; cf. Ariès 1981:465ff., 585.
[28] Walter 1990:63, 95 ff..
[29] Gorer 1965:111; cf Katz, Peberdy and Siddell 1993:55ff..

medical intervention. Kübler-Ross and Saunders showed that in the right atmosphere of openness and support from the medical staff and good communication with the family, death can be accepted more easily. There is less adjustment if death occurs in familiar surroundings, especially at home. If children are present and involved in the talking and grieving they develop a more balanced view of death "as a part of life".[30]

1.2. Bereavement[31]

Following Freud's work on mourning, bereavement studies have developed the concept of grief as a process which has to be worked through, with the possibility of recovery or adjustment. For Freud this involved the withdrawal of the libido, or emotional energy, from the lost object person and reinvesting it into a new relationship. This entailed what he called "grief work", in which the bereaved had to dwell on the past and review it until detachment was achieved. [32] For Klein and Bowlby recovery occurred with the internalising of the lost person,[33] whereas Worden saw it in terms of relocating the deceased.[34] The grief process is often thought to take place in stages or phases. Many writers suggest there are at least three, although not necessarily in a fixed sequence: shock and denial, pining, and reorganisation and recovery. These are seen as useful tools for understanding how the bereaved 'work' through the loss, by accepting it, experiencing the pain and adjusting to a newly ordered environment.[35]

Stroebe is critical of both the concepts of stages and grief work because of their assumption of universality, whereas in some circumstances and some

---

30 Kübler-Ross 1969:6.

31 The term 'grief' is to be understood as an emotion which arises in response to loss, and 'mourning' as the way in which this is manifested, often in culturally determined ways, and often for a specified time in a particular society, although Freud uses the latter term in both senses (Vol.II:251; cf. Parkes and Weiss 1983:2:2; Parkes 1993:292). Prior, in examining the social distribution of sentiments, tends to use 'grief' both as something that is felt and something that is expressed, which is confusing (Prior 1993:251ff.). Rosenblatt (1976:2) defines bereavement in terms of "both the period of time following a death, during which grief occurs, and also the state of experiencing grief... All grief behaviour by adults will ... be patterned, modified, and perhaps even coerced by culture, and any mourning act may be influenced by the biology or psychology of grief".

32 Freud 1917:253, 353.

33 Klein 1940:156; Bowlby 1980, 1981.

34 Worden 1991:16-18.

35 Kübler-Ross described five stages dying people go through: denial, anger, bargaining, depression and acceptance. They are criticised as inappropriate for the bereaved and because they are often used prescriptively; cf. Kübler-Ross 1969:38ff.. See Stroebe 1994; Walter 1994:70ff...

cultures repression of emotions and memories may have an adaptive function.[36] Rosenblatt also shows that repression of feelings in some cultures is quite normal, whereas in others it is important to retain ties with the deceased and maintain relationships.[37] In the Muslim cultures of Egypt and Bali there are contrasting cultural expectations as to how grief should be expressed - overtly in Egypt and controlled and contained in Bali. Stroebe suggests that the concept of grief work has to be seen in this wider context, and that counselling has to take into account such different adaptive strategies.

In Japan, China and other cultures the relationship with the deceased is maintained as an ancestor; this is an important feature of Hindu society, as we shall see. Walter, indeed, argues passionately for a view of the dead which brings them back into the circle of family and friends rather than banishing them, which lies closer to the views of Klein and Bowlby that they should be internalised, or Worden's that they have to be relocated, than to the Freudian position that the libido has to be withdrawn and reinvested in another 'object' or relationship.[38]

For Eisenbruch, grief has a biological basis which is not inconsistent with cultural variations in both normal and pathological grief.[39] How far different cultural groups vary as to what is considered normal grief and how long it should continue can only be assessed by ethnographic data on the post-funeral rituals, which show considerable variation. His study is of particular value in the present context because he examines, through secondary sources, bereavement in various ethnic minority groups in a Western society (the United States):

> Ethnicity entails, among other things, the use of a cultural system to make sense of the world, including its sufferings... Given the stress of bereavement, acculturated Americans can temporarily 'shift back' to their ethnic roots; not so much a pathological regression as an adaptive shift.... Differences in behavioural ethnicity give rise to variations in the public expression of mourning... Differences in ideological ethnicity will give rise to differences in the private expression of grief.[40]

The assumptions, psychological categories and terminology used in Western studies of death and bereavement may not be appropriate or relevant to a study

---

[36] Stroebe 1994.
[37] Rosenblatt 1993a, 1993b.
[38] Walter 1996.
[39] Eisenbruch 1984 I:286-8.
[40] Eisenbruch 1984 II:325.

of Hindu approaches. It is thus important to be aware of the way terms are used and understood, both by oneself and by informants, in order to ascertain as far as possible what they mean to different people, with reference to both rational explanations and feelings. Concepts such as 'death' will be affected by radically different views as to its meaning. If people *really* believe that when they die they are going to burn in the fires of hell or be with God, be born again in another miserable or better life, or be reunited with loved ones, it will make a difference not only to how they want to die, but how they live. Death may be viewed as a transition or as a final ending. If it is regarded as a familiar and normal happening, however painful, and in the context of some sense of continuity of belief and practice, it will have a different meaning, and a different effect on the bereaved than it would in a culture which sees it as something to be avoided, postponed or denied, so the psychological reactions as well as the cognitive ways of dealing with it may be very different. The researcher also has to be aware of different metaphors used to describe feelings, different body language, attitudes to gender issues and conventions of behaviour which may make understanding more difficult (9.1). It is important, therefore, to be aware of one's own presuppositions, attitudes and expectations, and to try to 'get inside the shoes' of the community being studied as objectively as possible.

Many Hindus, both in Britain and on the sub-continent, are influenced by Western concepts and language, particularly those who are bilingual or whose main language is English. English words such as 'guilt' may have theological overtones used by a British person with a Christian background, but different connotations for a Hindu, particularly in the light of concepts such as *dharma, karma* and *kismat* (Chs. 2, 3 and 9). Discussions in English with mainly middle class Westernised Hindus might miss nuances which would be present in discussions in Hindi, Gujarati or Punjabi. However, many informants were familiar with Western psychological terminology. Of particular value in India were discussions with a group of women lecturers at the University of Vadodara (Baroda), 'the Vadodara group', who had studied some psychology and who threw light on some of the questions I was asking. They had come to terms with fairly radical changes in lifestyle and attitudes by virtue of their education. Their understanding of the implications of these changes is pertinent to a study of British Hindus who are facing similar changes.

Interpersonal relationships vary between cultures, with different assumptions about, for example, mother-child or marital bonding since these reinforce and are reinforced by social expectations and cultural myths. The Indian psychoanalyst,

Sudhir Kakar, warns against ignoring mythological material and cultural influences in search of universalist theories, pointing to the different kinds of bonding that arise in the Indian extended family situation, in which a woman goes to live with her husband's parents upon an arranged marriage.[41] In particular, the intense bond which develops between mother and son owes its strength in part to the fact that his birth establishes and validates her identity as a mother, indeed, as a member of her husband's family. The emotional bond between marital partners may initially be much weaker than between those in a nuclear family, developing intimacy later in life. The life-long relationship between parent and child, which is maintained by the authority structure within the family, may make the loss of a parent profoundly disorientating to an adult Hindu. Kakar observes, "Autonomy arouses the most severe of the culturally supported anxieties: the fear of isolation and estrangement that are visited upon the completely autonomous human being."[42] As more British Hindus establish nuclear families with chosen partners these structures may alter, allowing for more independence and autonomy, but at the risk of losing the cohesion and strength of the extended family community.

Hindus establishing their own identity in Britain thus have to adapt radically in the way they deal with death in many areas of belief, practice, social life, family dynamics and self-awareness. Yet the dearth of cross-cultural education and research means that many medical and social work professionals have a Eurocentric bias. This means that although noting obvious differences in colour, custom and dress, they miss deep and fundamental differences in attitude and also forget the commonality of human experience in the face of loss, suffering and death. Anthropological perspectives shed light on the social aspects of death, grief and mourning, both for Hindus undergoing a process of change, and for Western culture which is struggling to find new ways of dealing with the issues. Similarly, an understanding of psychological aspects of grief and mourning in Hindu and other ethnic minority cultures not only benefits Hindus themselves and those who work with them, but provides a broader perspective than is possible in a monocultural context. The Hindu approach to death through the totality of belief, ritual and social structures is important to recognise and respect for their sakes, but can also provide stimulus to the discussion of religious and spiritual care taking place in palliative care and the hospice movement.

---

[41] Kakar 1990:433-434.

[42] Kakar 1978:36, 73-7, 89-91, 120, 133ff..

Chapter 2
Hindus in Britain

What it means to be a Hindu in India, a predominantly Hindu country, and what it means to be one in Britain where Hindus are in a minority, are very different. Hindus' sense of identity depends not only on their history, family, background and religious affiliation, but on a complex of religious beliefs and attitudes: their 'world view'. This chapter explores the meaning of the term 'Hinduism', followed by a brief history of the settlement of Hindus in Britain and in Westmouth in particular, and the role of the pandits in the community. While specific beliefs about life and death are discussed in Chapter 3, those concepts which are central to what might be called the Hindu world view, such as caste and *dharma*, are discussed here, as they are essential to an understanding of what or who a Hindu is.

2.1. The meaning of 'Hinduism'

The term 'Hinduism' is notoriously difficult to define.[1] The word 'Hindu' was applied by early Muslim invaders to dwellers in the area of the Indus. Cantwell Smith points out that "Hinduism refers not to an entity; it is a name that the West has given to a prodigiously variegated series of facts."[2] The term frequently used by Hindus themselves for their religion and culture (as they are not seen as separate) is *sanātana dharma*, the eternal religion (see below). Weightman suggests the term Hinduism should be understood as an 'umbrella concept' or a family of faiths embracing

> .... a vast diversity and variety of religious movements, systems, beliefs and practices. These have ranged in scale from major religious movements with sophisticated theologies and rich mythologies which have spread over great areas of the sub-continent and could, with justice, be termed 'religious' in their own right, to unsophisticated local cults which may be known only to one or two villages. There has also been continual absorption, interaction and readjustment to meet the needs of every type of person facing every sort of question in different ages and localities.[3]

---

[1] For example, Nesbitt shows that in areas such as the Punjab, the boundaries between what could be thought of as Hindu and Sikh are often unclear. Nesbitt 1991:8ff.; cf. Ashby 1974:8ff.; Knott 1986b:170-171; Burghart 1987:225ff..

[2] Smith 1978:50.

[3] Weightman 1984:4; cf. Nye 1992b:2-3; Vertovec 1992a:2ff.; Fuller 1992:24ff..

The regional and local traditions have sometimes been called by anthropologists, the 'Little Tradition' as against the 'Great Tradition' or 'Sanskritic Tradition', based on the vast range of Sanskrit texts which over the centuries were in the keeping of the Brahmin priests and accessible only to the *dvija*, twice born.[4] The texts were used in the *saṃskāras* or life cycle rites, and formed the basis of philosophical and religious learning. Hinduism has often been identified with the Great Tradition, particularly in the West, and it is this aspect of Hinduism which is most likely to be expounded by Brahmin teachers, pandits, or priests[5]. Nye argues that the dichotomy between the 'Great' and 'Little' traditions is misleading because it implies a value judgement. They do not exist in a pure form, but interact so that "... each 'universalises' and 'parochialises' other traditions in their own ways". This process may result in "dynamic equilibrium", but equally in a lack of balance and social change, which in turn may lead to tradition being reinvented and reinterpreted as different elements interact.[6] In British Hindu communities the *śāstrika* (from the *śāstras*) and the local or regional traditions are constantly being inter-woven particularly with respect to death and mourning rituals.

'Sanatan Dharm' (*sanātana dharma*), the eternal *dharma,* is the term Hindus often use for their religion, which, according to Basham, "is virtually untranslatable... It implies the idea of an eternally fixed and divine standard of conduct, a sacred law which is never to be altered, but only to be interpreted."[7] It has both a macrocosmic dimension, as a natural law maintaining the cosmos and all animate and inanimate things in proper harmony with each other, and a microcosmic dimension of moral obligation or duty for the individual, *sva-dharma*. The term *'dharma'* in the latter sense is often combined with *'varṇa'* and *'āśrama'* in a term often used for religion, *varṇāśramadharma*.[8] A virtuous life lived in accordance with *varṇāśramadharma* will ensure a good rebirth, particularly if the correct mortuary rites are carried out by one's son or

---

[4] Srinivas 1952:213ff.; Marriot 1955:197-201; Nye 1992b:4ff..

[5] Nye 1992b:4ff.; Burghart 1978.

[6] Nye 1992b:9; cf. Marriott 1955; Knott 1986b:87ff., 168.

[7] Basham 1967:244.

[8] *Varṇa* denotes colour, and is used for the four great classes which are known in Sanskrit literature from the Veda onwards. The four *varṇa*s are *brāhmaṇas* (brahmins), priests; *rājanyas* or *kṣatriyas*, warriors and rulers; *vaiśyas*, mercantile classes; and *śūdras*, peasants (Basham 1967:36). The first three are the *dvija*, twice born, and entitled to wear a sacred thread, invested at the *upanayana* or initiation (RV X.90). The four *āśramas*, or stages of life are that of *brahmacarya*, studentship; *gārhasthya*, householdership; *vānaprastha*, forest life; and *sannyāsa*, renunciation.

appropriate relatives.

At the individual level there are different kinds of *dharma*. *Jāti dharma* lays out obligations. The term 'caste' (*jāti)* refers to an endogamous social group associated with a particular occupation and ranked according to the purity of that occupation.[9] *Sādhāraṇa dharma* is a general *dharma* applicable to everyone. It includes two types of principles or moral obligations, according to Weightman. The first type relates to universal moral principles, such as prohibitions of murder and incest, as well as emphasising the obligation to honour parents, the gods, the Vedas and Brahmins, while those of the second type lead to the acquisition of merit *puṇya*, for the next rebirth. These include *ṛṇa*, the great debts to Brahmans, parents, the gods and the Vedas[10], as well as pious acts such as alms-giving and pilgrimage. The life-cycle rites, or *saṃskāras*, need to be seen in this context, particularly the final one or *antyeṣṭi*: "It is sādhāraṇ dharma... that the life cycle rites should be carried out properly, but jāti dharma that determines how and which saṁskāras, are celebrated by each or subcaste."[11]

An important doctrine related to *dharma* is *karma* , an automatic law of cause and effect, in which good and bad thoughts and actions store up a bank of merit, *puṇya*, or demerit, *pāpa*, (Hindi, *pāp*) which has consequences not just in this life but in the next (Ch. 3).

Connected to *dharma* are the concepts of purity and pollution, which are particularly relevant in the context of death and bereavement. Pollution can be voluntary, through breaking rules, eating the wrong kinds of food or with the wrong kinds of people, sexual intercourse, or touching impure objects or persons. Involuntary pollution includes bodily emissions, birth and death. As Weightman comments: "The opposed pair of concepts purity-impurity provide the scale by which castes are ranked, basically according to the extent that they are regarded as polluting", with the Brahmins at the top.[12] Purity thus refers both to an individual's state and to his station.

---

[9] *Jātis* are "characterized by heredity, endogamy, commensality, an actual or attributed common occupation, and actual or attributed peculiarities of diet. Jātis are ranked in a hierarchy, in which superiority of one jāti to another is marked by avoidance of contact of various kinds, notably acceptance of food and water" (Killingley 1991:9 and pp.7ff.; cf. Weightman 1978:10ff.).

[10] *Ṛṇa*: a Sanskrit word for debt, is used in a special sense to refer to dharmic obligations. TS V.I3.10.5 cites three debts "of Vedic study to the *ṛṣi* (sages), sacrifices to the gods and of offspring to the ancestors" (cited in Malamoud, 1983:26ff.; cf. Kane 1973 IV:550). In ŚB II.6.2.16 there is also a debt to death and ŚB 1.7.2.1-6 adds a debt to men, *manuṣya*, an obligation to offer hospitality (for further discussion see Malamoud 1983 and Dumont 1983).

[11] Weightman 1984:49.

[12] Weightman 1984:22.

While it is possible to follow one's *dharma* whilst being an atheist or agnostic, it is probably true to say that most Hindus are devoted to God in the form of Śiva, his consort Durga (or the mother goddess) or Viṣṇu, manifested as one of his avatars, particularly Rāma or Kṛṣṇa. Devotion to the latter is a prominent feature of the *bhakti* or devotional sects popular among Gujaratis and others in Britain, such as ISKCON, Pushtimarga, Swaminarayan, and Sathya Sai Baba. Such commitment may influence the way death rituals are performed, as in the example of Arya Samaj (below). The term *dharma* may thus be used in the more specific sense of the sect or *sampradāya*, which, according to Barot, is

> ... a particular body of traditional doctrines handed down through a succession of teachers. In other words the ideology and organisation of a *sampradāya* are invariably related to one particular teacher who demands exclusive allegiance from his followers.[13]

Unlike the Western sect which secedes from the parent body, the Hindu sect still regards itself as part of *dharma*, but a particular *dharma*.[14]

Pushtimarga (Path of Grace) is derived from the teaching of Vallabhacarya (1479-1531). Its leaders or *mahar$\bar{a}$jas* are householders in the direct line of descent from the founder and carry the name Goswami. Followers worship the *svarup* or image of Kṛṣṇa, particularly as an infant, serving him (*seva*), by attending to all his needs. The image is woken up, bathed and dressed, fed and played with and put to bed in the evening. It is not an ascetic movement but advocates a very strict vegetarian diet.[15]

Swaminarayan was founded in about 1804 by Sahajanand Swami (1781-1830). His title, Swami Narayan, implies that he was a manifestation of Viṣṇu (Nārāyaṇa).[16] A puritanical reform movement, particularly popular in Gujarat, it is open to all classes at lay level, enforcing the rules of commensality[17] and strict segregation of the sexes. The sect is administered by *ācāryas*, who are descended from the founder's family, but also has a strict order of ascetics. There are several sects, the principal branches being the Sri Swaminarayan Siddhanta Sajivan

[13] Barot 1980:19.

[14] Barot 1980:20; cf. Knott 1986b:10ff.; Michaelson 1987:34-35.

[15] Barz 1976; Bennett 1983; Michaelson 1987:36ff.; Dwyer 1994: 172.

[16] Cf.Williams 1984:60ff.; Barot 1980, 1987.

[17] Commensality refers to the rules governing with whom any given caste may or may not offer and receive food or dine together. Cf. f.n. 9 for ; Dumont 1970:123-9; Weightman 1978: 13-19.

Mandal at Ahmadabad, the Yogi Divine Society and the Akshar Purushottam Sanstha at Vadtal under Pramukh Swami. The latter branch has built a big temple in Neasden, north London (2.2.1).[18] Dwyer suggests that Swaminarayan and Pushtimarga have been influential in Gujarat and Britain because they were supported by wealthy merchants and also because they enabled followers to gain higher status through Sanskritisation.[19]

The Arya Samaj was founded by Swami Dayanand Saraswati (1824-83). He sought to reform Hinduism by a return to the teachings of the Vedas, and a rejection of the Epics and Purāṇas. He attacked the corruption of Brahmin priests and the worship of images and caste. The focal point of worship is the *havan*, the Vedic fire sacrifice, which a strict Arya Samaji does daily. This movement, particularly popular among Punjabis, rejects *mūrti pūjā*, the worship of images, and does not do *ārtī*, an offering made morning and evening with a lighted lamp before the installed images (below).[20] The Arya Samaj theoretically rejects the concept of death pollution, simplifying and shortening the death rituals. This and Swaminarayan have been the most influential of all the sects with regard to changes in death rituals.

Sathya Sai Baba (b.1926) claimed first to be the reincarnation of the Muslim saint, Shirdi Sai Baba (d.1918), then of Śiva-Śakti, and then the universal god, which meant that he received the devotions which were made to the godhead in any form. Sathya Sai Baba's teaching is strongly ethical, aimed at the promotion of *dharma*, but he is noted for the miracles which he is said to perform, particularly the manifesting of sacred ash, *vibhūti*, which he gives to his devotees. He appeals to Hindus from all regions as well as westerners.[21]

Smaller sects include the Radhasoamis, and devotees of Santoshi Ma(ta) or other forms of devotion to the Mother Goddess, Baba Balak Nath or Jalaram Bapa. There are also so-called 'neo-Hindu' movements which also attract British adherents, such as Transcendental Meditation, Ramakrishna Mission, the Brahma Kumaris and the International Society for Kṛṣṇa Consciousness (ISKCON), commonly known as Hare Krishna. The latter, founded by Bhaktivedanta Swami Prabhupada in the United States in 1965, has a considerable following among the indigenous white community. The temples in London and Hertfordshire are also important religious centres for Hindus.

---

[18] Cf. Williams 1984:25ff.; 187 ff.; Barot 1987:66-80.

[19] Dwyer 1994:171.

[20] Knott 1986b:16 ff., 128-140; see Jones 1976; Nye 1992a:103ff.

[21] Taylor 1987; Schulman 1971; Sandweiss 1975; Ganapati 1981.

Those Hindus who do not belong to a particular sect will describe themselves as 'Sanatan Dharmi,' followers of Sanātana Dharma, a term describing orthodox Hinduism in the keeping of Brahmin priests. The path of devotion, *bhakti yoga*, followed by the devotional sects described above, is one of three paths to liberation from the cycle of birth and rebirth. The second way is the way of mystical knowledge or enlightenment, *jñāna yoga*, which is followed by many *sannyāsīs*. The third is the way of action, *karma yoga*, particularly through the correct rituals and sacrifices; this was transformed by the *Bhagavad Gītā* into a doctrine of selfless action motivated only by devotion to God, Kṛṣṇa.[22] A Hindu may follow one, or any combination of the three.

2.2. British Hinduism

The beliefs and practices of Hindus in Britain, as in India, derive from many sources, combining regional and caste-based traditions, and sectarian commitments, with the Sanskritic or great tradition. There are varying degrees of familiarity with the scriptures and the Brahmanical rituals using Sanskrit texts, from which many of the beliefs and concepts about death are derived. Even when priests are not available, portions of Vedic texts may be recited at funerals, while the *Bhagavad Gītā* (BG) and *Garuda Purāṇa* (GP) are frequently read following a death, thus providing a thread of continuity from the past which continues to shape belief. Other sources of education are the great epics shown on film and television, family accounts and videos of, or participation in, festivals and life-cycle rites *saṃskāras* in both India and Britain.[23]

Some scholars have argued *varṇāśramadharma* cannot exist outside India, as it is tied to the social and structures of the subcontinent, and thus to Indian ethnicity. However, Knott observes that the concept is still relevant in Britain:

> Hindus are particularly aware of their allegiance, *varna* and *jati,* and, to a lesser extent, of their *asrama* or life-stage... In theory, the four stages of life, though not obligatory, provide guidelines on the duties and obligations of individuals according to their age. Both here and in India, it is the stage of the *grhastha* or householder that is of most importance to ordinary people... It is at this stage rather than at the ascetic stages ... that the social and religious obligations to deities and ancestors come into operation. These include temple worship, the enactment of life-cycle rites for family members,

---

[22] Weightman 1984:65; Brockington 1981:56 ff., Zaehner 1966:92 ff.

[23] Nesbitt 1991.

domestic religion, pilgrimage,[and] familial responsibilities.....[24]

Even though the system has altered because the old occupation-based hierarchies and interdependencies no longer exist, the affiliations are still powerful, which, together with sectarianism and regionalism, have prevented what Clarke, Peach and Vertovec call 'cultural homogenisation'.[25] It is these social ties which provide the "social meaning ... for organizations to develop, traditions to be transmitted to new generations, and communal rituals to be continued".[26] The diversity of the community is reinforced by the migration history of the different groups and the extent of ties with the extended family in India and elsewhere.[27] Thus, while white non-Hindus may view all Hindus as belonging to one ethnic group, Gujaratis, Punjabis and Bengalis, who speak different languages, perceive themselves as being different from one another ethnically, as well as experiencing their cultures as discrete in many ways.

At the same time, many Hindus in Britain are likely to perceive their religion in ethnic terms precisely because they are grouped together as 'Hindu' in the wider context of a non-Hindu society. The need to provide explanations and justification, Burghart suggests, has led to a perception that Hinduism transcends internal cultural divisions, and that "ordinary people, as bearers of their culture ... reliably know the beliefs and practices of Hinduism". In *An Introduction to the World's Oldest Religion*, Hinduism is defined in terms of the "Bhagavad Gītā, the message of Kṛṣṇa, non-violence, and vegetarianism... the hallmarks of urban, middle-class Hinduism".[28] Hinduism in Britain is thus seen as a universal as well as an ethnic religion. Knott argues that both are "legitimate forms of traditional Hinduism which have been given a particular impetus and form by the novel circumstance of their social, historical and geographical location".[29]

2.2.1. Settlement in Britain

Originating mainly from Gujarat and the Punjab, often via one or more generations in East Africa, Britain's Hindus have settled in all major British cities, often in large numbers, and have built temples or have adapted churches and other

---

[24] Knott 1986b:34, and also p.8.

[25] Clarke, Peach and Vertovec 1990:13, 21.

[26] Knott 1986b:158; cf. Barot 1980:11ff..

[27] Cf. Ballard 1994:219, 234.

[28] National Council of Hindu Temples,UK, cited in Burghart 1987:232, 247-8.

[29] Knott 1986b:9.

buildings for religious and community use.[30]

The earlier migrations to Britain after World War II were mainly from the Punjab and Gujarat to industrial areas where there was work, followed by relatives, peers and neighbours, and then their families in a process of chain migration. These were mostly agriculturalists, with some craftsmen and Brahmins from rural areas or small towns, forming 'village-kin groups'.[31] They lived in clusters near people speaking the same language, helping one another and setting up Indian shops. They sent money back to India, and arranged marriages there, thus maintaining many connections with the Indian economy and with their communities there. Unlike Sikhs and Muslims, Hindus did not initially build or adapt buildings for temples. This was partly because religious activity was regarded as a domestic matter, but also because temple rituals were forbidden outside India, and even in the 1960s, temple worship was declining among educated Hindus.

With the new immigration of Indians from East Africa in the late 1960s the pattern changed. These 'twice migrants' were the descendants of indentured labourers, tradesmen, businessmen and craftsmen who had gone to Africa from the 19th century onwards.[32]. Others came from Fiji, Mauritius and the West Indies, but in smaller numbers, with less close social and cultural ties with India than those who came from East Africa.[33] The Commonwealth Immigrants Act of 1962, which restricted entry for Commonwealth citizens for the first time, led to an influx before it came into force; the Commonwealth Immigrants Act of 1968 introduced further restrictions against East African Asians. The policy of Africanisation taking place in East Africa from 1965 onwards, followed by Idi Amin's expulsion of Asians in 1972, led to a big influx of South Asian refugees, mainly Hindus, into Britain.[34] There are currently about 760,000 Indians in Britain, 35% of whom were born in this country. Of this total about half are now Hindus and half are Sikhs.[35] About 70% of the Hindu population is ethnically Gujarati, 15% Punjabi and the remainder are mainly from Uttar Pradesh, Bengal, South Indian provinces and Maharashtra.

---

[30] Desai 1963:3ff.; Barot 1980:59ff.; Knott 1986b:10ff.; Burghart 1987a:1ff.; Clarke, Peach and Vertovec 1990:167ff.; Nye 1992a, 1992b; Vertovec 1992.

[31] Desai 1967:15.

[32] Bhachu 1986; Barot 1980, 1987; Michaelson 1983, 1987; Nye, 1995:46ff..

[33] Barot 1980:9; Clarke, Peach and Vertovec 1990; Clarke *et al.* 1990.

[34] Burghart 1987:9; 1986:9ff.; Michaelson 1983:10ff.; Barot 1980:65ff..

[35] Robinson 1990:274; Clarke, Peach and Vertovec 1990:19; Peach *et al.* 1988:592; Knott 1991; Vertovec 1992a:10.

Most of the Gujaratis have their roots in one of four regions of what is now called Gujarat; Jamnagar, Porbandar and Rajkot in Saurashtra or Kathiawar in the west, from which most of the Lohanas come; Vadodara and Ahmadabad in Gujarat proper; a cluster of villages around Bhuj, in Kachchh, from which many of the followers of the Swaminarayan sect originate; and the coastal area of Surat and Charottar. Each region has its own traditions and dialects. Dwyer notes that a number of *vaiśya* (mercantile) castes, who have achieved high status tend to be involved with Pushtimarga or Swaminarayan.[36]

The geographical closeness of East Africa to India meant that those who migrated there maintained very close links with India. Marriages were arranged in Gujarat, women went back to give birth and children were often sent to live with grandparents and were educated there. This led to religious conservatism and the maintenance of strong caste and linguistic bonds.[37] Many of the Punjabis come directly from the Punjab (Ludhiana and Jullundur), or from Delhi, although a number with Arya Samaj connections also came to Britain from East Africa in the early 1970s.

The tendency to settle in clusters has meant that the caste groupings in different British cities are quite varied. In Leeds one of the biggest Gujarati groups are Mochis or shoemakers (43%), most of whom came from Kenya. 30% are Kanbi and Leuva Patels, and 27% come from other groups such as the Brahmins, Lohanas and Suthars. In Coventry the predominant group are Suthars (carpenters), and in Leicester there are many Mochis, but also large numbers of Patels and Lohanas.[38] In Bradford, the largest group are Prajapatis, in addition to Mochis, Lohanas, Patidars and Kanbi Patels. Many of the latter, who were followers of Swaminarayan, settled in Bolton and Hendon. The bulk of the Lohana community settled in Greater London and Leicester.[39]

These and other groups began meeting in each other's homes to sing *bhajans* (devotional hymns) and pray, and various cultural associations were also formed. The first *maṇdir* (temple) was opened in Leicester in 1969, followed by many others. Knott suggests the lateness of this development was partly due to the size and economic strength of the communities, and the magnitude of the organisational task to set up a temple and import both priest and *mūrtis* (images).

---

36 Dwyer 1994:169; cf. Barot 1980:11, 62ff.; Michaelson 1987:33ff.; Vertovec 1992a:12.

37 Michaelson 1983:13ff.,120; Pocock 1976:345ff.; Burghart 1987:7ff..

38 Knott 1986b:40ff.; n.d.:6-7.

39 Barot 1980, 1986:73ff.; Michaelson 1983:34; Dwyer, 1994 in Ballard (ed), which contains a comprehensive series of articles on migration to Britain.

Many of these, such as the temples in Leeds and Edinburgh, were intended to attract Hindus from all regions and sectarian commitments; in other areas such as Bradford and Coventry, there were big enough groups to establish separate Gujarati and Punjabi temples. The development of temples as centres for community as well as religious activity, with regular Sunday services, is a feature of Hinduism in the diaspora. When they are organised for Hindus regardless of regional, or sectarian affiliation they both unite the disparate groups and define them as distinct from the majority white community. Members of Swaminarayan, on the other hand immigrated as an established sectarian group and now have their own temple in north London.[40] Arya Samaj and ISKCON also have centres in or near London.[41]

The focus of worship in a temple is on the *mūrtis* or images. In Westmouth, for example, the principal god is Kṛṣṇa, with his consort Rādhā; other *mūrtis* have been added and include Viṣṇu and Lakṣmī, Rāma and Sītā, Mātā, and Śiva in the form of a *liṅga*.[42] In sectarian temples the focus is on the deity of the tradition. In a Swaminarayan temple the central figure is Swaminarayan, with Rādhā and Kṛṣṇa on one side. In Sathya Sai Baba worship the focus is on photographs of Baba and Shirdi Sai Baba.

Knott identifies six elements of temple worship: *pranāma* (obeisance), *śuddhī* (purification), *prāthanā* (petition), *bhajana* (praise), *upacāra* (offering) and *prasāda* (sharing blessed food).[43] After the initial purification and obeisance, devotional songs (*bhajana*) are sung and offerings of food and other gifts are made to the deity. The *ārtī* hymn is sung, asking for deliverance from misery, for peace and for liberation. As this is sung a small tray with *ghī* lamps (*dīvas*) on it is rotated, purifying the deities, and at the close of the ritual it is taken around the body of worshippers for their purification and for personal offerings of money. The food that has been offered to the deity is shared among the worshippers as *prasāda* (blessed food).

Many Punjabis have been influenced by the Arya Samaj, even if they are not formally members. The worship of images was rejected by Swami Dayanand Saraswati, and the temple in Ealing has none, only the symbol, *Oṃ*. Arya Samaj

---

40 Barot 1980:70ff.; Knott 1986b:50ff., 60ff.

41 Burghart 1987; Carey 1987; Knott 1986b; 1987; Michaelson 1983; 1987.

42 *Liṅga*: a phallic symbol, in the form of a cylindrical pillar with rounded top, often set into a *yoni*,symbol of the female generative organs, representing the divine procreative energy of Śiva with Śakti, his dynamic energy. Cf. Flood 1996:150ff..

43 Knott 1986b:109ff..

influences the level of religiosity in the home of many Punjabis, as well as the life-cycle rites. Even if Arya Samaji pandits are not obtainable, Punjabi priests are preferable to those from other regions and traditions.[44]

Punjabis are more likely to form organisations such as a Punjabi Sabha for all castes, than to form distinct groups. They also observe different festivals, and the fact that many come from India exacerbates the differences with the larger East African groups. Some of the differences in attitudes between the two groups which were common in East Africa, seem also to be true in Britain.[45] Many Gujaratis, for example, do not consider Punjabis to be Hindus, especially if they are Arya Samajis. Where there have been temples established for all Hindus, there is the potential for some degree of conflict between them. However, there is also some syncretism, as is demonstrated by the Leeds temple, where both *ārtī* and *havan* are performed.[46] This is also evident in some Arya Samaji homes where there may be images or pictures of, for example, Kṛṣṇa or Sai Baba.

It is in the home that most religious activity takes place, particularly, as Knott found, in Gujarati homes. Most have a shrine, which can range from a room to a small purpose-built shrine in a bedroom or living room, or a shelf in the kitchen, the purest room in the house.[47] The women tend to keep the practice of *pūjā* (worship of the images) going, with regular offerings of food which is offered to the family as *prasāda*. Private prayer may include *jāpa*, the repetition of prayers and *mantras* while meditating on the deity or the guru. The home is also the locus of many life-cycle rituals, although the temple or some other public place is used for auspicious rituals such as marriage. Funeral rituals take place in the home prior to the cremation, as well as the tenth to twelfth day rituals, known as *ṣrāddha*, since these are associated with impurity and inauspiciousness.[48]

2.2.2. The community in Westmouth

In Westmouth there are approximately 2,000 Hindus, of whom approximately 60% are Gujaratis and 40 % Punjabis. A few others come from Uttar Pradesh, Bengal, Sind, and other areas. A small number come from Fiji, some of mixed Hindu-Sikh or mixed backgrounds. A few business and professional families

[44] Nye 1995:56ff..

[45] Nye 1993a:129, following Bharati 1967.

[46] Knott 1986b:116ff.; 1987:165ff..

[47] Knott 1986b:168ff..

[48] An exception in Westmouth was the *śrāddha* of an elderly Punjabi Brahmin woman which took place in one of the side rooms of the temple, but not in the sacred space of the main hall.

from India and East Africa had settled in the area before the big influx from Kenya and Uganda in the late 1960s and early 1970s. This small group, as well as some Sikhs, drew quite close and "treated any Asian family as a member of the community" (PBrM50).

A group of mainly Punjabi women, under the leadership of a devout elderly Punjabi Brahmin woman, used to gather regularly at each other's homes to sing *bhajans* (devotional songs). They also performed *havan*, using a Hindi and Sanskrit text compiled and written in Kenya by Arya Samajis. In 1970, when the Gujarati community was growing, the first *garba* (a Gujarati folk dance for the Navarātrī festival)[49] was held in the small hall of a Gurdwara, the Sikh place of worship. Members of both communities collected some money and decided to set up a formal organisation called 'The Vedic Society', to indicate a pan-Indian cultural association. Names and addresses of local Hindus were found in the telephone book, and a committee of Punjabis and Gujaratis was formed. They met in a school hall every Sunday afternoon, and began celebrating festivals and religious functions. There were disagreements and continual power struggles, which seemed to have some linguistic and regional basis, initially between a predominantly Punjabi group of men, and a group consisting of both Gujaratis and Punjabis. Later, the arrival of a Gujarati pandit led to the domination of a mainly Gujarati group; when he retired the Punjabis dominated once more. These differences were reflected in alternating committees, which seem to be symbolic of their respective sense of group identity.[50]

The committee leased a church hall in 1979 and set about raising funds to build a proper temple dedicated to Radhakrishna, which was formally opened in 1984 by Mathoor Krishnamurti, of the Bharatiya Vidya Bhavan. A Bihari pandit, who had been working in Southall, was appointed in 1985, but many members complained that he did not observe the rules of purity strictly enough, for instance by smoking on the temple steps, and he left before the end of his contract because of the mutual disagreements. In 1988 a Gujarati *śāstri* who had studied Sanskrit in India and worked in East Africa was appointed. Although well thought of among most of the Gujaratis, he was also criticised for not performing rituals properly, and for his approach to the non-Hindu community. On his retirement another pandit was appointed but resigned suddenly, it was said, at the instigation of the committee. Knott comments that "such complaints are an

[49] Nine nights in honour of manifestations of Śaktī; cf.Knott 1986:305.

[50] Cf. Knott 1986b:55-6.

integral part of Hindu culture, and accounts of contemporary Hinduism often mention priests who know little about the rituals, the Sanskrit language, and Vedic tradition or who are immoral and unreliable".[51]

Mūrtis of Mātā-ji, Viṣṇu, Rāma, Sītā and Lakṣmaṇ have now been installed in the temple, with the full *prāṇapratiṣṭhā* as well as a Śiva *lingam.*[52] When there was no pandit women bathed and dressed the images, and also led the *pūjā* and other rituals. Women have thus played a prominent role as bearers of the tradition both in the family and the temple, although only a very few have served on the committee in a public capacity. *Ārtī* is performed twice daily. However, since daily worship is normally conducted in the home in front of the private *maṇḍir*, these daily *pūjās* are sparsely attended. On Sundays there is a 'service' during the morning: the number of people attending and their ethnic background at any one time tends to reflect the committee currently in power. Such regular Sunday gatherings are an aspect of adaptation to life in Britain, partly because of the constraints of time, and partly because of a perceived need to create a cultural and religious identity.[53]

Many Gujaratis only take part in the life of the Vedic Society for festivals such as Navarātrī. The Lohanas, of whom there are now about 60 families, set up their own Lohana Mahajan. About eight of these families are Pushtimarga members. A couple of Patel and Brahmin families also belong to the sect. A number of the Leuva Patels, and more recently, Patidars, follow Swaminarayan. Several Jain families joined the Vedic Society and became very active, but avoided the *havan* in case insects might be killed. Other small groups have connections with the Hare Kṛṣṇa movement, with the Arya Samaj (all Punjabis), and a few are members of the nationalist Vishwa Hindu Parishad. There are two flourishing Sathya Sai Baba groups, with both Indian and white British members, and a vigorous Sai Baba class for children in the *maṇḍir* on Saturdays. The weekly *havan* in the temple has now become a Sai Baba *havan* "because it does not need a Brahmin to facilitate it". A number of families from the Darji (tailor) also hold their own functions but appear for the festivals, as well as a small number of Mochis (shoemakers) involved in the Indian shops.

---

[51] Knott 1986b:73.

[52] *Prāṇapratiṣṭhā*: a ritual calling life or breath into the image, which thus becomes the living god or goddess. The *lingam* (Skt *Linga*) is the symbol of generative power representing Śiva. It is usually displayed with the *yoni*, the female generative power; together they are "the supreme expression of creative energy" (Stutley and Stutley 1977:162-3, 351).

[53] Burghart 1987:236-7; Michaelson 1987:46 ff.; Knott 1987:161, 171.

2.2.3. The role of the pandits

During the years when the Hindu community in Westmouth had no pandit to perform life-cycle rites, a pandit would be imported from London or some other large city for auspicious occasions, but this was not so easy when it came to funerals. Weddings and the sacred thread ritual (*upanayana*), can be planned in advance, whereas funeral rituals have to take place as soon as possible. While the family priest (*purohita*) may perform aspects of the rituals, in some parts of India there are also specialist priests called *mahābrāhmaṇas,* whose function is to perform the death rituals up to the time of the cutting of the large *piṇḍa* (ball of rice) on the twelfth day (Ch. 5, 6). Parry describes the "apparently anomalous status" of the *mahābrāhmaṇa*s "as impure and highly inauspicious Brahmins, who by virtue of their work are identified with and are regarded as physical embodiments of the marginal and malevolent ghosts they serve".[54] The rituals are so inauspicious that in the Kathiawar region of Gujarat there is even a whose only function is to do the cutting, because this is symbolically cutting up the deceased.[55] Death rituals cause the priests to take on the sin of the deceased, since they receive the gifts on his behalf: they *become* the deceased. None of the pandits I interviewed had been specifically trained to perform funeral rituals or the impure *śrāddha* (post-mortem rituals), and only did so because of the need. Those willing to perform funeral rituals were uneasy about undertaking a task considered degrading, polluting and inauspicious. Their roles are changing; they now combine the roles of temple priest and family *purohita,* as well as developing, in some cases, a new pastoral role as parish priest.[56] Lay Brahmins also take on new roles. In Westmouth, if a pandit willing to conduct a funeral was not available when required, a senior member of the family or community might conduct a ritual, reciting *mantras* and reading from the *Bhagavad Gītā*. In some instances a senior Brahmin woman and early on, a local Sikh, also led some funerals in Westmouth. When the pandits were appointed they took on most of this work, although some of the local Punjabis still asked an Arya Samaji pandit to officiate.

According to Mathoor Krishnamurti, any initiated Brahmin can become a priest if he performs *sandhyā*, the regular prayer, and observes rules of purity, as long as he has faith *(śraddhā)*. The correct knowledge is also essential. The

---

54 Parry 1980:88, cf. 91ff.; Planalp 1956:617; Stevenson 1920:186; Raheja 1988:154.
55 Cf. Stevenson 1920:185.
56 Killingley 1991:3; cf. 6.2.1, 10.1.

priests have a big responsibility to ensure clients do the proper ritual so that the deceased goes to the proper place and gets *sadgati*, a good end:

> If a son is doing an incorrect ritual with all devotion, thinking it is a death ritual, the spirit, if it has knowledge, will suffer because it is not the right *mantra*. If I want to go to Oxford Circus you must not put me in a bus for Southall. If we don't perform the proper ceremonies what will happen to us? (personal communication)

In spite of differences in the pandits' backgrounds, training, experience and clientele, the *śrāddha* rituals I observed were very similar in broad detail. Even in India the rituals are being combined and condensed, with similar problems of time constraints and relatives arguing for tradition against the pandit's conviction of the correctness of his particular text.[57] Indeed, the texts themselves provide evidence of considerable variation in the rituals as well as exactly when to do them.[58]

The bereaved family may themselves be unsure what should be done, or have different views from the pandit, insisting on certain traditions which the pandit feels is incorrect. It is often the older women who argue how the ritual should be performed, as one Gujarati Kumhar explained; "I've a very bossy distant aunt in London who thinks she knows everything and there was a disagreement between her and the priest about what form the ritual should take" (GjKM32). This, of course, creates further tension for the priests between family customs, local traditions and the Great Tradition.

Menski reports similar situations regarding marriage rituals, and has also found that the older women and other senior family members are guardians of the tradition together with the priests. There are considerable variations in the marriage rituals because the pandits may choose to use or omit aspects of the rites, often according to the requirements of different groups, and by negotiation, so that there are no standard forms of rituals binding on all Hindus (6.2.1, 10.1).[59]

Some families only invite a pandit to facilitate the *śrāddha*. Many respondents felt the Brahmins were greedy and corrupt, or only interested in their prestige, so they preferred to send money to charities in Britain or India. For

57 Fuller 1984:135-161; cf. Nye 1992b:10ff.; Menski 1991:48-50.

58 Cf. Shastri 1963:63 ff.; Kane 1973 IV.

59 Menski, 1991.

this reason, or because a priest was not obtainable, the *śrāddha* was sometimes performed in India by a surrogate on behalf of the family (6.2).

The difficulties which Hindus in many parts of Britain experience with regard to funerals have led some communities to produce an order of service, and in 1987 the National Council of Hindu Temples (NCHT) published a standardised one in English, Gujarati, and Hindi with Sanskrit, which can be used without a pandit present (see Appendix).[60] The pandits interviewed for this study were very critical of this compilation on the grounds that it does not contain enough of the proper rituals for the release of the soul, but recognised its usefulness when a 'learned Brahmin' was not available.

Because the pandits, from whatever region, have to negotiate with clients from all parts of India, each with their own local traditions and individual circumstances, there are interesting possibilities for the development of ritual traditions unique to Britain, as the NCHT document indicates. It will be interesting to see how far these are localised, depending on learned (or strong-minded) leaders and pandits, or universalised. Regional and sectarian affiliations are still strong enough to divide communities, but as the Leeds example shows, and as many Westmouth Hindus hope, there are possibilities for co-operation and syncretism. The growing popularity of Sathya Sai Baba among both Gujaratis and Punjabis in Westmouth indicates one way in which different communities are coming together.

60 Firth, 1994: 524ff..

Chapter 3
Beliefs about Death and the Afterlife

Beliefs about life after death and the nature of the soul have a profound influence on how life is lived, particularly when they are rooted, as in Hinduism, in moral perspectives such as *karma* and *dharma*. The whole of daily life, the structures such as the *āśramas,* and spiritual and religious practices are conducted with this in view. Death is not the end of life, it is a process of transition leading to another life in which there is still contact with the living. The living, in turn, lead their lives in a continuous relationship with the unseen world of the ancestors and gods, however conceived. This chapter examines Hindu beliefs and concepts about what happens to the individual after death in terms of *who* he is, what becomes of him after death, and the means for attaining his goal. The first part of this chapter briefly reviews the sources of the multiple layers of concepts and ideas about death, heaven and hell, the soul (*ātman*), *karma* and rebirth, and then explores these beliefs in Britain, with reference to Indian ethnography and my own fieldwork in India when they throw light on the beliefs of British Hindus.

For most Hindus death is seen as a transition to another life, whether rebirth, hell or heaven, or liberation (*mokṣa, mukti*) from the cycle of rebirth (*saṃsāra*). For followers of *bhakti* (devotional) sects, this is understood in terms of existence in heaven with God, usually Viṣṇu or Kṛṣṇa.[1] For followers of *jñāna mārga* (the way of knowledge), this is understood in terms of absorption into Brahman, in which there is no longer duality. *Karma mārga*, the correct performance of actions, particularly ritual actions, in accordance with one's *dharma* leads to the acquisition of merit (*puṇya*), which guarantees a good rebirth (2.1).

Those who are not liberated are reborn again and again into for a high caste woman a better or worse position, depending on their *karma*. One may be reborn as a human with physical, mental or social advantages or disadvantages. For the sinful, rebirth may be as an animal or lower life form. The concept of *karma*, discussed below, explains the future consequences of behaviour and current

---

[1] When referring to a particular divinity as one among many, the term 'god' is used. 'God' refers to the being thought of and worshiped in the Western theistic sense as one supreme lord, who may be manifested in one form or another, and known as Bhagvān, Parameśvar, Paramātma, or Nārāyaṇa. Followers of Viṣṇu believe he appeared nine or more times as an *avatar*, the most famous and popular being Rāma and Kṛṣṇa. Other devotees worship Śiva, or the mother goddess in a particular form, such as Durga or Kālī. Many also worship several of these, as well as Ganeśa and Hanumān but recognise them as manifestations of the One, Bhagvān, Ātma, Paramātma, or Brahman. The soul within is the *ātman* (Hindi: *ātma*), sometimes identified with Ātman/Brahman.

misfortune - why, for example, one is poor, handicapped or a woman, or has a good or bad death.[2]

Such beliefs exist side by side with ancient concepts such as the notion that the ancestors exist in heaven and need constant nourishment. Although modern funeral rites owe more to later texts, many Hindus claim that their beliefs and practices are Vedic in origin, reinforced by the continuity in the basic structure of the ancestral rituals throughout India and throughout history. Knipe observes:

> This conformity across vedic, epic, puranic, and agamic periods,[3] and on into modern practice, is remarkable considering that the answer to the question, "Where does a Hindu go when he dies?" had varied considerably within each of these periods.[4]

Just as religious and cultural concepts have been transmitted through literature and tradition from earlier times, so too have ritual elements, not so much contained in whole texts as chunks of them, broken into pieces which then become reassembled in a new environment. Hindu beliefs about death today are thus a complex amalgam of old and new influences.

3.1 Historical perspectives

Hindu beliefs about life after death are derived from a number of important textual sources. Ritual parts of the Vedas, the most ancient, are still used in the death rituals; others, such as the Upaniṣads and the *Bhagavad Gītā* (BG), have had a profound influence on Hindu philosophy and devotion. One stream of concepts underlying rites of disposal and reincorporation has its origins in the funeral hymns in the tenth *maṇḍala* of the *Ṛgveda*, where the deceased is offered as a sacrifice to Agni (fire), and sent to heaven (*svarga*), ruled over by Yama, the first mortal to die.[5] *Svarga,* also called *pitṛ loka,* the abode of the ancestors, is

---

[2] Sharma 1978a:334; Kane 1953 V:1530ff..

[3] Knipe refers to various literary periods from the Vedas, the most sacred texts (approx. 1,500 to 500 BC), the *Mahābhārata* and *Rāmāyana*, the Purāṇas and the Āgamas, non-Vedic textS. Cf. Basham 1967:51ff., 59ff.; Flood 1996:21-22, 35ff., 103-113.

[4] Knipe 1977:111; cf. also Killingley 1985; 1991.

[5] There was no hell at this stage, apart from reference to a deep dark fiery hole into which the Aryans wished to send their enemies (O'Flaherty 1981:292; ṚV. VII.104, 1-3, 57. AV X.3.9) and the House of Clay from which Varuṇa is besought to save the worshipper (Ṛv VIII.89; X.18; X.152.4; IX.73.8; cf, Basham 1967:239). The name *naraka-loka*, which later refers to the many hells of classical Hinduism, appears first in the AV as the place where those who have injured Brahmins sit in a pool of blood chewing hair (AV II.14.8; cf. VS XXX.5; Winternitz 1927:125ff.).

where the ancestors and sages dwell, although they are also said to dwell in the three regions, earth, mid-space and sky according to their merit and when they died. As Knipe has shown, these concepts are firmly embedded in the contemporary *sapiṇḍīkaraṇa* rite on the twelfth day, where the father, grandfather and great-grandfather are called from their various locations so that the soul (*preta/ātman*), which has had a new body ritually created for it, can be incorporated into their society, after which each of them moves upwards into a new space with the other ancestors (*pitṛs*).[6] The ancestral concern for the welfare of their descendants in return for nourishment, is also reflected both in the daily ritual (*tarpaṇa*), which many Hindus, particularly Brahmins, still offer, and in the *śrāddha* rituals. The *Garuḍa Purāṇa* elaborates on this material, so that the soul on its year-long journey through various hells can only be released by the offerings of the living. Throughout this tradition there has been an emphasis on sacrifice and ritual action which gains rewards in heaven for the performer, but also on rituals on behalf of the deceased which have the power to improve or transform his status. The notion that ritual action affects the deceased is a fundamental aspect of contemporary death and post-mortem rituals, and some of these, at any rate, still depend upon the knowledge and sacred power inherent in the Brahmin priests to facilitate them.

A second stream of ideas flowering in the Upaniṣads, promotes spiritual knowledge as the determining factor in escaping the cycle of birth and death, *saṃsāra*, generated by *karma*, action, the moral law of cause and effect (2.1). It is *karma*, generated by desire, which determines the future existence of the individual.[7] Those whose minds are attached to action and to material objects and senses are doomed to return to the world of action. They take on a new body, just as a goldsmith creates a new form, or:

> As a caterpillar, when it has come to the end of a blade of grass, in taking the next step draws itself together towards it, just so this soul in taking the next step strikes down this body, dispels its ignorance, and draws itself together [for making the transition].[8]

The individual whose conduct is pleasant may enter the womb of a *brāhmaṇa, kṣatriya or vaiśya*, but those whose conduct is bad enter the womb

---

6 Knipe 1977.
7 Bṛ.Up. 3.2.13; 4.4.5-6.
8 Bṛ Up. 4.4.3.

of a dog, pig or outcaste, or take form as a worm or moth, fish, snake, or tiger or even a stationary thing.[9] Only he who pursues knowledge (*vidya*), austerity (*tapas*) and meditates on Brahman does not have *karma* adhering to him.[10]

The predominant view in the Upaniṣads is that the eternal soul (*ātman*) is identified with *Ātman* or *Paramātman,* the ultimate reality known as Brahman[11] and ultimate liberation, *mokṣa*, is union with, or absorption into Brahman in pure mystical awareness or knowledge, *jñāna*. Ritual action and sacrifice, on the other hand, lead to rebirth, albeit a good one.[12]

To this was added, in some Upaniṣads and in the *Bhagavad Gītā*, the concept of a personal deity. Devotion (*bhakti*), knowledge and *karma*, here interpreted as selfless action, all blend together as the path to liberation, understood as union with the divine rather than absorption. The *Bhagavad Gītā*, or 'Song of the Lord', is a devotional poem incorporated into the great epic, the *Mahābhārata*. It is probably the most loved and influential of all sacred Hindu texts. It is important in the context of the present study, not only because it is frequently read during various stages of the death rituals, but also because it has influenced beliefs about *karma*, death, and dying, and the nature of God and the *ātman*. It develops concepts from the Upaniṣads, such as the doctrine of *karma*, which is not just linked to action, but to motivation, stressing action without thought for its fruits. Human beings possess an indestructible soul which can neither slay nor be slain, but which is reborn in a new body: "Just as a person casts off worn-out garments and puts on others that are new, even so does the embodied soul cast off worn-out bodies and take on others that are new."[13]

Although the soul is eternal, it can be assisted on its way by focussing on God (Kṛṣṇa), at the point of death.[14] Following the Upaniṣads, the BG describes two ways in which the soul departs. There is the *uttarāyaṇa* (the northern path), the way of "fire, light, day, the bright half of the month, the six months of the northern path of the sun" by which the true *yogins*, those with knowledge of the Absolute reach the Absolute.[15]

The second way, *dakṣiṇāyana* (the southern path), is the way of darkness and

---

[9] Ch.Up. 5.10.7; Kauṣ.Up. 1.2; Kat.Up. 5.7; Bṛ Up. 4.4.5; cf. Ch.Up. 5, 3-10.
[10] Mun.Up. 2.2.8; Īśa Up.
[11] Bṛ.Up. 4.4.22; Ch.Up.6.9-16.
[12] Ch.Up. 5.10.3-6; Bṛ.Up. 6.2.16; Puligandla 1975:211ff..
[13] BG 2.22-24.
[14] BG 2.8-11, 8.5-6.
[15] BG 8.24; cf. Killingley 1997, pp.8-9

night, "the dark half of the month, the six months of the southern path of the sun".[16] These are dependent upon the spiritual state of the dying person but also reflect a concern for death at the right astrological time (cf. 4.1, 4.2, 5.3).

The *Garuḍa Purāṇa* (GP) is very important in this study, particularly the section known as the *preta-kalpa*. Evison observes: "With the exception of a few Brahmanical communities which still use the Vedic rites, the majority of Hindus claim that their funeral ceremonies are based on the *Garuḍa Purāṇa*."[17] The safe passage of the deceased is ensured by gifts before death, and in particular, the gift of the Vaitaraṇī cow which will take him across the river of death, the Vaitaraṇī Nadī.[18] The *ātman* "may escape through any of the nine apertures" of the body, the lower ones indicating that the person was a sinner, while the good person departs from the eyes, nose, mouth or from the top of the head (3.2.1; 4.1-2).[19] The soul, "as big as a thumb, is carried away by Yama's messengers".[20] As an inversion of the process of the dispersal of the physical body into the elements, *pañca-mahābhūta*, the microcosm absorbed into the macrocosm, the naked *preta* has to have a new ethereal body ritually *recreated* with food and water over a symbolic year, the time it takes the soul to reach its destination. The new body is formed by ten offerings of *piṇḍas* over a period of ten days "just as the foetus does in the ten months in the womb",[21] followed by further offerings on the eleventh day to strengthen it. Without these the *preta* remains a disembodied ghost, which "will have to wander in the ether without food, agitated by hunger".[22] In its new form the *preta* now has to journey for twelve months through a series of hells on its way to Yama's kingdom in the southwest before it can join the ancestors in *pitṛ-loka* in the final ritual, *sapiṇḍīkaraṇa*. This usually take place after a symbolic year, on the twelfth day, but can also be performed after twelve months real time (Ch.6).

Yama is no longer the benevolent king of heaven, but the terrifying king of the dead, Dharma Rājā, although he is "sweet to the virtuous". Citragupta, the

---

[16] BG 8.23-2. The dark half means the period from the full moon to the new moon, the bright half from the new moon to the full moon. The "northern path of the sun" is from the winter solstice to the summer solstice, the "southern path" is *vice versa* (Killingley, 1992, and personal communication). Cf. Bṛ Up. VI.2.1; Kauṣ.Up. I.2.

[17] Evison 1989:195.

[18] GP II 47:25-36; Ch. 4 below.

[19] GP I 11:9-11; II 31:27; Evison 1989: 209.

[20] GP II 2:44-45.

[21] GP II 34:44.

[22] GP II 34:34.

scribe, records all good and bad deeds.[24] Both heaven and hell are temporary abodes where an individual "reaps the fruits of his activities", and the wicked man undergoes the most frightful tortures according to his deeds.[25] The soul can only achieve release through offerings by the sons of the deceased to the ritual priests. Its fate is thus dependent upon others and not simply on its own *karma*, as is evident in the *śrāddha* rituals (Ch. 10-13). Death is a prolonged *process* requiring complex rituals and gifts to Brahmins to assist the departed on their journey; if they fail the they remain troublesome ghosts.

However, ideas about rebirth and liberation in the Upaniṣads, including the concept of an indestructible soul which cannot be destroyed when the body is burned, raise questions as to the purpose of death rituals, and even more, the post mortem rites for the progress of the *ātman*. Why, if the fate of the soul is determined by a person's *karma* and thoughts at the point of death, do the relatives have to make such efforts to ensure he moves on, and believe that their failure to do so can mean that the ghost (*bhūta-preta*) will harass them? The fact that these rituals fulfil the sacred debts (*ṛṇa)* to the parents and ancestors, and give the chief mourner merit (*puṇya*), does not account for this concern (2.1. f.n.6). The doctrines of transmigration and absorption into or union with Brahman also seem inconsistent with the earlier beliefs about heaven and the ancestors, or later ones about Yama's kingdom and hell, or with beliefs about the ritual formation of new bodies for the deceased. If transmigration is assured, Knipe asks, why is it assumed that the ancestors exist in another world, and why, in view of the laws of *karma,* do they need to depend on their descendants' ritual activities? "The doctrines of transmigration and liberation transformed the whole of ancient Indian speculation and practice, but the rites accorded the ancestors ... appear to endure beside the newer sentiments of saṃsāra and mokṣa."[26]

Kane also notes the problem of reconciling belief in reincarnation and *karma* with a belief that ancestors can be gratified with balls of rice. Whereas the doctrine of reincarnation states that the soul leaves one body and enters another, "The doctrine of offering balls of rice to three ancestors requires that the spirits of the three ancestors even after the lapse of 50 or 100 years are still capable of enjoying in an ethereal body the flavour or essence of the rice balls wafted by the wind." Furthermore, if there is immediate rebirth, how can food and drink be

[24] GP II 33:22-32.

[25] GP II 32:82, II 3, II 33:15.

[26] Knipe 1977:112.

transformed into substances for the use of ancestors at a distance?[27]

O'Flaherty notes another area of tension exists between "the desire to prevent rebirth and the desire to assure rebirth".[28] Sons are essential to perform the *śrāddha*, to ensure that the deceased will receive a new body for his next life. This is immortality "below the navel", in other words, via biological procreation. But in order to attain the other kind of immortality "above the navel", one should have no son, since "desire for sons is the desire for wealth and the desire for wealth is the desire for worlds", which prevents the ultimate liberation. This contrast reflects a tension between world rejection and asceticism on the one hand, and *varṇāśrmadharma* on the other. Since the severe asceticism which the way of knowledge demanded was a potential threat to the survival of society, the path became institutionalised within the framework of the four *āśramas*, encouraging withdrawal in old age after fulfilling the three aims of religious merit, wealth and pleasure and guaranteeing the production of progeny for posterity before renouncing the world. Individuals can also choose this path early in life as an alternative to the life of the *gṛhastha* (householder).

Contemporary *śrāddha* rites reflect both Vedic and Purāṇic attitudes to the body and the ancestors. The rites are performed *as if* the *preta* is going to join the ancestors, yet as we shall see, in practice Hindus usually talk *as if* the deceased is in heaven with God, liberated or reborn or, in a few accounts, in hell. Madan notes the considerable ambiguity about where the soul is:

> It would seem that in some symbolic sense, as an 'image' (*ākarā*), the *pit* remains in the 'land' of the manes [ancestors] but is at the same time reincarnated here on earth. Thus in the relationship between the living and the dead, the notions of the pitṛ (ancestor) and punarjanma (rebirth) negate the notion of death as a terminal event.[29]

3.2. Contemporary concepts of life after death

Contemporary accounts of beliefs about the nature of the soul and life after death reflect the scriptural traditions. While most informants in Westmouth were

---

[27] Kane 1973 IV:335. Parry also sees an inconsistency between the theory of the three cosmic layers of father, grandfather, and great-grandfather, each of whom is "steadily progressing towards a more etherealized state of being",... and the belief that "having thus expiated his sins or exhausted his merit, he is reincarnated on earth" (Parry 1989:509-510). It is interesting to note that Guru Nanak, the first of the Sikh Gurus, criticised the practice of making offerings to the ancestors, according to the Janam Sakhis. See Cole and Sambhi 1978:12.

[28] O'Flaherty 1980:4.

[29] Madan 1987:137.

familiar with the BG and many read publications from, for example, ISKCON or the Swaminarayan Mission, it was mainly older people, particularly women, who were familiar with the mythology of the GP. This is still read after a death, although many people expressed a preference for the BG, or in the case of Arya Samajis, a compilation called *Amṛta Varṣa* (8.3). However, as Part II shows, the changes which have taken place in Britain mean that there are fewer possibilities for traditional ritual practices, and thus for absorbing the knowledge which goes with them. Familiarity with English concepts and terminology means that terms like 'God' and 'heaven' are used in similar ways even though 'God' may have a variety of meanings, such as Brahman, Kṛṣṇa, Śiva, or *Mātā-jī* 'Heaven' can mean either the place in which one dwells with God, or a pleasant temporary resting place before taking rebirth. While the younger generation may be less familiar with myths about the journey of the soul, there is still obvious concern with what happens after death, the after-life, rebirth, and in particular about *karma* and explanations for suffering.

3.2.1. Departure of the *ātman*

There is some debate among Indian pandits as to when the *ātman* leaves the body. The obvious explanation is when the breath ceases, but according to some of Parry's Brahman informants in Varanasi it occurs at the moment when the skull is broken (*kapāla kriyā*) by the chief mourner, during the cremation of the body (5.3)[30]. My own learned informants took the view that the *ātman* departed from one of the nine apertures of the body when the breath ceased (4.4). What remains are ten "*śvāsas*, (*vāyus*, *prāṇas*, airs), which remain in the uppermost region of the head", which have to be released to enter the five elements, *pañca-mahābhūta* or *pañca-tattva-ghāta,* "from where they originate".[31] One of these, the *dhanañjaya prāṇa* or *vāyu,* remains in the skull and will create a ghost unless released by the ritual of *kapāla kriyā* at the cremation. Thus, although the *dhanañjaya prāṇa* is not identified with the *ātman*, the connection between them is sufficiently close for the release of the former to be a precondition for the separation of the *ātman* from the body so that it "knows it is dead" (HPBrM45). Another pandit, citing Lord Sivananda, thought that one could only assume the soul had left when decay started, and therefore it was a mistake to hasten the cremation. He knew of two cases in which people had recovered a day or so

[30] Parry 1982:79-80; cf. 5.3. below.

[31] GjPt65; cf. Padfield 1908: 200.

after being thought dead, so "maybe it doesn't leave it at once".

Most Westmouth Hindus believed that the soul departed when the breath stopped. However, several informants from UP and the Punjab, where there is a tradition of breaking a pot at the entrance of the cremation ground or at the pyre, thought the soul left when the pot was broken, and the sound enabled it to leave: "To put the body on the fire before that would be cruel" (UPKhM40; 5.2, 5.3).

The *ātman* was described in various ways. It is the life force, or energy, which has an upward rising tendency. It is trapped in the cerebrum, and has to be released by another form of energy, the heat of the pyre. That which survives death is the *jīvātman,* which can be distinguished from, and is a reflection of, the *Ātman* or *Paramātman* (MahBrM65; cf. f.n.1, above). A Gujarati pandit, referring to Bṛ.Up.5.5.1, said:

> It merges into it as like merges into like, absorbed into ultimate reality... Some part goes, some part remains, and some part is in *pitṛ-loka.* I don't understand this but pray about it and am comforted by it. At death we discard the body, including the *prān tattva*, which returns to the five elements, earth, air, fire, space, and water. In the *Gītā* Lord Kṛṣṇa says, "I myself bear all beings, my soul is there, just a reflection of it as *jivātman.*"

A doctor described the newly released *ātman* as a minute subtle body, the *sūkṣma-deha*, remaining when all the physical life is extinguished: "Your soul is liberated from the material body when you stop breathing, but you are still engulfed with your desires, *vāsanas,* and your thoughts. It takes birth according to your desires and greed" (MbrM55). It retained character or qualities, *guṇas*,[32] which survived, carried into the reborn existence, until the *ātman* ultimately merged into Brahman, when the character attached to it dissolved (PjKhM45).

Once the *ātman* has separated from the body it may be reborn immediately, or some time after a sojourn in hell or heaven, or attain *mokṣa*. One informant thought the soul travelled to the sun, which is cool, not hot, and colonised by *devas* and *devatas*, where they would see the thrones of Brahma and Viṣṇu and go to Viṣṇu's feet. Another thought it would go to another planet (PjBrF42). In line with the GP, many people believe the soul goes straight to Yama to ensure that the right person has been taken, and then returns to the house until the

[32] *Guṇas*: Three qualities or constituents forming the basis of matter or nature, *prakṛti*, in the Sāṃkhya philosophy; *sattva*, lightness, purity, subtlety; *rajas,* the principle of activity, motion and energy; and *tamas,* darkness, heaviness, dullness. In man the particular balance of these qualities influences the personality ; cf. Puligandla 1975: 116-117; Mines 1989:112ff.

eleventh day rituals prepare it to return to Yama for judgement. Indian ethnographic accounts of the journey of the soul follow closely the GP's description of the journey of the *ātman* through the series of terrible hells on the way to the kingdom of Yama, "the terrible Dharma Rājā". He is accompanied by the two dogs of Yama,[33] across the horrible Vaitaraṇī Nadī (river), holding onto the tail of the Vaitaraṇī cow, which, offered before or at death, takes the soul of the deceased across.[34] Usually Yama himself, or his servants, the Yamdūts, come to fetch those who have done bad things. They can make mistakes, and can be bargained with (4.4.1). Yama Rājā is not always seen as terrifying:

> Yama Rājā, the King, is very pleasant, dressed like Indra. Death is royal, and sends a divine vehicle for you. This is very consoling. Yama Rājā is very comforting. When people know they are going to die, they know they will sit in a nice vehicle, and will drop this body. This *vimān* [vehicle] will only go to good people and take them to *svarga*. This depends on how much *puṇya* [merit] you have earned, on how long you stay in *svarga*. (GjVF55)

Those who have been good are fetched personally by God. A Pushtimargi used similar images: "Lord Viṣṇu sends *puṣpaka vimāna*, an aeroplane, a royal vehicle and right royally takes you".[35] A Patel informant's grandfather, as he was dying, said, "Rāma Sītā, and Lakṣmaṇa have come to take me in a chariot."

Yama-loka is only a temporary stage. As in the GP, Citragupta acts as Yama's 'prime minister' or recorder.[36] One informant said that Citra and Gupta were two beings who sat on a person's left and right shoulders, recording good and evil deeds respectively. An evil doer can be cast into any of twenty-eight hells which have a purgatorial function, after which he is reborn according to his *karma*. A good person is sent to *svarga*, heaven until he is ready for rebirth, and if he has done both good and bad deeds, he will experience time in each location.

3.2.2. The ghost in the liminal period

During this period of ten days the soul is believed to remain around the house as a ghost (*bhūta-preta*), suffering the most terrible heat and thirst, which has to be

---

[33] Cf. RV X.14.10-12; X.180.

[34] Stevenson 1920:193ff.; Quayle 1980:20ff..

[35] *Puṣpaka vimāna* is also the chariot of Rāvana, the demon king of Lanka, captured by Rāma and used to transport himself and Sītā back to Ayodhya after Rāvana was killed (Monier-Williams 1899:640). *'Vimāna'*, the chariot of the gods, also means 'aeroplane' in modern Indian languages, which affects the way informants visualise it (Killingley, personal communication).

[36] Stevenson 1920:194; GP I 33:24-30.

quenched by daily offerings of water and milk (Ch.6). He also feels "cold, agony and weeps and talks, but although he can see everything, no-one can see him" (KanPt). He haunts the family, and is distressed if they are not performing the right rituals, or fulfilling his last wishes, and may curse them: "If a young man dies, his soul and the wanting of his wife and the wanting of his children, and his own wishes, or the things he wanted to achieve means the soul is bewildered and hangs around the family" (GjDM35). Because it is attachment to the family or material things of life which can hold the *ātman* back, it is particularly important to fulfil the wishes of the dying before they depart, and also the newly released *ātman's* demands. These might be manifested in dreams or through possession of a living person. This is particularly likely in the event of a sudden or unnatural death which prevents the *ātman* from going peacefully to heaven. A Gujarati woman described the death of her sister-in-law's nephew who had fallen into a well and died. On the twelfth day, he took possession of a female relative, and subsequently at a wedding she began shaking. The priest said, "What do you want?" and the *ātman* said in a deep voice, "I want to eat *śiro* (a sweet rice dish) - my big *phūī* (father's sister) must make it for me." The aunt made it and gave it to the relative, who was shaking with wild hair. She ate the *śiro* and drank a lot of water. Once the *ātman* was satisfied, there were no more problems (GjPF55).

Even when the rituals around death have been satisfactory, the deceased person may appear in dreams to indicate things he needs. A Darji woman used to dream of her father-in-law coming for dinner, which indicated that he required something, especially when the dream recurred on several nights. She would then prepare enough raw food-stuffs for two people, such as potatoes, butter, rice, oil, salt and sugar, and give it to a senior Brahmin woman. Sometimes she also gave a piece of cloth or a shirt, to ensure that the *ātman* was satisfied. Shortly after the death of Jaswant (7.1.2), a friend phoned his wife to say that she had dreamed that he had asked for blankets. Unknown to the friend he had actually asked for blankets in the hospital, so this was seen as an extraordinary coincidence, but also as an indication that he was unsatisfied and extra gifts, including blankets or money in lieu, should be given to the needy. A Punjabi Brahmin woman dreamed sometimes of her mother-in-law who had died recently. If she gave her daughter-in-law a gift in the dream this was considered to be a good omen; if she asked for something, this was considered to be a bad omen. Others dreamed of relatives who gave help and advice, and reported a comforting sense of presence (9.2.2.3). In one example a woman's father-in-law appeared in a dream while they were anxiously house hunting. He was carrying a boat on his head, which symbolised money from the bank, a sign that they would achieve their goal. Three days later they found the right house (PjSF40). One of Nesbitt's informants, when her mother died, was told by a neighbour that she had seen the soul going past as a *dīvā* (a *ghī* lamp). Subsequently she remained around her house for seven months as a pigeon sitting on the fence. Twice her deceased mother had saved her life. On one occasion she had been contemplating suicide after hearing insulting remarks about her husband, and her mother appeared and said that if she did so, she would be reborn seven times. On another occasion, she appeared in a dream telling her to wake up, and when she did so gas was found to be escaping from an unlit pilot light on the cooker downstairs (Nesbitt, personal communication).

The spirit of the deceased may indicate his needs in other ways, for example, if the *śrāddha* has been forgotten. In one instance, the small shrine (*mandir*) in the home of a Punjabi Brahmin couple was believed to have caught fire because the wife's guru had not been remembered on the *tithi,* the anniversary of his death.

Many informants said they did not really believe in ghosts or *bhūta-pretas*, but that this was what others believed. Nevertheless, it paid to remain on the safe side and observe the necessary precautions. An East African Darji said "We don't take risks; even if I don't believe it I have to follow the procedure. It doesn't mean it's not true. People say this because of accidents.". Another Darji revealed a similar attitude, but commented that if one ignored the rituals such as *śrāddha*, the rest of the community would assume that any ensuing troubles were due to this neglect. The fear of the ghost is so great that some relatives would not wish to sleep in the house in which someone had died (GjL45). However, an Arya Samaji woman rejected the concept of *bhūta pretas*, "because the priest, in the *havan*, says nothing harmful can come near if you keep your house like a temple. The *ātma* leaves at death, and only Sanatanis believe in *bhūt-prets*" (PKhF60). If souls were unsettled following a violent or unnatural death, the house could be made safe with incense and *ghī* lamps.

3.2.3. Heaven and *mokṣa*

As we have seen, according to the texts, the deceased may be reborn immediately, after a period in heaven or hell (or both), or attain *mokṣa (mukti)*, liberation or release from the cycle of birth and death, *saṃsāra.* The terms *mokṣa* and *mukti* are usually understood to mean final union with Brahman in which the individual personality is dissolved. However they are also used to mean being in heaven with God from which there is no rebirth.[37]

Most of my informants were devotees of one particular God (usually Kṛṣṇa), and belonged to a sect, such as Swaminarayan, so their concepts of heaven varied considerably according to their beliefs and affiliations. There are many heavens in popular mythology. *Akṣardhām* is the abode of the Supreme Person. Followers of Swaminarayan believe he is lord of *Akṣardhām* as Puruṣottam Bhagvan and that he manifested himself from there in the human form as Sahajanand.[38] In addition to Yama-*loka* and *Pitṛ-loka*, above, other worlds (*lokas*) are *Brahma-loka*, the world of Brahma; *Svar-loka*, Indra's abode; *Kailāsa*, Śiva's paradise; and *Go-loka* (cow world), Kṛṣṇa's heaven.[39] Vaikuṇṭha is Viṣṇu's abode or state of being. Outside the *śrāddha* rituals, '*Pitṛ-loka*' does not seem to have much importance, but is simply used as a convenient term to describe "wherever the *pitṛs* are".

A Swaminarayan follower, who had converted a lot of followers in Uganda, was said by Pramukh Swami to be resting in peace with God in Akṣardhām. A Punjabi woman believed her father, who had been a much respected community leader and loving father, was in heaven and "very happy, leading a nice luxurious life wherever he is, still loving and advising people". Her brother, who had drowned saving the life of a child, would also be somewhere in which he was held in high esteem (PjSF40). A Punjabi Brahmin thought heaven was a place above this earth, "somewhere with the Lord where there is no misery" (PjBrM40), whereas a Darji said he did not think it was "up there, although I haven't got the imagination as to where they have gone". However, he believed the final heaven was when "the *ātman* blends with God" (GjDM45). A Pushtimargi woman and a Gujarati pandit believed devotees went straight to Vaikuṇṭhadhām where they would see the divine beings:

> It is the best place to live because here there is perfect happiness, one has the company of Kṛṣṇa and Rādhā both aged eight - the best age. Also there are

---

[37] Bṛ.Up.II.1.5; Svet.Up.3.7; Stutley and Stutley 1977:193.

[38] Williams 1984:71.

[39] *Akṣara* is "the abode of the supreme person; an eternal state, thought to have an impersonal form as a state of being and a personal form as an abode of God" (Williams 1984:204). The term *loka* can mean heaven, as above, describe the three regions of earth, sky and midspace, or can be used to describe one of the three worlds to which one can aspire after death - the world of men, by means of a son; the world of the *pitṛs* by means of sacrifice, and the world of the gods by means of knowledge. Cf. Stutley and Stutley 1977:164, Monier-Williams 1899: 367, 906.

fires of diamonds. To reach Vrindāban or Vaikuṇṭhadhām is rare. (GjPlF50)

Suppose you have committed many sins and intuitively realise God is coming, you will go straight to Vaikuṇṭhadhām, where you will usually see Rādhā and Kṛṣṇa or Rāma and Sītā. In Vaikuṇṭhadhām a person, in rare instances, will be given the place of a *devata*. *Go-lokadhām* is the ultimate stage. It is the same as *mokṣa.* One is merged into Brahman but retains some difference. (GjB70)

The latter description reflects a (identity in difference)[40] perspective: one is part of God but not identical with Him, so that worship is possible. A pandit, who took an Advaitin perspective, distinguished between *moksa* and being with God. To be with God was to be in *svarga*

Where God is prime minister, his kingdom is very nice, where honey and milk flow and where I shall have a nice time and enjoy God. *Mokṣa*, on the other hand, is merging with Him. The Ganges flows, it merges in the ocean. Once you merge there you are gone, your identity is gone. That stage is not easy. As long as you worship God you consider that you and God are separate, *jivātma* and *Paramātma.* As long as there is an idea of He and me, it is always Viśiṣṭādvaita. There is a barrier between me and God because I have lust, anger and greed, so I have to defeat my weaknesses to merge in Him, and become *Paramātma.* (KanPt; 3.2.3)

The Swaminarayan tradition also follows Viśiṣṭādvaita, although in the following description there is loss of individuality:

The soul hasn't got any form. When you get to heaven all the souls are in the form of images of God himself, serving God; there's no "my father" or name or body, which are just related to the earth. If a particular soul has done something bad, or left something unfinished on earth, then God sends the soul back, to any of the life forms from bacterium to human body. There's a song that says the highest you can achieve is the human body and that's the

---

[40] Viśiṣṭādvaita Vedānta, modified non-dualism or identity-in-difference, was the school of Ramanuja (died 1137). Another school of Vedānta frequently referred to is Advaita, non-dualism, sometimes called monism, expounded by Sankara. They were both interpretations of the Upaniṣads; Ramanuja's teachings also reflected that of the BG. According to Ramanuja's philosophy, the created world is part of God's body, but allows the devotee to be sufficiently distant from God to make worship possible (Zaehner 1966:98-101, Puligandla 1975:191ff.). Sankara taught that ultimately everything was Brahman, and liberation was achieved when the individual recognised that the individual *ātman* and Brahman were the same thing.

time to pray to God and say you want to see Him. (GjPlM30)

The view that only in human form could one become liberated was reflected by a Darji woman who had been told that if she prayed and fasted during the month of Puruṣottam Mas she would achieve *mokṣa*, which would liberate her from going around and around 84 million times. *Mokṣa* was also attainable by calling Rāma or Kṛṣṇa at the point of death. Initially, *mokṣa* seemed to mean liberation from the round of birth and death, *saṃsāra*, in order to be with Puruṣottam or Kṛṣṇa. Later her daughter explained:

> She believes she would prefer *bhakti-yoga* to *mokṣa*, as she wants to be near God and do *bhakti*. She doesn't care for liberation. She doesn't know whether with *bhakti* she would come back but she would prefer that. She will have a body with *bhakti*. She is not going to ask for *mokṣa* or liberation.

This seemed to imply a distinction between *mokṣa* as liberation in terms of "having no body" and ultimate absorption, and being with God and serving him. She said at one stage in the interview that this would mean returning to earth for service, and at another that because one was serving God in heaven, one would not return (GjDF40). A Pushtimargi also rejected the concept of *mokṣa*. Salvation is found through the life of the householder, *gṛhastha*: "We don't believe in *mukti* (*mokṣa*). We want to be born in Gokul where He (the infant Kṛṣṇa) was born, and we believe He is still there and we can see Him. In Pushtimarg we want to come back, to give our God *seva* (service)." (GjLF35)

A Punjabi Brahmin woman said the spirit could either go to God or back into this world. If you died chanting the name of Rāma you would go directly to Vaikuṇṭhadhām: "*Rām, rām kahate marṇā, vaikuṇtha ko jānā.*" Her husband added, "You can achieve Him two different ways. You've got *bhakti mārga,* the way of devotion and the way of knowledge. For a householder *bhakti* is the easiest, as you don't have to leave your home to get to Him."

Attitudes to death are reflected in the euphemisms which are used. Examples are: *Svarga vas*, gone to heaven; *Bhagvān pāse gāya* (Gj), gone to God;*Dhām ma gāya* (Gj), gone to the divine abode; *Paramātma ke sath milna* (H), going to meet *Paramātma*, the great soul (Brahman). In ordinary discussions the assumption is made that the deceased have gone to heaven, *svarga*, are reborn or are liberated; there is no reference to them being in *pitṛ-loka* except during the annual *śrāddha*, the *pitṛ-pakṣa*. *Pitṛ-loka* was said to be wherever the *pitṛs* resided. A Brahmin woman distinguished between *pitṛ-loka* and *svarga:*

> *Svarga* is for demigods and *pitṛ-loka* is for other gods. They are not all in *Svarga* together, they are in different worlds. But we don't know what has happened because we can't go up there and look. It is written that when the God of Death is taking the soul away, if the deceased is sinful he is made to sleep on a bed of nails. When you go to *svarga*, the good things you have done determine how long you stay, and then when you finish you come back. In *pitṛ-loka* you don't come back. Most people don't ask for liberation, but ask to be reborn so that they can do *bhakti.* (GJBrF65)

Wherever the deceased have gone, according to a Punjabi Brahmin, there is still an attachment. He could not say where his own father was: "It's not for me to say he is reborn, to judge his merits, but we still remember him through doing *srāddh.*" Wherever the deceased happened to be, he would receive the gifts in the appropriate currency, earthly, heavenly or hellish currency (KanPt). The offering took whatever form was needed by the deceased, so that if he was a snake he received whatever the snake needed, and if he was a tiger he would receive whatever a tiger required. A Gujarati explained, "If you are suddenly very happy for no reason it is because someone from a previous life is doing something for you, and may be the reason why you win the pools" (GjKM30). According to a Darji couple, the offerings to the husband's parents enabled the deceased couple to have dinner together, wherever they were, implying that they were together in some post-mortem state - the only British Hindu informants to make such a suggestion. However the concept of *pitṛ* is understood, the newly deceased are still in a symbiotic relationship with the living, as the above descriptions indicate (cf.Ch. 6), and this is an important factor in the way in which Hindus approach their own deaths and cope with bereavement.

3.2.4. Hell

Hell, *naraka,* is both a place of punishment, the opposite of *svarga,* and misery on this earth. As a place of punishment, hell is temporary,

> Like having your driving licence suspended for a year, paying the penalty for your mistakes. I have to come back, getting the resultant life. The concept is that you are there in internment, detainment. Concepts such as dipping you in boiling oil or hot water are myths in all religions to create fear, but that is primary school education. Everything is temporary except *mokṣa.* (KanPt)

A Punjabi Khattri businessman used Western terms to describe his view of hell as a place where "souls who are absolutely demoralised go under Satan, they have no *mokṣa*, they are created like poltergeists". Hell, in more traditional terms, is ruled over by Yama, often identified with Dharma Rājā. No one would actually say that his father or mother had gone to hell, but would prefer to think of "an apartment with all comforts" (KanPt). Many informants saw hell in metaphorical terms, as a period of suffering and expiation in this life, rather than a post-mortem state, although it could also mean rebirth in "the lowest possible family" (GjLM65). It was also suffering through rebirth in an unsatisfactory life:

> Hell is in this world, not 'down there'. Everyday we see tragedies in front of our eyes, children without limbs, handicapped people, a sixteen year-old injured on a motorbike who becomes a mental patient for the rest of his life. If hell is not here for him, he can't have anything worse than that afterwards. (GjDjM36)

A lot of misfortune, including bad death, is explained by the *yuga*[41] theory involving the progressive deterioration of all standards. This age, the *kali-yuga*, is the age of suffering, where all mankind suffers (GjDF20; GjKF30).

3.2.5. Rebirth

Rebirth is commonly accepted, and along with the doctrine of *karma*, helps to explain the injustices of the world (9.5). The process was described by a pandit:

> The soul is very eager to be reborn, as it cannot remain too long as a vague, indefinite and unseen object. If it was, in life, a cheat or a murderer, it has no place to go and feels helpless. It enters man in food and water, where it is converted into semen, and then enters the womb. At the fifth month it becomes aware. (KanPt)

Rebirth is not always looked on with enthusiasm, and several informants said they would prefer to be with God instead of returning to this world, even in improved circumstances. For others the concept of rebirth is a comfort, and the image, from the BG, of the soul changing bodies in the way we change our clothes, is often used for consolation. It gives hope, so that death is less fearful

---

[41] There are four ages (*yugas*) of the universe, *kṛta* or *satya*, *tretā*, *dvāpara*, and the latest age, *kali*, descending in levels of moral corruption. The worst is the present age, the *kali-yuga*. At the end of each *kali-yuga* except the last, the world returns to the *kṛta-yuga*. The four *yugas* make a *mahāyuga*, and 1,000 *mahāyugas* make a *kalpa*. At the end of a *kalpa* the universe is destroyed and recreated in a cyclical pattern (Killingley, personal communication; Basham 1967:323; O'Flaherty 1975: 43; Stutley and Stutley 1977:351).

A young Darji woman was troubled about how to help a close friend whose father had died, but then read the BG which explained that "Life and death just come, you shouldn't grieve, but take it in your stride. It tells you the *ātma's* just going to transfer into another body, a fresher body. If I had read the BG I would have known what to say." A pandit commented: "Death is a blessing in itself. Unless there is death, unless there is winter, unless the leaves fall down, the new ones will not come. It is a cycle."

It is said that there are 8,400,000 lives (*caurāsī lakh yonī*) before one is reborn as a human being, and that those who are really sinful have to go right back to an amoeba state and evolve through all those millions of lives (PjBrM42: PjKhF40). Someone who commits suicide has to be reborn seven times. It is because the smallest creatures are souls who have been reborn that one should not harm them. Helpful animals may be born again as humans. Rāma is said to have told the victorious monkeys in the *Rāmāyaṇa* that in the *kali-yuga* they would be born as white people and rule the world (GjSM30). Pramukh Swami explained to some of his devotees that it was sometimes said that a bad person would return as a pig or a donkey, but that animals also had a right to live, and humans who ate them for meat were worse than the animals they were said to become. A Darji girl felt that when she looked into the eyes of dogs and animals: "I know we have the same soul, and I try to see the same thing in me as I see in them." One exception to respect for living creatures was a comment that intestinal worms were 'evils', which one could justifiably eradicate (PjBF42).

Rebirth is necessary to finish incomplete work. It was likened to starting a letter. When you go to bed you leave it unfinished, but when you get up you start where you left off. Some people are born with the letter nearly finished and ready to post. According to many accounts, one is reborn into the same family, or family group. It is sometimes said that this, rather genetics, explains physical and temperamental similarities. The roles of son and father might be reversed in the next life. A Gujarati Brahmin said that when Arjuna's son died, Arjuna was very upset. Kṛṣṇa told him he would show him his son but showed him a parrot. Arjuna was outraged and said, "How can this be my son?" The parrot said, "You were my dad only once, but I was your father several times." Stories were told of children who wanted to search for their partners or parents in a previous life, but these were all derived from books or television.

A spiritual awakening may be due to previous experience: "I went to an *āśram* in India and all the progress I had made in previous lives awakened and the answers began coming to me. I felt I was doing the right thing by doing *dīkṣā* [consecration, dedication]. I wanted to go to God" (GjKM30).

A child who has died may be reborn in another baby conceived soon afterwards, as might any other relative. A Punjabi Khattri father consoled his daughter when a much loved aunt died, by saying she was still alive somewhere, possibly reborn. The girl said, "I don't want her reborn as an animal, but as she is." He replied, "She will come back and you will find her some day."

There were many examples of dreams or signs that a person had been reborn in a particular family, or simply a belief that a pregnancy immediately following a death indicated the return of the deceased:

> When my brother died, my younger brother was in Fiji. We both wondered who could conceive in our family. When we found out his wife was pregnant he even picked the name of my brother. And a girl was born and they used the same name. I believe that my brother has taken rebirth, and she must have conceived immediately. The child was born prematurely under the same astrological sign. The child is very intelligent, very clever, very good, and in lots of ways she is so like him, I feel my brother has come into our own family. If she was a horrible child maybe I wouldn't think so! (PjBrF60)

Padma (9.3) had a dream about the father of another family, who had recently died. In the dream he said, "Don't worry, I'm coming soon, I'm here." Two days later his daughter-in-law gave birth to a baby boy, and Padma told them, "This is the soul of Papa-ji." Some informants, however, think it is unlikely that a girl would be born again as a boy, and have been distressed when a girl has not been conceived after one died (GjBrF26; PjBrF45; cf 9.3).

One of Nesbitt's informants made daily offerings to the photo of her deceased father-in-law, including gifts of 'food' in the form of raisins stuck to his mouth on his photograph. Nesbitt asked why she did this if she believed he was reborn, and she said it was partly to show respect, since she would feed him if he were alive, but also that he may have been reborn as her oldest son. She had become pregnant again after having two daughters and felt she could not cope, so she had arranged to have an abortion. Her father-in-law appeared and told her he would be taking birth in the child, so she did not terminate the pregnancy (personal communication).

Sudhir Kakar, the well-known psychiatrist, suggests that theories about where the soul goes - *pitṛ-loka*, heaven or rebirth - provide the Hindu with a choice. Rebirth is a way of getting rid of a person, because it deals with anger; the person gets his just deserts if he becomes a vulture or something like that. It would not be acceptable to think of a parent in hell. *Śrāddha* deals with guilt; it is very orthodox and allows a person to make restitution.[42] When talking about their own parents most of my informants assumed they were in heaven, either as a temporary sojourn or permanently. Aunts fared less well. Two families, in India and in Britain, described an unpleasant aunt being hauled off by Yama's servants, the Yamdūts, as a really bad death (4.2).

3.3. Attitudes to *karma* and suffering

Karma, as we have seen, is used to explain both good and bad fortune and why obviously evil and ignorant people appear to do well, while good people seem to suffer. Sharma's study of *karma* as it operates in a village setting shows that it is only one of three levels of explanation for suffering and misfortune. At the "ultimate karmic level" lies activity related to brahmanical rituals; at the intermediate level lies activity associated with the worship of gods, and the misfortune which occurs when they are offended; and at the third, mundane level, is interaction with other people, ghosts and spirits. *Karma* may be used as an explanation for present misfortune, but without any sense of culpability for offences which the sufferer cannot remember:

> Villagers do not show signs of deep anxiety or acute remorse over unknown offences committed in past lives. Such offences were theoretically committed by the same self incarnated in a different body, but in practice villagers seem to feel immediate responsibility only for offences committed in the present incarnation. Past incarnations are in theory the same self, but it is a rather remote kind of self, differently constituted.[43]

According to Sharma, both good and bad *karma* are transferable, although a wife can only be affected by her husband's *karma* and not vice versa. However, my own research indicates that the bad *karma* of a wife is thought of as transferable, since she may be blamed for the death of her husband (8.4-8.5).

Other explanations, Sharma suggests, such as the wrath of a deity or the malice of a relative indicate even less feeling of responsibility for the misfortune. She gives a timely warning to the researcher not to be too concerned about apparent discontinuities and inconsistencies, since these may not be a problem to the subjects. Such apparent inconsistencies appeared in my own fieldwork, the

---

[42] Sudhir Kakar, personal interview, 1986.

[43] Sharma 1978a:34

main one being the tension between a deterministic explanation of *karma,* in which bad fortune and especially bad deaths seem to be outside a person's control, and personal responsibility which is implicit in the concept of *karma*. It may be referred to in a deterministic way as *kismat*, fate. 'God's will' is also used sometimes in the same way as *karma* or fate, and at others as if God (usually Kṛṣṇa or Mātājī) is actually involved in events. The terms for God's will and fate are often, but not invariably, used interchangeably. Terms for God's will include: *Bhagvān kī marzī* (God's mercy); Bhagvān kī icchā (God's wish); *Bhagvān kī yahī icchā thī* (This was God's wish); *Īśvar kī kṛpā* (God's grace); *Yadī Īśvar ne chāhā to*... (If God wished, then....).

Terms for fate or luck include: *kismat, bhāgya, bhāgyavān, nasīb*. Bad luck includes *kismat hī kharāb thī, tagdir hī kharāb thī, bhagya hī kharāb thī* (It was bad luck indeed). If something happens such as a job loss, this is fate (i.e. bad *karma*). Yet "God is everything, he is fate and a provider. He gives life and air. He is fate, *kismat*, or *nasīb*" (PKhF17). One is not morally responsible for events which one cannot control: "If you can't get a pandit for a funeral, if you've tried and it's out of reach, then you can be satisfied that it's the will of God" (PjBrM45). God is also sometimes seen as being active, and as being forgiving. "Before you die people probably think of all the bad things they have done. People would probably ask for forgiveness from God for doing naughty things" (PSM32). Dharma Rājā (Yama) is regarded by some Hindus as a personification of *karma*.[44] Others regard this as unsophisticated: "To say 'don't do this or that because Dharma Rājā will punish you', is hypothetical. *Karma* is scientific: it is one basic theory which you can actually see and prove." (PBrM45)

A doctor was troubled by a friend's remark that "according to Hare Kṛṣṇas homosexuals would be reborn as rats", but he felt that from a professional point of view it was difficult to make such judgements. Was God saying it was wrong regardless of the circumstances? "People often do things as a result of other factors which aren't always their fault. In a Westernised society one has to be flexible and try to understand overall aspects of behaviour." (PjSM35)

Here two explanations are being used: the concept of a God who punishes wrong behaviour, and the automatic moral law of *karma*. For the doctor, his knowledge of psychology and of the influence of the environment on development made a straightforward explanation in terms of *karma* difficult, but also brought into question a view of a moral God.

---

[44] Cf. Sharma 1978a:27.

God uses people as instruments to help or take the life of another. If a drunken driver kills a pedestrian, this is be due to the *karma* of both parties. The driver is an instrument, a servant of God or a Yamdūt, a servant of Yama, yet at the same time has to expiate his own bad *karma*:

> God sends him this way because He doesn't want to kill me himself. He chooses someone to take the blame. The person who commits the offence is on a chain, and has to kill someone as an instrument of God because of the victim's own bad *karma.* (PjBrF42)

Her husband said that God also sent people to do good deeds on his behalf:

> If you say, "Please, God help me", you wouldn't see Lord Kṛṣṇa standing on the table and helping me. If I deserve the help, somebody like yourself will come along and help me out. We are all the instruments of God. This is the principle behind the saying, "love thy neighbour". Those who are the instruments carry responsibilities because of their previous *karmas*.

The concept of instrumentality contains a tension between the free choice of the actor, and being an agent or instrument, between free will and fate. The drunken driver was seen to be an instrument, yet he also had to make a choice to be that instrument (i.e., to drive). Here two people's *karmas* interact, yet the drunken driver is, in a sense forced to enact a deed which will give him even worse *karma* as a consequence of both his own and the other person's *karma*.

It may be difficult to regard one's own suffering or the suffering and bad death of a dearly loved parent or child, in terms of his or her bad *karma,* unless it is outside one's control. A Patel lecturer was distressed at being told by a fortune teller the cause, in a past life, of her present suffering. The reason she had been crippled by polio as a child was that she had been a Parsi lady in her former life, who had hurt her parents. This upset and alarmed her, but her mother said, "Don't worry, you didn't hurt *us.*" (GjPF35)

Many Hindus believe that *karma* can be altered by good and bad actions, especially by prayers, a changed life style, and the correct performance of rituals: "If you change your attitudes after 40 and become religious and give children sweets, your *karma* is washed out by God" (GjDM55). Chanting the name of God and thinking about Him at the point of death, and the post-mortem rituals, can also change one's *karma*. Such actions only affect minor *karmas* such as telling lies. An analogy was made of a blood-stained sheet, on which the smaller stains can be washed out, leaving a big one in the middle (GjKM30).

That *karma* is transferable is implicit in the formal and informal rituals after death, especially in the *śrāddha* (Ch.6). The offerings to the deceased benefit him both in kind, as when clothing and household goods are offered, and in an increased store of merit (*puṇya*), which the givers also receive. For some Hindus it is the gifts given on behalf of the deceased, rather than the rituals themselves, which are important. Merit is also obtained from helping others, especially when they are sick and dying, and according to a doctor, "this carries a lot of spiritual weight when you die yourself", although sometimes people boasted about all they did for the dying person.

Bad *karma,* as Sharma suggests above, can also be transferred, and other negative influences, particularly in the form of ill-wishing, are possible, either wittingly or unwittingly. An elderly Punjabi widow was taken ill at the time her granddaughter's marriage was arranged. She had never been happy about the arrangement. When she was taken to hospital after a stroke, she said, "I am going, I am half dead. He [the granddaughter's husband] came and pushed me out" (PjBrF80). This was not a case of conscious malice, but as an interesting postscript, a few years later the granddaughter died in a fire at her home. Her husband confessed to the police that he had set the house alight after taking their child to school. Subsequently he was tried and imprisoned for murder.

Not all Hindus accept that *karma* is transferable. A Darji man commented:

> *Karma* has no brothers, sisters, mother, anybody. My *karmas* are mine, and his are his [referring to his son]. My *karma* has no linkage with his. It wasn't anything to do with his *karma* that he was born in my family. If a child dies it is because of his *karma,* not the parents', even though they may feel they are being punished. My *karma* won't hurt anyone else. You can see drunken parents produce beautiful children because of the child's good *karma*.

Ill-wishing, though not ascribed to *karma*, is not unrelated in so far as it is action, and is sometimes seen as a cause of death. As a Punjabi Brahmin said, "Even if we think the evil eye is superstitious, it warrants doing *pūjā* and *jap* [repitition of *mantras*] to prevent or cure what may be a dangerous situation" (PjBrM45). Other harmful influences are the attachments, unsatisfied longings or resentments of the ghost of the deceased, either during the first twelve days after the death, or later if the appropriate rituals have not been performed (Ch. 5, 6). Two weeks before her father's death, the aunt of a Gujarati woman died. The young woman felt that the aunt had "taken my father" (GjBrF35), because of an excessive attachment (9.2.1). She also felt that one cause of her daughter's stillbirth was the ill-wishing of her sister-in-law (9.3). This was malice,[45] not just a question of one individual's bad *karma* or attachment having a bad effect on another.

We can see there are elements of continuity in Hindu beliefs throughout time, with evidence of the Vedic tradition still present in the cremation, with its concept of the last sacrifice to Agni (Ch.5, 6). The Vedic concept of the *pitṛs* is still an important feature of the *śrāddha* rituals, which for some Hindus are even more important than the funeral itself, although the concept of the *pitṛs* has become rather vague. Another stream of ideas, of *karma*, rebirth and *mokṣa* has continued since Upaniṣadic times, and has had a profound influence on concepts and beliefs about spirituality, death and the afterlife, as has the BG, which has developed these concepts in a theistic context. These influence attitudes to relationships between people and between people and animals, ethical behaviour and religious and spiritual practice. Many of the rituals around death appear to be heavily influenced by the *Garuḍa Purāṇa*, and its mythology is still an important factor among older Hindus. These beliefs and practices have an important effect on the way in which Hindus approach death, adjust to death and bereavement and find meaning in their experience (cf.9.5). However, the changes created by life in Britain may mean a shift in the belief patterns of younger Hindus as new generations lose contact with the bearers of tradition.

---

[45] Cf.Sharma 1978a:31.

Part II
Hindu Death Rituals

Chapter 4: Good and Bad Deaths

In Chapter 1 the concept of the good death was introduced. *Su-mṛtyu*, the ideal death, is one in which a person dies in old age, having lived to see his or her grandson or great-grandson. The person who has had a good death is *san-maraṇ* - "one who has left behind a lasting reputation for good deeds and has done what God has wanted you to do" (GjPt65). A person who is spiritually prepared for death may have foreknowledge of the day and even the time he will die.[1] He says goodbye to close friends and relatives, having performed any required rituals of penance, giving farewell gifts of land or money, and dying consciously with the thought of God in his mind and the name of God on his lips. It is normally painless. If such a death is accompanied by the appropriate rituals, which continue for 13 days, the person has a good end (*sadgati)*. The converse is a bad death (*ku-mṛtyu*), or untimely death (*akāla-mṛtyu*), exemplified by premature or sudden death from violence or by accident, or death at any age from certain diseases such as cholera. Death rituals vary according to the region, caste and the orientation of the priests. Changes are occurring: secularisation, urbanisation and consequent social mobility distance people from their roots. Refrigeration, allowing distant relatives to come to funerals, leads to delays, and electric crematoria are being built in major cities. The mourning period may also be shortened because of the demands of modern business. These both reflect and create a shift in attitudes towards death rituals, leading to adaptation and innovation. Nevertheless, there are still common traditional patterns of ritual, and priests are readily available to advise and help at the time of death and for the post-mortem rites. In Britain the emphasis in this model has shifted because of changes due to deaths in hospital, the delay and bureaucracy surrounding cremation, the need to return to work as soon as possible after the funeral, inaccessibility of knowledgeable priests, and sometimes to lack of knowledge on the part of the bereaved as to how their particular family or clan (*gotra*) would perform the rituals. The pandits have to adapt to circumstances by shortening and improvising services, and some communities have created their own order of service.

Part II explores the ritual aspects of good and bad death, comparing British

---

1 Parry 1982:82; 1994:158ff.; Carstairs 1957:233.

and Indian practice. In India the rituals around the death and funeral normally take place within twenty-four hours, and the subsequent rituals during the next 13 days. To illustrate the changes which have occurred in Britain, these will be discussed briefly at each stage, using a model of nine stages to compare the developments and changes which have taken place in Britain, and to highlight areas of continuity.[2] Stage I is preparation for death. Stage II, which may overlap with Stage I, involves rituals at the moment of death, and Stage III, which may overlap with II, is the preparation of the body. Stage IV is the procession to the cremation ground. Stage V is the disposal of the body, which for adults is normally by cremation.[3] Stage VI is the collection of bones ('ashes'), on the third or fourth day. Stage VII, *śrāddha*, involves the rites for the deceased's spirit (*preta*), covering the period up to the twelfth or thirteenth day, when various ceremonies enable it to take on a new spiritual body and become a *pitṛ* (ancestor). The first ten days of this time are a period of extreme impurity (*sūtaka*).[4] Stage VIII includes ceremonies marking the end of this state which can take up to a year. Thereafter, in Stage IX, the deceased, as an ancestor, receives daily oblations as well as annual remembrances.

In Britain there have been in major alterations to the pattern of Stages (see Chart) because most deaths are in hospital, so there are rarely rituals at the point of death. The cremation is usually delayed for up to a week, so Stage III, the preparation of the body, takes place at the undertakers' days after the death. The funeral itself is radically different in character, and Stage IV has virtually disappeared. Only stages VIII and IX bear much resemblance to those in India. Chapter 4 focuses on the concepts of good and bad deaths, preparation for death

---

[2] This is an expanded version of Evison's six stages: 1) rites at death, preparation of the body and the funeral procession, 2) disposal of the body, 3) rites concerned with the collection of bones or attention to the grave, 4) rites for the ghost, 5) the end of mourning, and 6) commemorative rites (Evison 1989:5).

[3] Burial is usual in certain circumstances, e.g. for *sannyasis* and infants, and water burial follows death from illnesses such as smallpox, or for the very poor (Das 1977:123; Kane 1973 IV:227-231; Parry 1980:90; 1982:81). Burial is also common in certain communities such as the Lingayats of South India (Evison 1989:39).

[4] *Sūtaka* (H,Gj, *sūtak*), is the term most commonly used by informants for death impurity, particularly those from Gujarat. Etymologically it has to do with pollution from birth or miscarriage as well as pollution in general (Monier-Williams 1899:1240; Stevenson 1920:17, 63, 157). The term *pātaka* (H,Gj, *pātak*), is applicable only to death pollution (Monier-Williams 1899:616). and was more commonly used by informants from Himachal Pradesh and the Punjab. *Aśudh* and *āśauca* are other terms meaning impure. Birth impurity is *jananāśauca* and death impurity is *maraṇāśauca*. *Śoka* (H *śok*) means sorrow, and the period of *śoka* and *sūtaka* overlap, but *śoka* will continue after *sūtaka* is over. Inauspiciousness is *aśubh*.

THE TIMING OF DEATH RITUALS IN INDIA AND IN BRITAIN

Timing	Stage in India	Period of sūtaka:	Stage in Britain
	I: Preparation for death		I: Preparation for death
Day 1	II: Death III: Preparation of body IV: Piṇḍa-dāna and journey to cremation ground V: Cremation	↑	II: Death; removal of body to undertakers'
Day 2			
Day 3	VI: Collection of bones (ĀS: end of rituals; end of śoka, with havan and pagṛī)		
Day 4			VIII: Some relatives may have to return to work
Day 5			
Day 6			
Day 7			III: Preparation of body at undertakers' IV: Domestic stage of funeral
Day 8			V: Cremation (ĀS: end of śoka, with havan and pagṛī)
Day 9			VI: Ashes received from crematorium
Day 10	VII: Ashes to river; śrāddha (10 piṇḍas)	Brahmin	
Day 11	VII: Śrāddha		
Day 12	VII: Sapiṇḍī-karaṇa; gifts to Brahmins; feast	Patel	VII: Sapiṇḍī-karaṇa (may be done in India). Ashes to river or sea; feast
Day 13	VIII: Gifts to Brahmins		VIII: Feast; gifts to Brahmins
Day 16	VIII: End of śoka for most communities; feast	Lohāna	VIII: End of śoka for most communities; feast
	IX: Annual śrāddhas		IX: Annual śrāddhas

Continuous lines indicate the period over which a stage normally extends.

Broken lines indicate the period over which a stage or group of stages may extend, or within which it may occur.

Adapted from Killingly Menski and Firth, 1991 p. 84

and the moment of death. Chapter 5 includes the preparation of the body, the funeral and cremation and disposal of ashes. Chapter 6 discusses the rites for the *preta* (ghost, disembodied soul) and ancestors.[5]

4.1. The good death

In the recent literature on death and dying there has been a good deal of discussion about the usefulness and relevance of the concept of a good or bad death. Bloch and Parry have noted that the distinction between good and bad deaths is related to control and choice over the manner, time and place of death. Good deaths provide for an adequate distribution of power, and reassure the mourners that the deceased has moved on to another life; they are associated with regeneration. The bad death is uncontrolled, at the wrong time and place, and does not allow for regeneration. Suicides and violent deaths are usually bad.[6] Ariès, in his survey of death in Western society, refers to the *ars moriendi*, the art of dying, which was important in the Christian tradition.[7] Bradbury, in a discussion of contemporary representations of death, distinguishes between a sacred good death, a medicalised good death and natural good death. The sacred good death is associated with belief in the continuity of the soul and an afterlife, and in contemporary culture may be linked to a medicalised good death, in which death is controlled to some extent by pain relief and prolonging life. The natural good death, is neither of the above, is often sudden, and characterised by lack of pain or fear, although Bradbury points out that some natural deaths, as in childbirth, are not particularly good. A "less medicalised" natural death allows for pain relief but no other intervention.[8] The natural good death has been legitimised to some degree by the Natural Death Society, which attempts to return death to the home, with home-made coffins.[9] Walter further distinguishes between "the good death of the therapists, with the person experiencing death as the final stage of personal growth, with death as the culmination of the self-aware human being", and the 'spiritual' good death based on Frankl's theory of meaning, in which the person organises practical affairs, says goodbye to loved

---

[5] A concise discussion of the material in Ch. 5 and 6 appears in Killingley, Menski, and Firth, reproduced here with permission. I am indebted to both my co-authors for their help with this material. For fuller details about the rituals see Firth 1994.

[6] Bloch and Parry 1982:15ff.; Parry 1994:158ff..

[7] Ariès 1983.

[8] Bradbury 1993.

[9] Albery *et al.* 1993.

ones and focuses on God or on external projects.[10] Mcnamara refers to a "good-enough death" which is as "close as possible to the circumstances the person would have chosen and a death in keeping with the life that person has led". However, the issue is complex, since "the process of dying in a hospice and palliative care environment will involve other moral, social and cultural dimensions" which have to be taken into account, including the ethical issues such as euthanasia, economic constraints and medical culture.[11]

The Hindu good death has features of the sacred and natural good death, but the ideal, or even a 'good enough death' is difficult to realise in Britain. It is a controlled death at the right time and place, which demands lifelong spiritual preparation, underpinned by the observation of *dharma* through proper religious, social and ethical behaviour throughout life (3. 1). As age progresses there should be a gradual detachment from worldly concerns, focussing on spiritual matters in the hope of liberation or *mokṣa*,[12] exemplified in the ideal of the four *āśramas*, the stages of life (cf. Ch. 2 f.n.8).[13] Many informants in both India and Britain have referred to this ideal, describing relatives who had gradually withdrawn in old age, emotionally and mentally, if not physically:

> Our life is divided into four *āśramas*, each twenty-five years long. But even if you assume your life will be an average of sixty, when you reach the third *āśrama* you start thinking of the journey to Him, so you [should] start thinking of the journey fifty years before you've got to leave this world. You're getting ready - it's as if you start getting ready for a holiday a long time before. You must be all ready, pack up your luggage and everything. On this journey you start renouncing your things in the world and people around you. You start living a simple life - only your shirt and *dhotī* and a shawl, and then you take *vānaprastha* [the forest-dweller stage]. (PjBrM45)

Truly spiritual people are conscious of impending death and enter it willingly; such deaths are 'willed deaths' (*icchā-mṛtyu*) or conscious deaths (*caitanya-mṛtyu*). Ideally, according to Parry, the dying person fasts before death to enable the 'vital breath' to leave easily and also ensure there is no "foul faecal matter" to prevent him being a "a worthy sacrificial object". Then, "Having previously predicted the time of his going and set all his affairs in order, he gathers his sons

---

[10] Walter 1993:115.

[11] Mcnamara 1997a.

[12] ŚBX.63,1,2; Drury 1981:115; Bṛ.Up.4.4.7; Kat.Up.6.14; Mun.Up. 3.2.1ff..

[13] Stevenson 1920:139, Basham 1967:159-160; Brockington 1981:92.

about him and - by an effort of concentrated will - abandons his body. He is said not to die, but to relinquish his body."[14]

Many of my informants in India and Britain provided accounts of relatives who were aware of impending death. Often they knew the exact time they were going to die, called for their relatives, and prepared for it by bathing, putting on clean clothes and lying on the bed or purified floor, quietly chanting. A Punjabi Brahmin woman in Westmouth described a conscious death:

> My mother was like a saint and she died in just 5 minutes at 103. She was able to thread a needle and walk without a stick. She asked for a bed on the floor and asked for a light. (When someone dies we give a *dīvā*, like a candle, made of flour and *ghī* - into her hand to show her a way to God). Then my sister and her son came and said, "What's happening, Bibi?" She said, "Oh thank God you have come. Come and give me a *dīvā*, on my hand," and my sister started crying and she said, "Don't cry, I'm going to God. Don't stop me, your tears will make a river for me to cross." He did everything, then she said, "Put my head in your lap, I want to go to God".

When a ninety-nine-year-old Pushtimargi was dying, his grandson asked him whether he should read the BG or some books by Vallabhacharya. He replied, "The *Gītā* has gone through my mind throughout my life so you need not do it." Having called his sons and daughters the previous day, he announced that he would be leaving this world the next morning at 6:00 a.m.. As he was dying he asked, laughing very loudly, "Do you want me to carry a message to the next world? To whom?" Then he died, chanting the name of Rāma (GjPM70). An elderly Gujarati Brahmin in Westmouth asked his wife to make *prasāda* (food for the deity) the following day because he was going to die. She said "Don't talk like that - there's nothing wrong with you", but on the following day she made the *prasāda* as requested. They offered it to Saraswati, ate it and then he lay on a white sheet on the floor and died. The father of a Gujarati Brahmin woman, without acknowledging he was going to die, set all his business affairs in order, and wrote letters to all his children, nephews and nieces. He wrote to his daughter in Westmouth to congratulate her for her forthcoming anniversary, which lay two months ahead. On the morning of his death, he told his wife where his money and insurance policy were, and in the evening, he asked her to stay with him instead of going to a party at the neighbours. After going into the kitchen to get

[14] Parry 1982:82; cf. Madan 1987:122ff.; Carstairs 1957:233.

some milk, she came back and found he had pulled the sheet up over his face, and when she looked at him "his face really shone. He looked so beautiful, so happy, and he was really clean, he hadn't wet or anything, [which] meant his soul had gone from his mouth. That's really good". The *ātman* of such an individual does not take rebirth but will reach *akṣardhām* or *vaikuṇṭha* or attain *mokṣa.*

Premonitions of death such as these are common, either on the part of the person who subsequently dies, or of his relatives. There may be omens, often only recognised in retrospect, and astrologers and swamis may also recognise death is impending. A dream that a friend or relative is about to die is generally seen as a sign that the person dreamed about will have a long life; however, there were a number of informants whose dreams came true. A Swaminarayan follower in Westmouth wrote asking Pramukh Swami if he could go to a major ceremony in Bombay and the Swami said no. The devotee died unexpectedly shortly afterwards. Subsequently the family learned that the night before the death a close family friend had dreamed that she and the father were at the ceremony in Bombay. Everybody was saying goodbye to the father, and someone asked her if she also wanted to say goodbye. As she stood up he fell off the stage, and she awoke. Her husband, who was in Bombay, told Pramukh Swami about the dream. Pramukh Swami said he had witnessed the death. My informant's father rested in peace "up there with God" so the family need not worry about him.

The good death is characterised by being at the right time (*kāla*) and place (*sthāna*). The ideal place to die is on the banks of the Ganga (Ganges), especially in Varanasi (Kāśī), or on the ground at home rather than in hospital. There are times to die which are better than others. *Uttarāyaṇa,* the six months of the year following the winter solstice, is a good time to die, and *dakṣiṇāyana,* the path of those who will be reborn, is a bad time to die.[15] The dark half of the month in the five days known as *pañcaka,* or even at night are bad times to die. Although the time of death is said to be fixed in advance and nothing can be done about it, some informants believed that Yama could be bargained with (4.41). People are said to have died and gone to Yama-loka but returned after a mistake was admitted. One pandit said his mother's aunt was returned to life because she had been mistaken for someone of a similar nature, and henceforth she led an especially holy life, withdrawing from social activities In averted deaths a person recovers unexpectedly from a serious illness, or the death is averted by particular

[15] 3.1, 4.2; BG 8.23-26; Killingley 1997, pp 8-9.

rituals designed to create a 'second birth'.[16]

For most Hindus Kāśī[17] is the place *par excellence* to die; this enables one to go straight to heaven or attain liberation, *mokṣa*.[18] To die in Kāśī is a sign of good *karma* - even if one has been quite wicked in this life - so that one could not die there without deserving it. In Varanasi and Haridwar, also on the Ganga, there are hospices where the terminally ill may come to die.[19] This is impossible ideal for most British Hindus, but Hindus with terminal illnesses sometimes try to return to India to die, and even unexpected death while on a visit is satisfying.[20]

The other important place to die is at home. According to Madan, this is even preferable to dying in Kāśī (Varanasi). The home, for most people, is the place where they came into the world, and is a "microcosm of the universe" where the householder "pursues his legitimate worldly goals (*dharma-kāma*), and seeks to improve the moral quality of his person or self".[21] For women the home is where they have lived since marriage, and borne their children. It is also important for Hindus to die on the floor or the ground, with the head to the north (4.4).

Since hospitals are regarded as a place to get better, and home as a place to die, many hospitals in India send patients home when death is imminent; as a Gujarati Brahmin doctor said, "We do not consider hospital to be a very holy place." Death in hospital creates its own problems of disruption and, for Hindus, inauspiciousness and impurity. Two other doctors working in sophisticated hospitals in Pune and Calcutta were reluctant to inform patients and their relatives who were not already aware of the fact, that death was imminent, for fear the family would create a scene in the hospital, or the patient would be disturbed, thus placing the efficiency of the hospital, and the immediate comfort of the dying person, above the longer term religious requirements of the patient and family (4.4.1; Ch.7). Dying at home, in addition to the psychological advantage of being surrounded by the family, enables them to facilitate a good death.

4.2. The bad death

A bad death, *akāla-mṛtyu*, is one which is sudden or premature, particularly a

---

[16] Madan 1987:133.

[17] Parry describes Kāśī as "the 'Luminous', the City of Light... the sacred city of Banaras, now officially known as Varanasi...As the site of cosmic creation, it is the place where time itself began...Kashi is both the origin-point and a microcosm of the universe." (1994:11)

[18] Quayle 1956:595; Parry 1982:75; Eck 1983:324ff.; Firth 1994:136-7.

[19] Cf. Parry 1994:52-3.

[20] Rees 1990.

[21] Madan 1987:122-123.

violent death or suicide. It may be painful, showing negative signs, such as a contorted expression or the discharge of urine, faeces or vomit (4.4). The polluting discharges are said to be signs of bad *karma* in a previous life, and suggest an unfortunate post-mortem destiny. Parry describes this as the death "for which the deceased cannot be said to have prepared himself. It is said that 'he did not die his own death'".[22] It is an uncontrolled death - whereas the good death implies a degree of control - it is a willed death. Because sudden death takes the person unprepared it may be bad even for those who would otherwise be ready to die.

According to Madan the bad death is usually explained by bad *karma* in a previous life and "certifies the existence of the cosmo-moral order just as the good death does". He regards this as an anomic situation, which is referred to as "pralaya, the dissolution of the cosmo-moral order, for it upsets the natural-moral ordering of things", particularly when it refers to the premature death of a young man, who would have supported his elderly parents, and whose wife is now stigmatised and excluded from auspicious ceremonies.[23] The concept of *karma* makes such a situation bearable (3.3; 9.4).

Suicide and death in childbirth are particularly bad, except for religious suicides.[24] If the death is a violent one or a suicide, the spirit of the deceased remains a ghost and causes problems for the family. After death in childbirth the mother will still be attached to the child and unable to move on to the next life. Bad deaths are buried or given a water burial, rather than cremated. Such deaths require an elaborate remedial ritual called *nārāyaṇa bali*.

If someone, especially a young person, dies during *dakṣināyana* or during the last five days of the waning moon, *pañcaka* (3 f.n.15), it is a very bad omen and it is even worse if the cremation has to take place during this period.[25] Five more people may die unless a six hour long ceremony, the *pañcak vidhi* or *pañcak śantī* is done. This involves burning five effigies on the pyre along with the corpse and performing *nārāyaṇa bali*. In Britain older Hindus may be anxious about deaths during *pañcaka*, and may ask the pandit to perform the remedial rituals quietly but to say nothing to the rest of the family to avoid great anxiety (5.3; 5.5).

---

[22] Parry 1982:83-84; 1994:162.

[23] Madan 1987:126-7.

[24] Kane 1973 II:924-928; III:939, 948-949; IV:603 ff.; Parry 1982:96-97. For a different perspective see Carstairs 1955:37; Madan 1987:131.

[25] Cf. GP II:35.17ff.; II.4:176ff.; Parry 1994:79.

Not surprisingly, informants were reluctant to discuss bad deaths in detail. One Westmouth family described an aunt who had been very unpleasant, bad tempered, and shrill and critical of everyone. She died in the lavatory, and was found with a hideous grimace on her face. This was seen as a deservedly bad death, as the Yamdūts had come in the worst possible situation (GjPlF60).

Even if the death was otherwise a good one, failure to perform the appropriate rituals at the time of death can cause the deceased to have a bad end (*durgati*). If hospital rules prevent the rituals, as sometimes happens in Britain, this can cause great concern among more traditional families (4.4.1; Ch. 7).

4.3. Stage I: Preparation for death

In addition to spiritual preparation for death the examples of good deaths discussed above indicate the importance of dealing with unfinished business and family affairs, sorting out inheritance and overseeing marriage arrangements for unmarried daughters, granddaughters and nieces. Reparation should be made to people who have been injured. As death approaches an act of penance (*sarvaprāyaścitta*) should be performed with the help of the family *purohit* (priest).[26] Although the custom is said to be dying out, many Hindus follow the scriptural injunction to offer five gifts, (*pañca-dāna*),[27] including land, money and a cow or cow and calf (*go-dān*). The cow is the Vaitaraṇī cow, which is said to tow the *ātman* across the terrible Vaitaraṇī Nadī (river), full of blood and pus, which lies at the threshold of Yama's city. The cow is be given to a *brāhmaṇa* with a sugar cane boat or raft, which the cow walks over, also symbolising the crossing of the river. The donor holds on to the tail after milk and water have been poured over it, reciting a *mantra* dedicating the cow to Viṣṇu, requesting permission to cross the river.[28] A silver surrogate image of a cow, or money of equal value, with a ritual statement of intention, is an equally meritorious gift.[29]

Other gifts, offered by the son or nearest male relative if the dying person is too weak, include money and gifts in kind to Brahmins and charities; wealthier ones give land (*bhūmi-dāna*) and the father of one of my informants built a *dharmaśālā* (a hostel for pilgrims) at Rishikesh.

---

[26] Kane 1973 IV:183-4.

[27] Some texts suggest ten gifts. For further details see Stevenson 1920:140; Kane 1973 IV: 182ff; Dubois 1906:482; GP II 4:3-8; 36:23-32; Planalp 1956:598; Monier-Williams 1884:296; Quayle 1980:9.

[28] Pandey 1969:420; Madan 1989:134; Planalp 1956:598; Stevenson 1920:141; Kane 1973 IV; Evison 1989:12-14, 207, 308-9; GP II 4:12-14; 47:2 ff.; 47:25-35.

[29] Stevenson 1920:78.

4.3.1. Stage I: Preparation for death in Britain

While the model of the good death is very important to British Hindus, who, as we have seen, stress the importance of spiritual preparation, many of the practical and ritual preparations for death which feature strongly in India have less emphasis in Britain. Life here is seen as being very different from life in India or East Africa, and only older informants could remember specific details of what should be done. A Gujarati Brahmin woman said, "In India people used to know when someone was going to die - they didn't have diseases like cancer. In England no one knows - they could die anywhere." This seems to be related in part to the fact that people rarely live in extended families which not only care for the elderly, but are also more likely to deal with death in the home. British Hindus have less control over the processes of death and dying in hospital. Deaths which occur outside hospitals are likely to be sudden, and there are fewer pandits available to advise or perform pre-death ceremonies.

It is important for British Hindus to know in advance that death is impending so that they can prepare for it, both spiritually and materially, ensuring that the welfare of the family is guaranteed. As the Case Studies of Ramesh and Maya in Chapter 7 make clear, one of the most distressing aspects of their fathers' deaths in hospital was the fact that they had not realised they were going to die, and in Maya's case her father had not been able to prepare spiritually or arrange financial matters for the family.

All the priests interviewed in Britain regarded the rituals before death as important, especially the act of penance (*prāyaścitta*) and various prayers and *pūjās*, such as the Viṣṇu Pūjā. While they were willing to go several days before death if necessary, they were rarely, if ever, called upon to attend a dying patient. Gifts should also be offered. One Gujarati pandit said there should be gifts of land (*bhūmi-dāna*) and cows (*go-dāna*), or their value, in order to compensate for omissions, but this was difficult in Britain. Another Gujarati pandit said that the dying person should be sprinkled with *pañca-gavya*,[30] and then he should offer a *ladū* (ball) of uncooked (*kachchā*) wheat flour, *ghī* and *jāggarī* (raw brown sugar), to the priest, with gold or money in the middle. The dying man should perform *saṃkalpa*, taking water in his hand with the appropriate *mantras*. "If he is weak he just touches the *ladū*, and the son then gives it to the pandit. As long

[30] *Pañca-gavya*: a particularly sacred and pure mixture of cowdung, urine, milk, *ghī* (clarified butter), and curds.

as *dakṣiṇā*[31] is given to the priest, *go-dān* and *bhūmi-dān* are unnecessary."

For non-Brahmins an act of penance and reparation before death may be made, but not necessarily in the presence of a *purohit*, even if one could be obtained. A Gujarati Brahmin woman who often took the place of a pandit thought that a *purohit* was unnecessary, but when she had gone to a deathbed to read from a text, she was "frightened by the sorrow and the pain and couldn't speak". Informants did not mention gifts before death, but the gifts after death are of great importance and may include the miniature cow.

At a practical level some elderly people keep clothes previously dipped in Ganga or Yamuna water ready for their funerals. Some keep pearls for the eyes, gold for the mouth and sticks of sandalwood for the fire. Many families have a *tulasī* plant, and a small sealed pot of Ganga water (*ganga-jal*) is kept ready for various functions.

For British Hindus the emphasis is upon long term preparation of a spiritual nature, practical arrangements, and saying farewell, rather than upon specific rituals, such as the *prayāścitta*, although it will be evident (below) that some rituals at the moment of death are still very important.

4.4. Stage II: The moment of death

The rituals which should ideally be performed at the moment of death may not be possible until afterwards, for the obvious reason that a person may die suddenly. Some of these may therefore take place as part of preparation of the body, which in India is immediately after the death (Ch. 5), but in Britain may take place much later.

Evison suggests that the rites before death are concerned both with processing the corpse and "putting the spirit into a fit state to leave the body." The readings, chanting of divine names and almsgiving on behalf of the dying person are attempts to improve his *karma* so that his *ātman* leaves from the *brahmarandhra*, rather than through "the anus, the gateway by which a departing spirit enters into the terrible fortress of the damned".[32]

When death is imminent, the floor or the ground of the courtyard or outside should be purified with cowdung, covered with the sacred *kuśa* grass and

---

[31] *Dakṣiṇā*: the gift given to the priest by the sacrificer. In Westmouth the priest was expected to hand all such gifts to the temple, but one pandit felt this ignored the significance of such gifts, which is the transfer of merit to the sacrificer, and in the case of funeral gifts, also transfers the sin of the deceased to the priest.

[32] Evison 1989:17-18.

sprinkled with sesame seeds.[33] Having said goodbye to his family and friends, the dying person is purified with Ganga water and *pañca-gavya* and placed on the floor or ground. This can also be done immediately after death.[34] If the death occurs indoors, the doors should be opened, as open spaces "allow the *ātma* to merge with Brahman more readily"(BnBr42).

The most common reasons given by my informants for placing the person on the floor or ground were to be near Mother Earth, to allow the *ātman* to escape more easily, or to allow the person to breathe more easily. The concept of earth as a mother protecting the dead is an ancient one.[35] According to a Bihari pandit, death outside is a sign of freedom, indicated by the loosening of all knots in the clothing, whereas death under a roof signifies bondage, as does death on a bed (below). Furthermore, death on the ground signifies the return of the *ātman* and the body to the elements from which they came. Contact with the earth may be compared to holding the tail of the Vaitaraṇi cow. Both the earth and the cow are symbols of universal motherhood for Hindus; the word '*go*' means both 'cow' and 'earth'. The use of cowdung and *pañca-gavya* (above) reinforce this symbolism (4.3).

From a more negative perspective to die on a bed is dangerous because, as Evison notes, "*Rākṣasas, piśācas, bhūtas, pretas* (types of evil spirits and ghosts) and Yama's followers enter a cot above the ground." This is a bad death which causes the deceased to become a permanent ghost unless the remedial *nārāyaṇa bali* is performed (4.2).[36] Dubois' account suggests that the dying Brahmin, if he expires on a bed, "would be obliged to carry it with him wherever he went, which, it may easily be supposed, would be very inconvenient".[37] It is interesting to note Kalsi's observations that many Sikhs follow this Hindu tradition, regarding death on a bed as an indication of family neglect, resulting in social stigma and inauspiciousness.[38] Kaushik points out that the thing most Hindus

---

[33] *Kuśa* or *darbha* grass, strewn on purifying cowdung, releases the dying person from sins and takes him to heaven (GP II 2:7-9, 19), and sesame "can destroy the evil spirits [and] can burn all sins committed by the deceased" (GP II 2:16-17, 29, 35; II.29:6ff.; Evison 1989:99; Pandey 1969:246).

[34] Kaushik 1976:270, 276; Padfield 1908:194-6; Stevenson 1920:142; Kane 1973 IV: 184.

[35] ṚV 10.18.10-11; TS 1.4.40; Evison 1989:197,305.

[36] Evison 1989:198; see GP II 4:104-112; II 2:10; II 15:6; II 29:9.

[37] Dubois 1906:499, Padfield 1908:194-6. A *charpoy* (bed) is traditionally a net of knotted cords stretched on a wooden frame, and knots are associated with bondage, so that who die on it are caught in a web of future lives (cf. Planalp 1956:59). The clothes on the corpse also have to be free of knots.

[38] Kalsi 1996:32.

adhere to most strictly is to die on the ground rather than on one's bed; as can be seen below (Ch. 7) this concern remains important for many Hindus in Britain.[39]

Most informants said the dying person should be placed with his head to the north, the direction of men, or more rarely, to the east, the direction of the gods: "Being in the right direction enables Yama Rājā to swoop up and grab you as he comes up from the south" (PjKhM; cf.3.2.1). By placing the body with the head to the north, his face is turned to the south, which, according to Evison, starts him "on his journey from being a man through death to the status of Ancestor by being pointed towards the region occupied by the Ancestors in the ritual cult."[40] According to many educated informants the north-south orientation allows the magnetic currents of the earth to pass through the body and ease the passing of the *ātman*, but a pandit described this as "scientific mumbo jumbo".

Immediately before death, or if the moment is missed, afterwards, Ganga water (or Yamuna water in the case of Pustimargis), *pañca-gavya* and *tulasī* leaves are placed in the mouth.[41] Gold, which should be put in after death, is sometimes placed in the mouth before death, and one informant claimed that forcing a coin into the mouth of a dying patient sometimes actually choked him.[42]

It is very important for the family to be present even if the dying person wants to be alone, so that they can say goodbye, ask forgiveness, and so that he can "speak kind words". The family may also need to help the dying person fix his mind on God, because the last thoughts determine one's status in the next life.[43] The BG is frequently cited by informants as the basis of this belief:

> And whoever, at the time of death, gives up his body and departs, thinking of Me alone, he comes to my status of being; of that there is no doubt.

---

[39] Kaushik 1976:270-271, 283.

[40] Evison 1989:306; GP II 32:88; Stevenson 1920:14. In some regions the body is placed facing south. Since a body with the feet to the south may be said to face south, these are two ways of applying the same principle, that the south is the direction of Yama and the *pitṛs*. See Pandey 1969:246; Parry 1994:173.

[41] *Tulasī* is said to be pervaded by the essence of Viṣṇu, Kṛṣṇa and Laksmī. The worship of the plant wipes away sins from various births (GP II 38:11) and it should be placed near the dying person (GP II 2:21-25, II 15:10, 14-15). Today the placing of a leaf of *tulasī* in the mouth of a dying or dead person is one of the most important things relatives can do for them. A Hindi film, *Tulasīvivāh*, "The Marriage of Tulasī", about a young woman pursued by Viṣṇu who changed herself into the *tulasī* plant, is popular in Britain and seems to reinforce belief in the importance and efficacy of the plant.

[42] Cf. Evison 1989:8; Stevenson 1920:143 f.n..

[43] Cf. Br.Up. IV.3.35-36; GP II 49:108; Kane 1973 IV:185-6; BG 8.5-6; Chand.Up II.14.1, Madan 1987:124; Monier-Williams 1884:297.

> Thinking of whatever state (of being) he at the end gives up his body, to that being does he attain ...[44]

Those who are present must remain quiet so as not to distract the dying person with emotions or worldly thoughts. The only sounds should be of readings from, for example, the BG, especially chapter 15, chanting the *Gāyatrī Mantra*, or the singing of *bhajans* (hymns). At the point of death it is helpful to say "Rām", "*oṃ*" *or* "*śrī kṛṣṇaḥ śaraṇam mama*" (Kṛṣṇa is my refuge), if Vaisnavite, or if Saivite, "*oṃ namaḥ śivāya*" (Homage to Śiva) in the dying person's ear. This is particularly important if the dying person is in a lot of pain.

According to the GP, death is due to Kāla, time:

> At the appointed hour, without a single exception ... the breath is pushed by Yama's messengers standing nearby. The person assumes a terrible form and the breath lingers to stay in the throat... Just at the moment when every body [*sic*] is lamenting, the soul, as big as a thumb, is carried away by Yama's messengers, even as it looks towards its home.[45]

The *ātman* leaves through any of the nine apertures. For sinners the subtle soul escapes through the anus (3.2.1; 4.2). In the case of someone who has done good deeds, however, it departs from "the upper holes". The best of all is from the top of the head, the *brahmarandhra,* which signifies holiness, indicated by positive signs such as a peaceful expression and shining forehead, as in examples cited above.[46]

Many informants thought it wrong to cry at the point of death, since it prevented the soul from moving on. However, various sources describe the wailing that occurs at the moment of death. In villages, professional mourners may still be called, but the practice is said to be dying out. Men are expected to keep much more in control of their emotions, and be 'stone-hearted', although they too may weep. Padfield reports that it was not considered seemly for men to weep and wail, "but females abandon themselves completely to their sorrow ... they tear their hair, beat their foreheads and roll their bodies about as if in great agony".[47] Madan, writing of the Pandit community, reports that once death has occurred the event is publicised by loud wailing of women and children:

---

44 BG 8.5-6; cf. BG 2. 8-11.
45 GP II 2:35, 43-45.
46 GP II 11:9-10.
47 Padfield 1908:197; cf. Dubois1906:484; Stevenson 1920:145.

> The stylized wailing is associated with death and is very distinctive, and announces the death to the neighbourhood. Intense activity is thus generated; neighbours (kith and kin) rush in, messengers rush out to carry the news to all concerned and to perform other chores. The family priest arrives ... and preparations for the last life-cycle ritual begins. In short, it is a situation of emotional stress, much movement and much talk.[48]

From now on the role of the men is "to get on with the serious business of begetting an ancestor", while the women "refuse to bow to the inevitable separation of death, and they try - like the *preta-ghost* itself - to hang on to the corpse".[49]

4.4.1. Stage II. The moment of death in Britain

While most of the rituals at the point of death do not occur in Britain, older Hindus stressed the importance of death taking place on the floor if possible, as we have seen. However, most deaths are either unexpected or take place in hospital, so this is very difficult to put into practice, which causes considerable anxiety. A Punjabi Brahmin commented:

> The belief is that you should die on the floor. In India, when you are near death you are sent home and put on the floor, but here people are more scientific and have hopes and would rather leave him here in the hospital's care. Here a lot of people die in hospitals and a lot of us families are very shy to ask for what we want. We feel out of place, like a Muslim praying towards Makkah on the factory floor. When someone is near death he must have his next of kin with him because there are a few religious rituals to be performed.

There is also great emphasis on dying with the name of God on the lips and in the heart: "If you have committed minor sins and at the time [of death] your thoughts are filled with God, if you say God's name then you will obviously go to heaven, because God is there"(GjDM35).

The dying person or, if he is comatose, the family, may read the BG or other favourite texts, sing devotional hymns or chant "Rām, Rām", the sacred syllable "*oṃ*", or the short Sanskrit prayer, the *Gayātrī Mantra* (4.4 above). This means that the family must be present to facilitate a good death. If rituals such as giving Ganga water or *tulasī* are not performed, then the survivors may be affected, since the dissatisfied ghost may create problems for them:

---

[48] Madan 1987:135.

[49] Parry 1991:22.

> Nurses should let the family be present when the soul leaves, because if the person dies without the family there, then that person will not be thinking of God, but of his family who weren't there. Not only would the family be affected, but the dying person, who would have to take rebirth. The family couldn't take part in any social occasions or anything because it would always be hanging over them that they hadn't been present at the death, so no good omen will occur for them to perform [auspicious rituals] for a very long period. The person's whole extended family would be affected, uncles, aunts, distant cousins. (GjSF35).

The family of this woman had been prevented from giving an aunt Ganga water at the point of death in hospital and believe they have been affected for seven generations (7.1). However, a pandit commented that the ritual could have been done immediately afterwards by the son, the wife or the nearest relative: "[offering] two or three grains of rice, the most symbolic food we can offer, with *til* (sesame) and *gingely* oil" (KanPt).

Allowing the family to be present also enables the dying person, if conscious, to make final arrangements and say proper goodbyes. Last words are very important, especially those of someone who has died a good death, and these are spoken about and remembered for years afterwards. Lack of understanding and communication here cause more distress than anything else. Maya (Ch. 7) was denied the opportunity to say goodbye to her father:

> I kept on saying "is there anything to worry about?" and they said, "Nothing, we'll take care of him, pneumonia is nothing nowadays." And at 3:00 a.m. there was a phone call and this doctor said, "Your father has passed away." If he had known he would have had everything done. He would have prayed in his last time, but really he would have worried about us.

Sometimes people report visions at the point of death, particularly with reference to the Guru, Yama or his servants, Yamdūts, coming to fetch the dying person:

> When my uncle died my cousin brother saw Guru Dev come to take my uncle. The Guru was in a white robe. The whole family were around his bed. He had concentrated on his prayers throughout his last few years. If Yamdūts come for you, the soul leaves from the lower part of the body, or there is blood from the mouth. If the Guru comes for you the soul leaves from the *brahm*, the forehead. My uncle was breathing at the last moment, and his forehead was moist. The *ātma* is heat, so the moisture was a sign that it had

come out of his forehead (GjCF32; cf. 2.4.2)

A pandit saw two Yamdūts coming from his sick wife's room, saying, "No, we've got the wrong one" the day before his wife died. He was greatly relieved, but she died the next day (3.2.1; 4.1). Sometimes these visions have the nature of a judgement. A Gujarati man said that a person saw all his good and bad deeds "as if he had a video film, he can see himself and say to people why he is suffering. If he has really bad *karm* he can't talk" (GjSM45). Another Gujarati saw Yama as he was dying and began shouting and talking about his past.

The model of the good death is as important to British Hindus as to those in India, although it is being modified in accordance with what is likely to be possible. The rituals at the point of death do not require a pandit, but may involve dying on the floor in the presence of the family, with *tulasī* and Ganga water in the mouth, and the name of God on the lips and in the heart. Narratives of such deaths are very important to the relatives, providing inspiration and a source of religious teaching, as well as comfort (9.5). Many of the rituals performed in India are regarded as dispensable in the present circumstances, but there is anxiety if the basic observances are impossible. This can create obvious problems in a hospital setting, as there may be tensions between the need to fulfil obligations on behalf of the departing soul (and secure the subsequent safety of the family), and the comfort of the patient as perceived by the medical staff. There may be blank incomprehension as to the requirements of the Hindu patient and his relatives, like the old man (Ch. 1) who lay on the floor because he thought he was going to die (cf. 7.1.1). The major difficulty for British Hindus is that control is taken from the patient and family, both by hospital staff, and by the professionals after death (Ch. 7). The good death is not just a matter of what happens at the moment of death; it depends on the post mortem rites provided by the chief mourner, from the cremation (Ch.5) to the final *śrāddha* on the thirteenth day (Ch. 6). If this is made impossible by the medicalization of death and officialdom and bureaucracy afterwards then it may not even be 'good enough'.

Chapter 5
The Funeral

In India the procedures after death are part of ritual process which forms a continuum from the moment of death: the preparation of the body (Stage III), offerings of *piṇḍas* in the home and on the procession to the cremation ground, (Stage IV) and the cremation itself (Stage V). Normally these all take place within twenty-four hours of the death; the same day if it is still daylight and the chief mourner can get there, or the following day. The primary focus of the rituals is the release of the soul, although they also protect the body and the mourners from harm. In Britain there is a marked change. The preparation of the body takes place, not at home after the death, but at the undertakers before the funeral, which in Westmouth is usually about a week later. Many rituals have disappeared altogether, or exist in truncated form. The cremation itself has changed because of time constraints and there is an obvious contrast between the open pyre and an electric cremator. The ritualised procession has vanished altogether, to be replaced by the hearse and following cars and buses. Space does not allow a detailed discussion of the funeral rites in India, but a summary at each stage will highlight the changes with which British Hindus have to deal

5.1. Stage III: Preparation of the body in India

From the moment of death the chief mourner is the principal functionary in all the rituals on behalf of the deceased, including the *piṇḍa* ceremonies on the day of the cremation, cremation itself, the subsequent rituals up to the thirteenth day, or whenever the mourning is concluded, and also the annual *śrāddha.* Ideally, this is the eldest or youngest son who is old enough to have had the *upanayana*, the sacred thread ceremony. He should be someone whose own *preta*, after death, will join those of the deceased's ancestors, or if the deceased is a married woman, her husband's ancestors, since she is no longer part of her father's lineage but has joined that of her husband.[1] A husband does not have to perform the ritual for his wife if there are sons or nephews who are old enough perform them. If there is no son, then the man's brother can act; he can also act for his brother's widow.[2] A man's father or male cousin can take that role, as can an adopted son. This is often a nephew, for reasons of lineage and to keep property

---

1 Dumont 1983:6ff..

2 See Kane 1973 IV for details, especially 220; 256ff..

in the family.[3] A son-in-law can only act for his father-in-law in the absence of anyone else, since he is not a member of the deceased's lineage. In some cases a daughter-in-law or wife may be the chief mourner if no suitable men are available. An informant explained that the *ātman* may return to the house in order to be born again in the same lineage, and would be confused by rites conducted by someone who was not part of the lineage (GjBrM). The crucial role of the chief mourner in enabling the deceased to move on to his next life was explained by analogy. A pandit explained that it was like buying a train ticket for someone who had to go to a particular destination (because of his good *karma*) and seeing that he got on the correct train (the rituals). This ensured he achieved *sadgati*, a good end.

As soon as the person has died, the body is placed on the floor if it is not there already. *Ganga-jal* and *tulasī* are placed in the mouth the moment a person has died if not offered before. A gold or silver coin is placed in the mouth, either immediately death occurs or after the body has been dressed.[4] This is usually said to pay the ferryman while crossing the river of death, Vaitaraṇī Nadī, but also ensures rebirth in an affluent family. According to several informants, it is also a germicidal agent (hence *pavitṛ*, 'purifier'). A lamp is placed near the head and kept burning until the final rites on the 12th or 13th day.

Experienced relatives may be contacted for advice on the preparation of the body and subsequent procedures. There are local and family traditions as to how things should be done (*laukika* or *kulācāra)*, as distinct from regional traditions (*deśācāra*) and what is perceived to be correct according to the Śāstras (*śāstrika*), in the Brahmanical tradition. These can give rise to fierce negotiations with the pandits supervising the rituals, It does not seem to be usual for a pandit to go to the home immediately after the death except for Brahmin clients. He may go to the cremation ground with the mourners.

The body is prepared by relatives and friends of the same sex and caste, who have previously bathed. The *Garuḍa Purāṇa* states that this should be done immediately.[5] It is bathed in Ganga or Yamuna water and dressed in new clothes, which may be bought in advance and dipped in water from the holy river beforehand. Generally a man is dressed or wrapped in a *dhotī* with no knots; a

[3] A son, *putra*, is said to be called *putra* because he saves (*trāyate*) from a hell called *put* (Manu 9:138; GP II 34:9; Monier-Williams 1899:632). A man who has no son can adopt one who is then called *dattakaputra*, 'given son'. Cf. GP II 21:32, f.n.; II 34:9, f.n.; Kane 1973 IV:161.

[4] Stevenson 1920: 143.

[5] GP II 4:44.

Punjabi may be dressed in a *kurtā pajāmā* (suit) if that is what he normally wears. A woman who has the good fortune to die before her husband, is dressed in her wedding sari or suit, and if her husband dies first he may be covered with her wedding sari, or with a red cloth (GjPt). A widow is dressed in white, an unmarried woman in white or red, depending on her age.[6] Silk cloths may be laid over the body. The toes are tied with a seven-coloured holy thread called *nālā chadi* to prevent the legs from spreading but also to immobilise the ghost and prevent it walking back to the house.[7] The body is placed on a ladder-like stretcher and decorated with garlands and ornaments. A coconut may be tied to each of the four corners of the stretcher, which, according to a Gujarati Patel woman, symbolises the four ambassadors of Yama (Yamdūts) who come to carry the dead. Gujarati Brahmins are usually tied on to a single pole, with just two coconuts tied on it.[8]

All the individuals in the house are in a state of ritual impurity (*sūtaka*) from the moment of death, according to my informants, although Parry's Varanasi informants stated that pollution began after the *kapāla kriyā*, because that was when the soul was released.[9] The length of time varies according to *varna* and caste. The commonly cited periods are ten days for *brāhmaṇas*, twelve for *kṣatriyas*, fifteen for *vaiśyas* and a month for *śūdras*, but there are caste variations. The chief mourner is subject to more severe restrictions than anyone else, and the severity and length of time also varies according to age and sex of the deceased, and the relationship of the mourners to the deceased.[10]

The corpse has an ambiguous status being both highly inauspicious and auspicious, as it is both a source of pollution and a sacred object about to be offered to the fire, Agni, as a sacrifice.[11] Evison observes that "It is treated as a god/goddess in the house and circumambulated in the auspicious direction (with the right shoulder to the corpse), while the mourners at the same time are wearing their threads in the inauspicious direction i.e. over the right shoulder."[12] Various

---

[6] Planalp 1956:599; Kane 1973 IV:212; Dubois 1906:484; Quayle 1980:10; Stevenson 1920:144.

[7] Evison 1989:21,28.

[8] Stevenson 1920:146.

[9] Parry 1982:79.

[10] Manu V.83; Kane IV 1973:271, 277ff..

[11] Evison 1989:5; Parry 1982:79-80; 1991:26.

[12] Evison, 1989: 26. The sacred thread (*yajñopavīta*)is given at the *upanayana* (initiation) to boys of the top three classes, who thus become 'twice born'. It is normally worn over the left shoulder and hangs down towards the right hip (the auspicious direction). This is moved around according to who is being addressed. For the gods it rests on the left shoulder, down to the right

Gujarati informants said the body was regarded as Viṣṇu, Lakṣmi, Śiva or Kṛṣṇa. It has to be guarded against objects and animals and cannot be touched by anyone outside the caste.[13] The family then circumambulate the body from one to seven times:

> You have to walk around the body four times clockwise with millet and sesame seeds in the palm, sprinkling it and saying "*śrī kṛṣṇaḥ śaraṇam mama* [I yield to thy feet, Lord Kṛṣṇa]". After the four revolutions the person will touch the feet, and others will, in turn. [The dead person] is like a devata, almost a god, so revolving around four times is like a pilgrimage of four *dhāmas*.[14] It is the person, not the body [you are honouring]. This is not to protect the soul but to discharge an emotional debt. (GjPlM)[15]

The circumambulations seem to have several functions. There is the discharge of a debt (*ṛṇa*), which would be especially important if the deceased is a parent or grandparent.[16] Secondly, like the circumambulation of a god, the mourners take *darśana*, receiving the blessing of the deceased, by being "in his sight". At the pyre the circumambulations create a boundary around the corpse, which protects the newly released soul (*bhūta-preta)*, and the body from ghosts on the one hand, and separate the mourners from the *bhūta-preta* on the other, as it may still be attached to the family. Finally, they may be a rite of separation of psychological significance to the mourners (5.3).[17]

5.2. Stage IV: *Piṇḍadāna* and procession to the cremation ground in India.

Offerings of balls of rice, wheat or barley (*piṇḍas*), should be placed at the place

---

(auspicious); for the sages it hangs around the neck, and for the ancestors it hangs from the right shoulder towards the left. It is moved to the right shoulder at inauspicious times during the funeral and *śrāddha* offerings to the deceased. Mathoor Krishnamurthi and Hemant Kanitkar state that it should be worn as a *mālā*, i.e. like a necklace or a rosary, over *both* shoulders and around the neck, when making the offerings to the deceased, and at the pyre (personal communication). Stevenson 1920:143-4, 152; Das 1977:122. 253; Planalp 1956:602.

[13] Das. 1976:253; Stevenson 1920:145; Pandey 1969:248; MS.5.104.

[14] *Dhāma*, Skt. *Dhāman:* the 'abode' of a god. The four *dhāmans* are the four points of the compass, and also (since a sacred place is a microcosm of the universe) four points around a place of pilgrimage which are visited in turn by pilgrims. Cf. Firth 1991:65; Eck 1983:288-89.

[15] Cf. Das 1976:253; Stevenson 1920:145.

[16] T.S.VI.3,10.5; Malamoud 1983:26ff..

[17] The ambiguous status of the corpse is reflected in the are conflicting views as to whether it should be circumambulated with the right shoulder to it (clockwise) in the way deities in the temple are circumambulated, which would suggest it is pure and auspicious, the view of Parry's Varanasi informants (personal communication; cf.1994:177). Kane says the CM circumambulates the corpse with his *left* side towards it (anti-clockwise; 1973 IV:206).

of death and at various strategic locations on the way to the cremation ground. Most Brahmin informants said there should be six *piṇḍas* offered, beginning at the home and ending at the pyre, but in some areas only five are made, the sixth offered when the ashes are gathered.[18] They have the dual function of protecting the *bhūta-preta* from dangerous spirits, and of satisfying it so that it does not wander, enabling it to become fit to be a *pitṛ*.[19]

These are the first of a series of sixteen *piṇḍas*, the remaining ten being offered, one each day, for ten days to enable the newly released *preta* to form a new body, although many people offer all ten on the tenth day (Ch. 6, below). The chief mourner, having been shaved, bathed, and wearing his sacred thread in the inauspicious direction over his right shoulder should offer the first, the *śava* (body) or *sthāna piṇḍa*, on the spot where the person died.[20] The family *purohit* usually directs this, although when available a specialist priest, a *mahābrāhmaṇa* or *acharāj*, may be called. Subsequent *piṇḍas* are offered at the doorway (*dvāra*) or threshold (*pānthika*), and may be offered in the courtyard (*tṛtīya*) or at the edge of the village, halfway to the cremation ground at a halt or at the crossroads (*khecara*), outside the cremation ground (*viśrāma*) and at the cremation ground. The last, *śmaśāna* or *sādhaka piṇḍa*, is offered for the *kṣetrapāla*, the protector of the area who is sometimes identified with Mahābhairava (Śiva), to ask his permission for the cremation (VarBrM.42).[21]

The ritual procession to the cremation ground, with its pauses and *piṇḍa* offerings is an important rite of separation of the deceased from the family and the deceased, and of the soul from the body and its old environs. The stops also allow the mourners to check that the person really is dead.[22] The procession should be on foot, with male members of the family and caste peers carrying the body as a sacred duty, although it was mentioned with some outrage that nowadays bodies are sometimes taken by Jeep or ambulance. Normally women follow as far as the edge of the village or the crossroads and then return to bathe and clean the house, although in urban areas, and according to Punjabi informants, in the Punjab, women may go too. The chief mourner may assist in

---

[18] Kane 1973 IV:219; Planalp 1956:600ff; Quayle 1980:10. The GP specifies five, the sixth to be offered when the bones are collected on the third or fourth day. GP II 4:48-9; 15:30ff; 35:33-34; cf. Parry 1985:615ff..

[19] GP II 4:61.

[20] Evison 1989:26; Planalp 1956:601.

[21] Cf. Evison 46, 1989; cf. Firth 1994: 528ff., for a full transcription of the *piṇḍa* ritual from *Śrī Śrāddhakaumudī Sūraka Nirṇaya Saṃhitā*, by Dvivedi, 1973, tr. Sheila Laxman, with comments by Hemant Kanitkar,

[22] Dubois 1906:485; Evison 1989:41.

the carrying of the body or walk in front of it carrying a brass or clay pot, bound with vines, containing fire from the domestic hearth (GjPt; GjVM.32), or water (PjBrM.65; UPKhM.60).[23]

Most informants said that the body left the house feet first, and after a halt outside the cremation ground at a special platform, called the *viśrāma,* it was turned so it could enter the ground head first. At the *viśrāma,* the chief mourner may make a number of rounds sprinkling water from the clay pot, which is then broken on a step at the foot of the platform. The pot breaking may also occur after circumambulating the pyre, or just afterwards (below).

5.3. Stage V. The cremation in India

During my fieldwork in India I visited three cremation grounds (*śmaśāna*). The Vadodara ground was located in a beautiful garden, with an electric crematorium, of a tasteful modern design, at some distance from the open pyres. The cheapest cremations took place on pyres built in concrete pits. There were also pyres on iron crib-like structures, which presumably burned faster but used more wood, and an elaborate roofed structure which provided shade from the sun. The electric crematorium made provision for rituals by means of a platform just outside the cremator, allowing the mourners to circumambulate it. The second one was at the *ghats* in Chandod, near Vadodara, where three sacred rivers join, and the third was in Varanasi; at both these pyres were built on the river bank in a manner more typical of village India.

There is considerable variation in the details of the cremation according to caste and region - for example, whether the fire is made of wood or cowdung according to availability and cost, whether the circumambulations are clockwise or anti-clockwise, and the number and way the *piṇḍas* are offered - but there also seem to be common elements. At least one *piṇḍa* is given as an offering, circumambulations are made around the pyre with water and fire, and there is a symbolic, if not actual, breaking of the skull.[24]

On arrival at the *ghat* the chief mourner cleans an area with cowdung (this is not done in Varanasi, it is already so sacred), makes a boundary with nails or *kuśa* grass, and then washes the first piece of wood with water and puts it in place. Friends and relatives make up the rest of the pyre, although in Varanasi the Doms, an untouchable caste who look after the cremation *ghats*, prepare and tend

[23] GP II 15:12-13; Padfield 1908:198; Stevenson 1920:146; Shastri 1963:28; Pandey 1969:248.

[24] Evison 1989:52

the fire. In some traditions the face is uncovered for a last farewell, before being covered with *ghī* and sprinkled with Ganga water, and placed on the pyre with the head to the north or south, depending on the pandit's textual tradition.[25] The cloths covering the body may be removed as the cowdung and wood are placed on it, preserving decency. These are then given to the *śmaśāna* attendants, although at Varanasi I saw the wrapped bodies, tied to the stretcher, being burned as they were.[26] It is at this point that the last *piṇḍa* is offered on the ground at the head of the body or on its folded hands or stomach.

The chief mourner circumambulates the body, but there is considerable variation as to how this is done. He may circumambulate the body carrying a clay pot of water before the fire is lit. A hole is made in the pot for the first *pradakṣiṇā* (clockwise circumambulation), a second hole for the second and a third hole for the third. The circles of water purify the soul, enable it to rise upwards in the direction it is supposed to go (Evison 1989:53), protect it from the dangers of the cremation ground, and create a boundary between the living and the dead, thus symbolising both separation and farewell. It also assuages the thirst of the ghost and pain of the fire.[27] If the chief mourner has brought fire from the domestic hearth in a pot, he may carry this around prior to lighting the fire. The pot may be broken now, or after the cremation. There may be a shout at this point, or later: "Many people shout when the fire is being lit, to make the chief mourner cry and also to scare away evil spirits. After that, when doing *kriyā* you are not supposed to cry, but at this stage you should cry so as not to get too depressed." (GjBrM.)

A number of informants said that the circumambulations here had to be clockwise (*pradakṣiṇā*), indicating a view of the body as sacred: "I move around thee, please forgive me. May whatever sin I have committed in this life and the previous life be forgiven by doing this *pradakṣiṇā*."[28] Other informants said emphatically they should be anti-clockwise, suggesting that the body was impure and inauspicious.[29]

The chief mourner lights the pyre with camphor, burning cowdung from the domestic fire, and a brand of burning *kuśa* grass or wood, carrying it around the

[25] Padfield 1908:199; Shastri 1963: 29; Gold 1988:83; Dvivedi 1973.

[26] Cf. Eck 1983:249.

[27] Padfield 1908:200; Srinivas 1965:151.

[28] BihPt. cf.Padfield 1908:200; Parry 1982:78.

[29] A tantric Brahmin in Varanasi said there should be five or seven half circles which did not cross at the feet. Cf. Firth 1991:69; Das, 1977:122; Parry 1982:79; Kaushik 1976:277; Evison 1989:30.

body. Halfway through the cremation, in some regions, the skull is broken (*kapāla kriyā*, literally 'skull action'), with a bamboo. Brahmin informants said this was because the *dhanañjay prāṇa* or *vāyu* remains in the skull and will create a ghost unless released (GjPt; UPBrM; GjVF; cf. 3.2.1). However, many of Parry's informants defined death "as the instant at which the *prāṇ* or 'vital breath' leaves the body ... this occurs - not at the cessation of physiological functioning - but at the rite of *kapāla kriyā*, which is performed mid-way through the cremation", before which it is "commonly said to be completely inappropriate to use the term 'preta' meaning 'a disembodied ghost'". The implication of this is that the corpse is, in some sense, animate: "As another informant spontaneously put it, 'he does not die but is killed. He dies on the pyre.'" The cremation is thus a sacrifice, in which the chief mourner becomes a homicide, and the subsequent purifications are performed in accordance with this.[30] Regarding the body as a sacrifice would, of course, mean that it would have to be circumambulated clockwise, in an auspicious direction (cf. f.n. 17). Although my own informants, including four Varanasi pandits, did not regard the cremation as a true sacrifice despite the implication of the term *antyeṣṭi* (final sacrifice), it seems that the *ātman* becomes disconnected at some level from the remaining *prāṇa* in the skull, either through the *kapāla kriyā* or the pot breaking, so that it "receives a message" and "knows that it is dead" (VarPt.42). In either case the postponement of the cremation for a week or more, as in Britain, has extremely grave implications for the *ātman*, and according to the Indian pandits, the soul will not rest.

In some regions the *kapāla kriyā* is not done, as the heat of the cremation is thought to be enough to break the skull spontaneously. It is difficult to watch and very traumatic for the people doing it; some men pass out. In the Punjab and Uttar Pradesh the chief mourner leaves when the body is nearly burned, and "three or four stone-hearted" men perform the task on his behalf. In Varanasi the chief mourner can buy a pot from Dom Raj, the head of the Dom community, and break it instead of the skull by throwing it backwards, and then walking away without looking back.

The pot-breaking ceremony, with its variations, seems to be common in most parts of India.[31] It occurs at the entrance to the cremation ground after the *pradakṣiṇās* but before the body is cremated, towards the end of the cremation,

---

[30] Parry 1982:79-80; cf. Evison 1989: 53ff..

[31] Cf. Evison 1989, 52ff..

as above, or after the cremation. According to Raheja, the breaking of the pot, which in her account contains four *piṇḍas,* outside the cremation ground, transfers the inauspiciousness of the dead body "to the proper recipient, here, simply the space outside the village and the animals who may eat the *piṇḍ*".[32] It may also, as above, be a substitute for the breaking of the skull, symbolising (or actually enabling) the release of the *ātman* (UPKhM). It also seems to have the function of finally breaking the bond between the deceased and the chief mourner: "to have any further contact with the corpse would encourage death and the denizens of the funeral ground to follow the relatives back to the village".[33] Parry sees the pot as symbolizing both the womb and the body; the last thing the *mahābrāhmaṇa* does as he walks away on the eleventh day after conducting the *śrāddha*, when the new body for the ghost has been formed, is to break a pot.[34]

Should the death occur during *pañcaka*, the five inauspicious days each lunar month, then drastic action has to be taken, especially if the person is young; otherwise more people will die within five days (4.2). According to Evison, this time is dangerous because "the distinction between the world of the living and that of the dead becomes blurred and the barriers which separate the two realms are at their weakest". The result is that " the force of death cannot be repelled and claims other victims before a proper distinction between the two worlds is restored as the moon waxes".[35]

Cremation during *pañcaka* is more dangerous than death, as four or five more people will die, or as many as there are days left in *pañcaka*. If it cannot be delayed, the family have to make five effigies of barley flour (PBrM) or *darbha* grass (UPBrM) and cremate them with the dead, in a special ritual called *pañcaka śānti*.[36] Effigies also have to be burned if the householder dies away from home, especially if no body is found. If bones are found these are used; if not, and also in the case of unnatural deaths, effigies are created and burned instead of the body.[37]

While the men go to the cremation the women return to the house, which they sweep and clean, and then bathe. Either now or before the rituals on the tenth day they throw away fresh foodstuffs and may throw away the bed. Some Gujaratis place red powder or flour on the floor where the body lay, and place a basket

---

32 Raheja 1988:148.
33 Evison 1989:56; PjKhM62;
34 Parry, personal communication; cf. 1994:167ff..
35 Evison 1989:169ff cf.GP II 4:176ff; 35.17ff..
36 GP II 4:179ff..
37 ŚB XII 51; Parry 1989:507; Evison 1989; cf.4.2; 6.2.1.

over it before the procession leaves. When the male mourners return it is raised to see what pattern there is underneath, as this will indicate the kind of rebirth the *ātman* has taken (somewhat at variance with the view that it will take ten to twelve days for the *preta* to form a new body). A Darji said, "If the flour is plain, that is good, he has gone to heaven, but if you see signs then it is his *karma.*" Informants claimed to have seen the figures of a man, Kṛṣṇa, Oṃ, and a snake. A Darji woman saw 'photos' of Kṛṣṇa, Rāma and Oṃ when her father-in-law died, which indicated he had gone straight to heaven, to God.

In some families the widow's bangles are broken on the body, in others they are smashed after it has left the house: "...the ladies will be collected and the one who has become a widow will be sitting in the centre, and her bangles will be broken by a stone, and it is very pitiable...they all make her aware that 'now you are a widow'." (GjPlF.60; cf. 8.4 below)

The returning men wash or bathe at the cremation ground and wash at home and purify themselves in the smoke of a lighted incense stick. Some communities touch an iron object, and step over a stone symbolising strength and permanence, as a rite of re-entry into the house. Evison sees the stone as a "channel through which the dead person receives offerings but also a temporary body for the ghost until a new one can be constructed from *piṇḍas*", used as the focus for the offerings to the *preta*.[38] A new fire is lit in the courtyard and people will walk around it before going inside (PjKhM62). The lamp, placed where the person died, may also be offered *piṇḍas* every evening. Mourners normally fast until the cremation is over, unless there is a delay. There is no cooking in some households, so food is brought in by friends and relatives.

5.4. Stage III: Preparation of the Body in Britain

In Britain there is a radical transformation of the stages from the moment of death. All the deaths in my study occurred suddenly or in hospital. From the moment of death most of the control and decision-making about the disposal of the body was taken out of the hands of the family, especially if a post mortem was necessary. Once the body was released from the hospital, it was taken to the undertakers'. Instead of bathing it immediately after death when it was still warm, it had to done a week or more later after being refrigerated.

In the early days of the community the body was sometimes prepared in the hospital mortuary shortly after death. This was changed because the body needed

---

[38] Evison 1989:348.

to be in a state of ritual purity for *agni saṃskāra* (cremation), so that it would need to be prepared immediately beforehand (7.3). The chief mourner with his male relatives or caste peers bathes and dresses the body of a male relative. Participating in the preparation of his father's body can be quite traumatic for a young son who may not have seen a corpse before. Older female relatives or caste peers prepare the body of a woman, sometimes assisted by a retired nurse. Young women, even if married, are not allowed to participate.

There are caste traditions as to how the body should be washed - some use water, either washing fully or sprinkling, while others use yoghurt or milk. Senior members of the family or caste peers give guidance; relatives in India may be telephoned for advice. When the father of a Punjabi man died suddenly in the street from a heart attack, an uncle visiting from India was able to give guidance. He, another uncle and the three sons prepared the body, which was "quite terrifying, quite traumatic. We were just chanting religious things at the same time, trying to keep my mind off it" (PjKhM). Sometimes the mourners are so upset they ask the funeral director to bathe and dress the body and just give a symbolic sprinkling with Ganga water afterwards.

The body is dressed in the sort of clothes the person normally wore. A man is dressed in a new suit if it can be afforded, and socks and shoes, so there is a shift from the ideal of the *dhotī* or loose covering. A woman, as in India, will be dressed in a white sari or *salvār kameez* if widowed, and her wedding sari or *salvār kameez* if she is fortunate enough to die before her husband (8.4-8.5). The body is placed in the coffin covered with a cloth or beautiful shawl, especially if the deceased is elderly. A piece of gold or a coin is placed in the mouth "to pay the ferryman", either at the undertakers' or during the funeral. The body is then taken to the family home in a hearse for the first part of the funeral.

5.5. Stages IV-V: The funeral in Britain: the domestic ritual

For convenience the ritual in the home will be described as the funeral, which is how it tends to be referred to, reflecting the changing pattern of events, and the service at the crematorium will be referred to as the cremation. The rituals in the house are adaptations of domestic rituals which would have been performed immediately after death in relation to the body, such as its preparation, the circumambulations (Stage III), the offering of the first two *piṇḍas* (Stage IV) and those which, in India, would be performed at the cremation ground (Stage V), but which would be impossible in the crematorium, for reasons of both design and time. The ritual procession (Stage IV), with its halts, the offering of *piṇḍas*, and the breaking of the pot, has been reduced to a drive in the hearse from the undertakers' to the house and then to the crematorium. If *piṇḍas* are offered at all, they are offered in the home and placed in the coffin. Thus Stages III, IV and V, which in India normally form a continuum with Stage II (death), within twenty-four hours, are separated from it by as much as a week, and in Stage IV the rituals have been detached from the procession. To an observer, the ceremony at home seems to be the most significant part of the funeral, not least because the whole family is present, including women and often children. There is more time than the 25 minutes permitted at the crematorium, and more freedom to perform whatever rituals are possible in the circumstances. Because it is usually possible to display the body, various substances can be placed on it which would have been placed on it prior to the procession and at the pyre in India. All the funerals I observed in Britain had a pandit conducting them, with considerable variety in the ways this was done, but there were many accounts of funerals conducted by a local Brahmin, and in the early days of settlement a Sikh conducted a Hindu Punjabi funeral. There may be a eulogy or a homily. While the chief mourner is usually the son or a male relative, several pandits have permitted daughters to act as chief mourners claiming there was scriptural backing for it,[39] although more conservative pandits have frowned on this practice.

A Gujarati pandit sends a list of what he will need to the family in advance, advising them as to what materials should be prepared. He tries to arrive at least half an hour early to start the prayers and *mantras*, and if it can be arranged suggests the family gather for a private ritual before the body arrives from the undertakers'. He has found havoc on occasion, so he asks the mourners to be quiet and orderly. *Thālīs* (circular trays) are prepared with all the necessary ingredients: *piṇḍas*, *tulasī* leaves, flowers, Ganga water, various powders, incense sticks, *chandan* (sandalwood), yoghurt, and sesame seeds. Arya Samajis and many other Punjabis also have *havan sāmagrī*, herbs for the sacred fire. A small bit of gold is needed, which may be taken from the wife's *mangalasūtra* (marriage necklace), if she has just been widowed, but some priests do not like to take this and prefer new gold, which the Indian goldsmith gives for no charge. The furniture is removed from the living room, and white cloths spread on the floor, sprinkled with *pañca-gavya* (the five products of a cow) and Ganga water.

The body is carried into the house in its 'box' - a disparaging term reflecting dislike of the coffin - by male relatives and friends who 'give shoulder' to it as

39 AGS IV 2:4-9; GP II 34:23; Evison 1989:319.

a sacred obligation. Sometimes, in a small house it is brought in through the window, or turned on end to negotiate the front passage. This can shift the body, to the distress of the family. It is brought in feet first, since people enter the house feet first, and placed on trestles in the living room. The body is oriented as it would have been in India. There may be disagreement as to the correct direction, especially if the pandit and clients come from different regions with their own traditions. A Gujarati pandit carries a compass to ensure the head is to the north; a Bihari pandit insists it should be to the south. There may also be procedural wrangling over other aspects of the ritual as older members of the family argue with the pandit, especially the women who wish to maintain family traditions, but one pandit found senior men who served on the temple committee quite difficult at times: "There is always someone who wants to show they know more than anyone else" (GjPt70).

At all the funerals I have attended the living room was packed with friends, relatives and community members who stood as the coffin was brought in, and began chanting the *Gāyatrī Mantra*. According to several pandits, no Vedic *mantras* should be chanted during *sūtaka* (the time of impurity).[40] "It is only done because people don't know; they do it to purify the place and make it holy, but it is not part of the old tradition" (PjPt55). A Gujarati pandit, however, commented that the rituals themselves were from the ṚV and AV, and incluced the word "*Oṃ*".[41]

Other phrases which may be chanted include "*rādhe kṛṣṇa, gopāla kṛṣṇa*" (Rādhā Kṛṣṇa, Kṛṣṇa Gopāla),[42] "*śrī kṛṣṇaḥ śaraṇam mama*" (Kṛsna is my refuge), "*oṃ namaḥ śivāya*" (homage to Śiva), "*om namo bhagavate vāsudevāya*" (salutations to Bhagavan Vāsudeva, Kṛṣṇa), and "*śrī rāma, jaya rāma, jaya jaya rāma*" (victory to Rama).

The coffin is opened, with the family standing on the right side of the body and the pandit on the left. A *dīvā* (lamp) is lit and placed near the head, on the right. The sons and the rest of the immediate family perform *ācamana*, sipping water, and then touching themselves, from head to neck, neck to waist, and waist to feet, as a purification. This symbolises the three *lokas*, heaven, earth and below

---

40 Cf. Stevenson 1920:164 and 8.2 below.

41 If one took the view of some of Parry's pandits that the corpse was not impure until after the soul was released by the *kapāla kriyā*, the use of Vedic *mantras* would not be a problem, but the time delay in Britain would doubtless necessitate a reinterpretation of this position. The funeral rituals for non-Brahmins are said by some pandits to be Purāṇic, not Vedic, but the NCHT ritual includes Vedic verses.

42 Kṛṣṇa in the form of Gopāla, the cowherd.

the earth. Then the chief mourner performs *saṃkalpa*, a declaration of intent, naming the day, date, and month, as well as the name and *gotra* (lineage) of the deceased, explaining what is to be done and for whom:

> This is my prayer for the departed soul that I am offering, may this soul have *sadgati*, the happy ending. "O my father or mother, you were here all these days with us, now you have left the body - may I offer my prayer to see that your soul journey will be happy, and I, as a son, will perform my duty to see you have a safe journey." (KanPt)

The chief mourner then moves the sacred thread from the left shoulder (the auspicious side) to the right, the inauspicious side. If he has no thread, one is made on the spot from white cotton. The chief mourner or priest may chant eight stanzas of the *Gangā Stotra* or *Puruṣa Sūkta*, and then the chief mourner places Ganga water in the mouth of the deceased, with *tulasī*, gold, yoghurt, *ghī*, or *pañcāmṛta* (a mixture of *ghī*, honey, sugar, milk and yoghurt), although one pandit (Bihari) felt the latter was not *śāstrika*, and was only appropriate for bathing a deity. Other members of the family follow suit if there is time, and put a *tilak* of sandalwood paste on the forehead, or *sindhur*, a red paste, in the parting of a married woman. Rice, sesame and *darbha* grass may be put on top of the body; pink and white powders are also sprinkled on, and flowers or petals will be scattered over it. The family should do this, but if time is short they will touch the chief mourner as he does it. The body may be garlanded. Four or five coconuts may be given by the sons, one for each direction, (although at one Arya Samaji funeral only pieces of coconut were placed on the body), and the widow may, either now or later, place one on the chest.

When the body has thus been decorated, six *piṇḍas* should be offered, although at some of the funerals I attended only one or none were offered. Most of the pandits interviewed said they insisted on six, and often had to argue their case with the older members of the community, explaining the *piṇḍas* were necessary to protect both *ātman* and body against *bhūts*, evil spirits (5.2). The Westmouth pandit thought this part of the ritual was the only thing that really mattered. Three *piṇḍas*, according to a Gujarati pandit, should be placed on the right, and three on the left, near the hands. While most of the experienced pandits read from one of their *karmakāṇḍa* (ritual texts), one Punjabi pandit simply read a large portion of the *Bhagavad Gītā* and then directed the chief mourner to make the *piṇḍas* and place them in the coffin. Various other items may be placed in the coffin: a *kuntī* (rosary), sandalwood, *agarbattī* (incense sticks),and *ghī*, which may be applied to the feet and hands, or applied all over. Some communities just put in packets of butter. *Havan sāmagrī* may also be sprinkled on the body. One pandit said if the funeral occurred during *pañcaka*, he quietly took five effigies with him and placed them in the coffin, only telling the chief mourner or senior relatives to avoid causing pain and anxiety (5.3).

The family now do four *pradakṣiṇās*, or five if the wife is alive, the widow in front carrying a coconut with both hands unless the eldest son is there to lead the family. A Gujarati pandit commented, "She entered marriage with a coconut in her hand, so this is the moment when it should be returned. It is a very holy and auspicious thing, used in all religious ceremonies." The Bihari pandit thought this was a new tradition which had arisen in Britain for her consolation, but since his clients were mainly Gujarati this may simply reflect regional differences. Since it is impossible to circumambulate the pyre with a burning brand, some pandits suggest that the mourners take lighted incense sticks around the body and touch them to the lips of the body (*mukhāgni*) as a substitute. Other pandits feel strongly that this is inappropriate in the house as it is not the cremation, although pushing the coffin into the furnace is no substitute for the rituals at the pyre: "We are living in a culture where we are not in control" (BihPt.65). Those who do take lighted incense around touch the right toe and sometimes the head and sides as a symbol of lighting the fire, then circumambulate four times and place the sticks in the coffin. Some communities such as Mistrys take a clay pot, containing incense and rice and other substances, to circumambulate the body. At a Punjabi funeral the eldest son carried a pot of water round the coffin and broke it just outside the front door as the coffin was removed from the house. If the pot is copper the water is poured on the wheels of the hearse before it departs.

As the family circumambulates, starting from the feet, they take sesame, flowers and other substances, and on the fourth round, bow low and touch the feet of the corpse:

> This is the highest honour you can pay to a person. I do not know whether it is to the body or the soul but I think it is the soul as it is the last honour. When a young boy goes on a journey to a foreign land, or undertakes an examination, you do a *tika* and give him a coconut, so similarly this is to say goodbye and send him on his journey. (GjDj35)

This was described by another Gujarati as "*antim darśana*" the last *darśana*, but he believed it was only the *darśana* of the body: "The *ātma* is not there; some people think it hangs around the house, but that is all in the mind" (GjL70; 5.1).

Finally, after the outsiders have paid their respects, the eldest or youngest son will go around again, chanting God's name. If his father has died he bows low, crying "*Bābūjī, Bābūjī*"; for a mother he cries *"Mājī* or *Mātājī"*. According to one pandit this is *lokācāra*, a local tradition. The priest, meanwhile, reads a passage such as BG 2, 8 or 15 or recites the "Thousand names of Viṣṇu". A cloth (*kafan*), is placed on the body; if the deceased is a married woman, her family will provide this. This may be white, or for an older person, an embroidered shawl, or for Brahmins it can be a richly coloured silk. Then, if the husband has died, the widow is brought to the coffin to say goodbye, and this may be the stage at which she will take off her coloured bangles and place them in the coffin, although some communities force them off or break them for her, which the pandits find very distressing: "The widows want to bring her into their own camp" (BihPt; 8.4-8.5). The lid is closed as the mourners chant something such as "*oṃ namo bhagavate vāsudevāya*".

A Swaminarayan informant had been told by Pramukh Swami that a pandit was unnecessary except for the *śrāddha*; "the only ceremonies of concern were the coconut, doing *ārtī* and saying goodbye to the body". At the funeral of the informant's father there were three principal features. The BG was read as "God's message that the person has not really died but has gone to his place, to heaven". A water offering was made to make sure "the soul goes to heaven or rests in peace, so that it doesn't come back to earth because he didn't get food or water" (4.4.1; Ch.7). Finally the eldest son made a vow to fast on the eleventh day (sacred to Viṣṇu) for two months, "so that whatever sins [his father] had done got washed away".

A number of Westmouth informants have not brought the body home but have had a simple ceremony in the undertakers' chapel, sometimes with no pandit, either because none was available or from choice. A senior family or caste member or local Brahmin has read portions of the GP or BG, recited some *mantras* and prayers, and the family circumambulated the coffin, placing various substances in it according to tradition. A Darji told me he did not have a pandit for the funeral, prepared the body of his father himself, and made four big *piṇḍas*, which he placed on each side of the body "as food for the journey".

An Arya Samaji funeral will be greatly simplified in principle, without the use of *tulasī* or *gangajal*, or the purificatory rituals, but "many half-baked Arya Samajis demand it", according to one leader in London. Mourners circumambulate in a clockwise direction placing *havan sāmagrī* and flower petals on the body, and then leave. He reads from ṚV X.16.3 and then suggests that the

Gayātrī Mantra be recited five to seven times to prevent people shouting and screaming.

Where there has been a Sikh-Hindu intermarriage, or where elderly Punjabi Hindus are involved in Sikh devotional activities, there may be a Sikh funeral. An elderly Brahmin woman was given both a Hindu ritual at her home and a Sikh funeral in the gurdwara. Both the pandit and the granthi (reader) led the cremation service, with two eulogies, one in Punjabi and one in Hindi.

5.6. Stage IV: The procession to the crematorium

The ritual procession has virtually disappeared in Britain, although important remnants of it, such as the *piṇḍa-dāna*, may be preserved in the domestic ceremony. While the body cannot be borne to the crematorium on foot because of the distances, it is carried by the sons, male relatives and caste peers from the home into the hearse. The hearse is followed by the family in a limousine and mourners in double-decker buses. There are usually no stops on the way, although at recent funerals the hearse has driven past the temple. This may be a new tradition imported from elsewhere, or have evolved as a result of Sikh influence, as Sikh bodies are taken to the gurdwara for prayers. The elderly Punjabi Brahmin woman (above), who had both Hindu and Sikh funerals, was driven past the temple after the procession left the gurdwara. The effect of this detour is to return to the procession a religious element which has been absent.

On arrival at the crematorium, the mourners wait outside for the coffin to be carried in by relatives and friends, so that they can follow the body in.[43] This has caused difficulties in the past with the undertakers who usually carry the coffin in after the mourners have entered the chapel. Women enter first after the coffin has been carried in by the chief mourner, male relatives and close friends, followed by the rest of the men who may have to stand if the chapel is overcrowded. At all the funerals I observed in Westmouth, Punjabi women attended but Gujarati women did not normally go, although younger women are changing this.

5.7. Stage V: The cremation in Britain

In the Westmouth chapel the cross is replaced by the symbol of *oṃ*. There are a few prayers and *mantras*, and the BG may be read, although this is regarded as quite inappropriate at the cremation by some pandits.The funeral prayer should

---

[43] Cf. Stevenson 1920:148.

be directed towards two things: one for the elements making up the body, the *pañcatattva*, the other for the elements making up the spiritual body, the *prāṇatattva*. The correct rituals should be obtained by a suitably learned priest from a *karmakāṇḍa* (book of rituals). The short service produced by the National Council for Hindu Temples (Appendix) has been criticised by the pandits because of its use of the *Bhagavad Gītā*, which a Gujarati pandit says is

> ...not for the soul. It is for the comfort of the mourners, but this isn't a proper funeral prayer. The *ślokas* from the *Gītā* [2.22] about casting off our clothes are for our knowledge but God, Agni or Yama will not accept that as a prayer. It is all right to read the *Gītā* at home, but it is not appropriate at the cremation.

A short eulogy or homily may be given, although the pandit, above, was told in no uncertain terms at one funeral that "We have brought you here to pray, not to give us a sermon." If the pandit knew the deceased, some remarks about his or her good works and character will be made, and the mourners reminded of the ephemeral nature of earthly existence and the inevitability of birth and death.The following homily was given in Westmouth by an Arya Samaji priest at the cremation of a Punjabi Khattri:

> Man's life is very uncertain. It is beyond our power to say when it comes and goes. God gives us this life in trust out of his own wealth, and for this reason we have no authority over this life. He who gives us this wealth and sustains it has authority over it. After some time he who is the owner takes back his own money and we will have to give it back. Today Mr. X is no longer with us. His earthly body will, after a few moments, turn to ashes. But he who does not die for his own sake, selfishly, never dies. He who dies for the benefit of society, for the benefit of the people of society, gives his life. As long as the sun and the moon remain he remains alive. His 'name' certainly remains alive. From your presence here I can tell that Mr. X made his home in your hearts in the form of service done for society.

After the prayers the chief mourner presses the button for the coffin to disappear, and then the CM and male relatives [44] go down below to ignite the cremator or to push the coffin in, which is difficult for some. A Śiva shrine may be set up outside with a pile of rice, a *dīvā* and *agarbattī* where the sons and

---

[44] While women have been allowed to conduct both the domestic funeral rituals and the *śrāddha*, I know of no situations where they actually pushed the coffin into the cremator.

other mourners do a short *pūjā* offering money before returning. [45]

Outside the house there is a large bowl or bucket of water, and mourners and visitors sprinkle themselves with water before entering, although strict members of strict Swaminarayaṇ or Pushṭimarga bathe and change in a friend's house before returning to their own home. For a time everyone returns to the house and sits quietly on the sheet-covered floor, before returning to their own homes, except for the relatives. Friends and neighbours bring in simple, spice-free food to feed the visiting relatives, of whom there may be a great number from various parts of the United Kingdom, India, East Africa or the United States.

In some Punjabi families the pandit returns with the family for a havan immediately after the funeral. This seems to be a modified Arya Samaji tradition. In East Africa, the Arya Samajis completed all the ceremonies by the fourth day, when traditionally the ashes are collected, because Swami Dayanand Saraswati rejected the concept of *sūtaka* and the conventional *śrāddha* ceremonies.[46] The local pandit refused to perform *havan* with Vedic verses during *sūtaka* for a recent funeral, so the family invited a priest from London instead. Following the *havan* the eldest son was presented with a turban (*pagṛī*), by his wife's family, as a sign that he was now responsible for younger members of the family, unmarried sisters, and his mother. The pandit gave a little homily, telling him that he was now the head of the household and should take his responsibilities seriously and not provoke his younger brothers, while they were told to obey and respect him. They then presented their mother with gold bangles and saris as a sign that they would care for her. This completed the Arya Samaj rituals, although another *havan* may be offered on the 12th day with gifts to the Brahmins.

The constraints of time mean that only the minimum of rituals can be done, with some of the *saṃkalpa*, *vidhis* (prescribed ritual acts) and *piṇḍas* offered at home instead of at the cremation. There is clearly a tension between the pandits' need to use as much of the traditional ritual as possible, regardless of the significance of the text to the mourners, and the mourners' desire to provide a good send-off, often resulting in inventive compromises.

---

[45] An image of Śiva was formally installed at the Gilroes crematorium in Leicester in July 1997. Some pandit informants said worship should not occur in *sūtaka*, but some of my informants said it was justified as Śiva was Lord of the Cremation ground. A spokesman at the installation said, "The soul goes to Lord Shiva when it parts from the body."Leicester Mercury, July 31, 1997.

[46] Saraswati 1975:337: 419-423.

5.8. Stage VI: *Asthisañcayana*: disposal of the ashes in India and Britain.

While there may be a great contrast between the procedures and the timing of the gathering of the bones and ashes in India and Britain, there may be little difference in their disposal, especially if mourners deposit the ashes in the Ganga or the Yamuna. If the journey takes place shortly after the death, the ritual forms part of the *śrāddha* rituals, usually performed on the tenth day, but in both India and Britain the taking of the ashes often forms part of a longer pilgrimage much later. This is not just a simple journey to a particular site at a holy river. With the *śrāddha*, it is the culmination of the process beginning before or at death, symbolising the final departure or 'seeing off' of the *ātman* on its journey to the next life, affirming ancient beliefs, as well as following family traditions. As Parry points out, "The saying is that the deceased will reside in heaven for as long as any portion of his mortal remains is sanctified by Ganga water...as the Sanskrit verse proclaims: 'those whose bones, hair, nails and flesh fall in Kashi will reside in heaven even though they be great sinners'."[47] Its importance lies not just in the symbolic and religious significance of the Ganga or a sacred river identified mystically with it, but in fulfilling a duty to the deceased.

In India the bones and ashes are usually collected on the third day, although in busy city crematoria, especially electric ones, they may be collected the same day. The term used is *phūl chānnā* (picking flowers). The bones are picked out, washed in water or water and milk and hung in a pot from a tree or from the roof of the house, or kept at the cremation ground until they can be taken to a sacred river. The ashes are thrown into the nearest river. Ideally, the bones are divided into three parts, with one each going to Allahabad, Varanasi and Haridwar. For Gujaratis, the confluence of the Yamuna, Ganga and Saraswati at Prayaga (Allahabad) is particularly sacred.[48] In Varanasi the ashes and bones are thrown into the river straight away; the holiness of the city and the river makes elaborate procedures unnecessary.

The gathering of ashes in Britain is not attended by any rituals since they are already packaged by the crematorium. They are taken to India or to the river or sea locally, usually just before the *śrāddha* rituals, or sent to India with friends or even posted. The Divine Society will do the appropriate ceremonies in Haridwar for a small payment, although the current government project to clean up the Ganga makes this more difficult. Where possible the family make the

---

[47] Parry 1981:351; Kane 1973 IV:243.

[48] Cf. Stutley and Stutley 1977:233.

journey to India to perform the rituals themselves with the *śrāddha* rituals. Gujarati and Punjabi Hindus in Westmouth tend to go to Haridwar. For many Hindus this is where their ancestors went, and they will visit a pandit who has their family's names written in a huge ledger, thus maintaining ancient links and continuity with the past. Tandon describes this:

> There our family has its own panda .... who at his death is succeeded by his son. He maintains the family records in long, old-fashioned Indian ledgers, covered in red cloth, in which he writes down the length of the page. Every time someone goes he brings these records up to date by entering births, marriages and deaths, migrations and other information about what has been happening in the family. When I first visited Hardwar I had only to say I was a Tandon from Gujrat, and from a crowd of pandas our priest came forward and reeled off our whole family tree for several generations. He had met my father, uncles and elder brother when they had visited Hardwar. ...The family ledgers are the precious stock-in-trade of these pandas, and they know the genealogies by heart.[49]

A Gujarati Brahmin took his father's ashes to Haridwar after arranging for an evening of prayers and *bhajans* in his ancestral town, Porbander in Gujarat, and collecting money for cows and for a temple. He performed the *śrāddha* at Haridwar: - "It is cleaner than the water at Banaras, and nearer to Delhi. Putting Dad's ashes in the Ganga purified his soul, dipping in the Ganga cleansed my sins and made me feel better, softer, changed my way of doing things."

Some Hindus think it unnecessary to go to India, since all rivers run into the sea. According to a Punjabi Khattri, "If you have faith it doesn't matter where you scatter the ashes. The world belongs to you. The idea of going to the Ganga clashes with *karma*. As long as you believe in God and fear God and know whatever you do you will pay for that is all that matters". Others are concerned that the length of time it would be necessary to wait to go to India could affect the fate of the soul. A Swaminarayan family said that the ashes should not be kept beyond a full moon as the *ātman* would not have any peace. Some members of the family had previously taken ashes to the Thames, which they said had the sacred attribute of three rivers merging, but was also rather unclean. They solved the problem by approaching Lord Montagu of Beaulieu, who allowed them to use the bank of the river at Beaulieu. This was sanctified by the head of the sect, Pramukh Swami, so that this is now a holy river, and like the Ganga runs into the

---

[49] Tandon 1961:9.

ocean. In a sense, this is 'bringing India' to this country, by bringing the estuary into the domain of an *avatar* of Viṣṇu. Others take the ashes to an estuary, such as the mouth of the Severn or Thames (7.3 below).[50]

There is thus a shift in both the pattern and emphasis of the funeral rituals. The cremation procession with its halts, the offering of *piṇḍas*, and the breaking of the pot have disappeared or lost their emphasis; the cremation itself has altered radically, with no open pyre, circumambulations at the crematorium, or *kapāla kriyā*. The fire can only be offered indirectly, and many of the last rites are performed in the home instead, sometimes without a pandit. For some Hindus this seems to be the focal point of the funeral, especially for those Gujarati women who do not go to the crematorium. Despite the efforts of the pandits, the purpose of the service at the crematorium may be shifting towards the consolation of the mourners in this world, rather than concern solely with the welfare of the dead in the unseen world. The long term effect on belief of losing the *kapāla kriyā*, with its implications for the soul, and the different context of the *piṇḍa dāna*, may create a shift in understanding of the nature of the departing soul. As some of the rituals disappear or alter, such as the pot breaking and the *kapāla kriyā*, the beliefs that go with them may also change. The pandits are adapting the rituals to the circumstances. Whether there is eventually a standardised form, or a variety of forms as at present remains to be seen.

Taking the ashes to India connects with ancestral, religious and cultural roots. Performing at least some of the *śrāddha* rituals in India gives the satisfaction of having done the best they could for the peace of the soul. It is a journey *home* of both the deceased and the living, a spiritual as well as an emotional pilgrimage, in which contact is re-established with distant relatives and holy places visited to gain merit and for renewal. It is thus more than an expression of the desire of every Hindu in India to have his/her ashes in the sacred Ganga - it is the return to and maintenance of his/her deepest roots, reinforcing and confirming, for those in the diaspora, the umbilical link with India.

---

[50] Poulter 1989:82-85; 1990:124ff; cf. 7.3.1 below.

Chapter 6
Stages VII-IX: *Śrāddhas*: Offerings to the *preta* (ghost) and *pitṛs* (ancestors)

From the earliest Vedic times death has been seen as a transition to another life (Ch. 3), and the deceased have been nurtured and cared for in various ways. Furthermore, the relationship between the living and the dead, the ancestors, *pitṛs* or *pitaraḥ*, is a symbiotic one, depending on the regular sustenance of the dead by the living. In return for the performance of their duty the living receive merit for progeny, health and well-being. When it separates from the body the soul is no bigger than a thumb, naked, hungry and thirsty. It has to go through a painful intermediate period in which it has to have a new body created ritually by food offerings over a period of ten days. During this time the family are also dead to the world, leading an ascetic life style in a state of extreme impurity, and socially isolated from outsiders.[1] The newly formed *preta* is nourished and strengthened on the eleventh day before it embarks on its journey to Yama's Kingdom.[2] The process by which the deceased becomes a fully-fledged *pitṛ* (ancestor) takes up to a year, but nowadays the rituals are often condensed to a symbolic year of twelve days in the final ritual, *sapiṇḍīkaraṇa* (3.1).[3] Thereafter he is nourished at regular times.

These rituals are known as *śrāddha*, the word derived from the term *śraddhā*, faith. There are three main groups.[4] The first group, Stage VII includes the *nava* (new) *śrāddhas* consisting of the first ten days of offerings. These are the *malina ṣoḍaśī*, or impure *śrāddhas*, as they are offered during *sūtaka* and *aśauca*, a time of impurity and inauspiciousness.[5] There are sixteen of these: six *piṇḍas* offered on the day of the cremation (cf 5.2 above) and one each day on the following ten days, or ten on the tenth day. The second group, are the semi-pure *śrāddhas*, known as the *nava-miśra* or mixed *śrāddha*.[6] These take place from the eleventh day up to a year and include those given on behalf of one ancestor (the deceased), *ekoddiṣṭa*. These release the deceased from the rank of *preta* and give it the strength for its journey through Yama's kingdom. The third group, the pure

---

1 Das 1976:256-257; Kaushik 1976:278-279.

2 Kane 1973 IV:267ff.

3 GP II.5; II. 34.53; Kane 1973 IV:262, 520; Knipe 1977:114; Parry 1989:509.

4 Müller 1969:136; Evison 1989:84.

5 Stevenson 1920:159; cf. Knipe 1977:520.

6 Also known as *madhya ṣoḍaśaka* or *madhyama* (middle) *śrāddhas*.

śrāddhas, includes those given for all the ancestors, especially the three generations of father, grandfather and great-grandfather (*pārvaṇa śrāddha*). The climactic one on the twelfth day (Stage VIII) is the *sapiṇḍīkaraṇa* in which the spirit of the deceased joins the ancestral ranks. Those performed after the *sapiṇḍīkaraṇa,* when the *preta* has become a *pitṛ,* are known as the *uttāra or purāṇa śrāddhas* (Stage IX).[7] Subsequently, *śrāddhas* are performed throughout the first year and on the *tithi*, the anniversary of the day of death according to the lunar calendar.[8]

6.1. Stages VII-VIII. *Śrāddhas* in India

For the first ten days after death, the chief mourner, often accompanied by the family priest and perhaps by a *mahābrāhmaṇa*, the specialist funeral priest who acts as the surrogate for the deceased, goes daily to a tank or river bank.[9] He makes offerings to the deceased, sometimes represented by a stone (*jivkhada*) or *darbha* grass.[10] He offers a *piṇḍa*, which both represents the deceased and forms part of its new body, while the Brahmin recites the name of the deceased's *gotra*, the month in which he died and his name.[11] A cup of water containing sesame is poured over the ball, increasing by one more cup each day.[12] Each day a *piṇḍa* is offered to create a new part of the body, the chief mourner repeating after the pandit: "May this create a head", "May this create eyes, nose and ears", and so on. These provide "a new body just as the foetus does in the womb."[13] Each *piṇḍa* is divided into four parts, two parts going to the creation of the new body, one part for the messengers of Yama, and one to be consumed by the chief mourner, or offered to nourish the preta.[14]

The *piṇḍas* were a substitute for the animal sacrifice according to

---

[7] Kane 1973 IV:261-2; Gonda 1980:441-3. There are diverse opinions in the texts as to how many there should be after the tenth day: sixteen is the minimum, but some texts, such as GP II.5.49-50, indicate three sets of sixteen beginning on the twelfth day after the death. Cf. Kane 1973 IV:518; Evison 1989:326; Parry 1989:508; 1994:191ff.; GP II.35.39.

[8] Kane 1973 IV:261-2, 517ff.; Shastri 1963:63ff..

[9] Cf. GP II.15.63; II.4.77.

[10] Evison 1989:72, 77; cf. Dubois 1906:490-492; Padfield 1908:201ff.; Planalp 1956:613.

[11] Planalp 1956:619.

[12] Cf. Planalp 1953:616; GP II.34.44; II.5.33-37; II.15.69-71.

[13] GP. II.15. 69-71; 34.48-51; variants in II 5.33-37; Parry 1989; 233; GP II.15.67; Kane 1973 IV:266.

[14] GP II.65-66, 68.

O'Flaherty, and have other fertility and seed symbolism, the term *piṇḍa* also meaning embryo.[15] In view of the symbolism of both sacrifice and regeneration, along with the belief that the cremation itself is a sacrifice (5.3 above), it is not surprising that the offering of the *piṇḍas*, made of elemental materials, came to be seen as a means of reconstituting the body which has been distributed into the elements. It is about the size of a large apple, made of rice, wheat, barley or a mixture, depending on region or caste. Stevenson also mentions sesame, sugar, milk, curds, honey and *ghī*.[16] Few people nowadays offer the full sequence, but usually offer all ten balls on the tenth day, often following the disposal of the ashes in the river.[17]

In addition, a *ghī* lamp is kept burning in the house at the place of death, and if it goes out it is a bad sign requiring remedial action. Another lamp, to show the way to the ghost, may be kept burning in a pot hung from a pipal tree near the burning ground, from the eaves of the roof or in the courtyard. A pot, with a tiny hole, is filled with water or water and milk, sometimes also with *kuśa* *(darbha)* grass, sesame and barley, for the purpose of nourishing the ghost until the tenth day rituals: "The water goes into the mouth of the ghost which is very thin and as small as a needle, and its body is very wide" (VarBrM45).[18]

On the eleventh day, when the extreme impurity is over, a much more elaborate series of sixteen *śrāddhas* is performed with *mantras*. These are the *ekoddiṣṭa* (for one ancestor) *śrāddha*.[19] They are very lengthy and therefore usually condensed to two hours; often combined, as in Britain, with the twelfth day rituals.[20] There is great variation as to how these are done. The purpose of the ritual is to give the newly formed *preta* a *piṇḍa* to give him strength and appease his extreme hunger, so that he can eat his fill on the eleventh day before embarking on the terrible year-long journey to Yama. Gifts are made to Brahmins representing the needs of the deceased, including a bed, a gold image

15 ŚB. 1.2.3.8; O'Flaherty 1980:4 8; cf. Parry 1989:497ff; 508.

16 Stevenson 1920:160.

17 cf. Stevenson 1920:159; 278; Planalp 1956:618; Kane 1973 IV:263; Kaushik 1976; Knipe 1977:115 cf. Quayle 1980:11ff...

18 Quayle 1980:12; Khare 1976:176. According to the theory in the GP, the mouth and digestion are formed last of all so that it is only on the tenth day that the *preta* can feel hunger and thirst (Knipe 1977:115). In practice there is a belief that it is desperately hungry and thirsty and needs constant nourishment. Padfield 1908:202; Evison 1989:80; Planalp 1956:613-6.

19 Kane 1973 V:261; GP II.5.38.

20 Knipe 1977:116; cf. Planalp 1956:624.

of Viṣṇu and Lakṣmī, various spices and toilet articles, clothes, gems, grains and ornaments.[21]

Prior to the offerings on the eleventh day is the *vṛṣotsarga* or bull release ceremony. The bull, marked with Viṣṇu's *chakra* on its left side, and Śiva's trident on its right is 'married' to one to four heifers, worshipped, and released. The bull represents *dharma*, and is asked to help the deceased over the ocean of existence, or to intercede with Dharma Rājā.[22] Like the Vaitaraṇī cow this enables the deceased to cross the terrible Vaitaraṇī river. This is also associated with maintaining the fertility of the herds, and thus the prosperity of the community.[23]

If there has been a bad death, particularly one during *pañcaka* or *dakṣiṇāyaṇa*, the *nārāyaṇa bali* must be performed on the eleventh day. Knipe describes this as "in its full form a rite of tremendous power ...designed to promote the deceased, after the sapiṇḍīkaraṇa, to the Vaikuṇtha heaven of Viṣṇu".[24]

The *sapiṇḍīkaraṇa* is the climactic ceremony, in which the *preta* is promoted to the rank of ancestor or *pitṛ*. As Knipe points out, this has its basis in "the ritual world view of early vedic religion" with little evidence of change in ethnographic studies by Stevenson, Quayle, Gold and Evison, although there are regional variations.[25] It is usually performed on the twelfth day, with a year's rituals condensed to a ritual year on the eleventh and twelfth days[26], although in India it is still sometimes performed after one year.

The *sapiṇḍīkaraṇa* has several functions. It enables the *preta* to become a *pitṛ*, removing the deceased from the environs of the house, which Gold observes "neutralizes his specific nature, simultaneously transforming a hovering threat of inauspicious interference into part of a peaceable and generalized source of potential benevolence".[27] For the chief mourner, it also "affects the combined legal and ritual assumption by the surviving son of the position of head of the family and heir to the property and community status of the

---

[21] GP II.15.73ff.; 34.73-89.

[22] GP II.5.40, 44-45; Kane 1973 IV:539ff..

[23] GP II.6.22-6; II.14.27; Dubois 1906:493; Stevenson 1920:174ff.; Kane 1973:IV:539-542; 10.2; Evison 1989:90, 246, 249-250 Parry 1989:508-9; Quayle 1980:15.

[24] Knipe 1977:116; cf.. Kaushik 1976:279.

[25] Knipe 1977:121, Stevenson 1920 Quayle 1980, Gold 1988 and Evison 1989.

[26] Cf. Stevenson 1920:181; Kane 1973: IV :262. 520; Knipe 1977:114; Parry 1989:509.

[27]. Gold 1988:90-91.

deceased".

The *sapiṇḍīkaraṇa* ritual involves joining the *piṇḍa* of the deceased to those of his father *(pitṛ)*, temporarily resident among the Vasus in the earth, grandfather *(pitāmaha)*, who dwells in midspace with the Rudras, and great grandfather *(prapitāmaha)*, who dwells with the Adityas in heaven, who depend on the ritual offerings of their descendents.[28] The day before the ritual five or three Brahmins should be invited to attend, according to Kane to represent the *preta*, one the Viśvedevaḥ and one each of the ancestors, or one for all three of the latter.[29] However, because of the inauspicious and still polluting nature of the role, bundles of *kuśa* grass may be used as substitutes.[30] The officiating Brahmin is usually a *mahābrāhmaṇa* or *mahāpātra*. In some parts of Gujarat, especially in Kathiawad, a specialist caste called *kāṭaliyā* (cutting) Brahmins actually cut the *piṇḍa* on behalf of the mourners.[31]

Four *piṇḍas* representing the father, grand-father and great-grandfather are made from wheat flour, cooked rice, or barley or rice flour, depending on caste and region, mixed with milk, sesame, honey, yoghurt and water. It is divided into half for the *preta piṇḍa*, representing the deceased, and half for the three ancestors, moulded into shape, and placed on a leaf plate. After various *pūjās* the CM gives fuel to the sacred fires, and then fills four pots, *ārghya*, representing the four generations, with water.[32] The water in the pot representing the deceased is mixed with the water in the other three pots, giving their names and stating that they are united, reciting verses from RV X.191.3ff. and VS 19.45ff., calling the ancestors to receive the offerings.

After making offerings to the *piṇḍas* and naming them, the CM (or the *Kāṭaliyā* Brahmin), with a piece of gold wire, a golden skewer,[33] silver wire (GjPt35), or *darbha* grass (GjPt75), then cuts the *preta piṇḍa* into three and blends it with those of the three ancestors, naming them: "Go to your father

---

28 Knipe 1977:118ff.; cf. RV 51.1; AV XVIII.4.5.78ff.; ŚB 2.6.1.1-3, 4-7.

29 Kane 1973 IV:522; cf.. Stevenson 1920:182.

30 Stevenson 1920:182; Quayle 1980:16; Evison 1989:113, 385.

31 Some informants used the term '*kāratiyā*'.The *kāṭaliyā* Brahmins are called in because it is believed that the preta really is cut into three parts. A Gujarati pandit explained that it was believed that "the dead body lies there, and by dividing the body it is dissolved into the *pitṛs* and the soul is merged with the *pitṛs*". GjPt65; GjBrM45. Cf. Stevenson 1920:186; Parry 1994:204ff..

32 Kane 1973 IV:523; Knipe 1977; Evison 1989:381; Shastri 1963:94.

33 Stevenson 1920:185; Quayle 1980:16.

(grandfather, great-grandfather)", according to Knipe, or "I will now effect the union of the *preta* with my ancestors in the presence of Viṣṇu and these Brahmins".[34] The son of another pandit commented, "Cutting the *preta-piṇḍa* really hurts us because we are cutting the body of our father. It is the last farewell, and is thus very painful. If you don't perform these ceremonies the soul will be wandering around" (GjBrM40).

The deceased now replaces his father in the tripartite ranking, and the grandfather now becomes the great-grandfather. The new *piṇḍas* are blended with sugar, *ghī* and sesame.[35] Knipe comments:

> And in *that moment* the deceased has passed from the preta to the pitṛ stage and has joined the revered company of the ancestors at home in the three worlds, his father and grandfather having advanced to new levels and divine groupings in the cosmic and ritual hierarchy, and his great-grandfather having been regenerated into the realm of the remote dead as one of the Viśvedevāḥ.[36]

After the ritual the Brahmins are offered food and gifts, and one should receive daily offerings for a year.[37] The *piṇḍas* may be thrown into the river or offered to crows, a cow or a dog. Offerings to the animals may also be made at the time the ashes are gathered and on the tenth and eleventh days. They are "representatives of the *pretātma* and know where it is." If they do not eat the *piṇḍas* it means the *ātman* is not detached and the *nārāyaṇa bali* is necessary (GjPF55).[38]

The *sapiṇḍīkaraṇa* does not seem to be universal throughout India. For many lower caste groups *piṇḍas* are offered during the funeral rites, but at the fourth stage (the rites for the ghost) the *preta* is offered food in other forms.[39]

Some communities follow this ritual with the giving of a turban to the CM, *pagṛī bandhan kī pūjā*, others offer it on the thirteenth day.[40] Some Punjabi informants have described a simpler ceremony in which the CM's in-laws present

---

34 Knipe 1977: 121; Stevenson 1920:185; Parry 1994:205..
35 Gold 1988:93-95.
36 Knipe 1977:121.
37 GP II.37.12; Evison 1989:262-3.
38 Cf. Stevenson, 1920:188.
39 Evison 1989:106.
40 Stevenson 1920:189; Raheja 1988:155; Gold 1988:97.

him and other brothers with new turbans, which may be simply placed on the head. This acknowledges the heir as head of the household. [41]

The thirteenth day, *śrāvaṇī śrāddha,* is often the day when gifts of the necessities of life are given to Brahmins, as surrogates for the deceased, who, as one of the ancestors is now addressed by his caste name[42]. Prior to the giving of the gifts there is the, *Lalitā śrāvanī śrāddha,* the main feature of which is the worship of thirteen goddesses, the most important of whom is Lalitā. This is important for women. It is followed by the sixteenfold Viṣṇu *pūjā.* A Śiva temple may be visited that evening.

On the twelfth (Gj. Barmu) and thirteenth days (Gj. Termu), when *sūtaka* ends for some castes such as Patels, there may be feasts, to which Brahmins are invited. A calf, or cow and calf, may be produced, have milk poured over their tails, and be offered food. Cows or their full value may be given to a Brahmin. Further feasts are held up to the sixteenth or seventeenth day, when *sūtaka* ends for some communities such as the Vanyas, Lohanas,and some Khattri castes. Offerings, including *piṇḍas*, and gifts may be made monthly up to the first anniversary.

6.2. Stage VII. *Śrāddha* rituals in Britain

Hindus in Britain also usually condense the tenth to thirteenth day ceremonies into one, chiefly because of the difficulty (and expense) of obtaining the pandits for all three occasions, particularly in the absence of *mahābrāhmaṇas*. However, the pandit in Westmouth, when his wife died, arranged for all the rituals to be held, conducted by his son who was also a temple pandit. The combined ritual is usually held on the twelfth or thirteenth day. The local temple pandit, or a visiting one, will attend for this. If the ashes are to be taken to the river or sea nearby, the pandit may accompany them prior to the ceremony. It is interesting to note that the combined *piṇḍa* ceremony will be held for non-Brahmin castes before their *sūtaka* period ends on the sixteenth, but after the ten-day minimum period for Brahmins.

Because the pandits have to combine four days of ritual into a few hours, they have to be very selective. Lengthy *sūktas* and *pūjās* may be omitted or

[41] Cf. Parry 1994:206.

[42] Stevenson 1920:189.

condensed. However, I found a surprising level of conformity, even if details and order change from one pandit to another. All the pandits referred to the difficulty of getting enough time for the ceremony, since their clients were often unprepared to spend more than a few hours on the rituals. The total number of *piṇḍas* used varies according to the pandits, who have to cut various aspects of the rituals to fit the circumstances and the requirements of their clients. Bargaining may be necessary to ensure that there is the minimal amount of ritual necessary to guarantee the safe passage of the soul. Even this may last up to four hours, and there is considerable preparation involved beforehand.

The performer *(pūjak)* is usually the eldest son, but sometimes several sons perform jointly, and two pandits permit daughters to act if there are no sons, and they are ritually pure (5.1). The following brief description is derived mainly from a Gujarati pandits in Leicester and Westmouth.

During the ten days following the death the pandit asks the mourners to observe the *kṣirodaka nidhān*, by offering *piṇḍas* daily, or two on alternate odd days, and give water libations daily after bathing. The *ghī* lamp should be kept burning but changed daily, and morning, noon and evening water and milk should be offered to the birds *(dūdhokadāna)*, saying, "You have been suffering from the fire, so take your bath and drink this milk", adding, "*pretya tāp upśāntiḥ* - may the *preta* rest in peace". In addition food should be put out between one and two p.m.

The pandit asks the mourners to prepare materials beforehand, including bowls, spoons and *thālīs*, various herbs and spices, cooked rice and other ingredients for the *piṇḍas,* which may be made in advance or on the spot, and red, white and black clothes for three altars. He brings the low tables, copper vessels, and a silver cow, calf, miniature sandals representing Viṣṇu, a silver boat (to cross the river) and ladder (to climb up to heaven). Five Brahmins should be invited in advance, but since they are unlikely to come, they can be represented by *kuśa* grass or a banyan plant. The pandit asks the mourners to prepare themselves by inner purification, avoiding foods such as cereals, aubergine, onions and garlic. The house should be purified and the deceased's clothing disposed of. If conditions permit, the ritual may be held outside.

The three altars are set up for Viṣṇu, Maheśa (Śiva) and Satyeśa (a form of Kṛṣṇa). The pandit begins the ritual by telling the mourners that their bodies are nothing but a *piṇḍa*, therefore it is their duty to keep them pure and holy. In order to create the right kind of peaceful atmosphere and concentration he recites some *śānti mantras*.

The first ritual is the *nāva śrāddha*, to perform the *daśgātra* (ten organ) *vidhi*. After the purification (*ācamaṇa*) the chief mourner puts on a new temporary sacred thread over the left shoulder[43], and then says the *saṃkalpa*, the declaration of the aim of the ritual. After worshiping the three gods and the *pitṛs* he performs the sixteen-fold Viṣṇu *pūjā* "to relieve the *preta* from anxiety and give him *sadgati*, a good end", and if time, the Rudra *pūjā* and Satyeśa *pūjā* with Śakti *pūjā*. It begins with *dehaśuci*, the purification of the *pūjak's* (performer's) body and inner self; only then does he obtain the right to perform the *śrāddha*. Further *pūjās* are offered, with *mantras* for self-reproach, penitence and forgiveness.

The ten *piṇḍas* are now offered. Each *piṇḍa* is laid on its prepared place with a mantra, beginning with the head: "I am offering the first *piṇḍa* for the formation of the head of the *preta*", until the whole body is formed (6.1).[44]

A short *pūjā* is performed, with as much of the sixteen-fold *pūjā* as there is time for, and then each *piṇḍa* is offered water in ten small cups, which are placed on the floor in front of the *piṇḍas*, together with, flowers, betel nut, water, sandalwood, sesame, and coins.

Once the deceased has received a complete new body he is given offerings to give him strength for the symbolic twelve-month journey confronting him through Yama's kingdom. These are made to him alone, *ekoddiṣṭa śrāddha*. Even in India, the twelve monthly offerings tend to be condensed into a single two-hour ceremony on the eleventh day or combined with the *sapiṇḍīkaraṇa* on the twelfth day. The ritual, as we have seen, is for the purification of the *preta*, and involves *prāyaścitta sadgati prapti artham*, penance to enable the deceased to achieve a good transition, or a 'good end'. In its full form it is very lengthy, and only the bare essentials can be included in the one day ritual. It consists of the offering of eleven *piṇḍas* and the *nārāyaṇa bali* if needed. *Ādya śrāddha*, for *pretmukti*, the liberation of the *preta*, ensures freedom from bondage and lasting tranquillity. The marriage of the cow and bull (6.1. above), and the release of the latter, the *vṛṣotsarga*, should precede this, but it is not done in Britain, although in principle it could be performed with two silver images. After the *piṇḍas* and water are offered to the deceased, with further *pūjās*, they may be taken outside with food

[43] For details see Ch.5, footnote 10.

[44] GP II 5.33-37; II.15.69-71; II 34.48-51.

offerings and left on the grass or flung onto the roof for the crows. An earthen pot should be filled with water, and carried on the shoulders and poured at the foot of a tree.[45] It is only after this ritual, reinforced by the symbolic nurturing of animals and plants, that the preta, who has travelled for eleven symbolic months represented by the eleven *piṇḍas*, is in a fit state to become ạ *pitr* in the *sapiṇḍīkaraṇa* ritual.

6.2.1. *Sapiṇḍīkaraṇa* in Britain

In Britain the *sapiṇḍīkaraṇa* is usually part of the combined ritual on the twelfth day. One pandit does not often include it unless requested by informed participants, either because of the shortage of time his clients are willing to give, or because they insist on their own tradition which does not include the full Sanskrit rite.

The *piṇḍas* are formed of freshly cooked rice blended with honey and *ghī*. If they were prepared in advance they would have been placed on the lower table with the eleven (above) in the front row and included in the earlier *pūjās*. The manuals often used by the Gujarati pandits suggest different numbers of *piṇḍas* for the ritual. Joshi recommends four, but Sharma recommends five, one each for the *preta*, his father, grandfather, great-grandfather, of the size of a medium potato, and a fifth one the size and shape of a coconut, also for the *preta*, to be cut and blended.[46]

Tarpaṇa is offered first. Water, milk, sesame, barley and flowers are placed in a basin or wide-mouthed vessel. With both hands water is scooped up and offered to the Gods, the Vedas, Nature, Time, the *ṛṣis*, the *pitṛs*, and the unknown people in the *gotra* who have died without sons.

Viṣṇu *pūjā* should follow, but in the combined ritual this has already been done. The chief mourner invokes the preta, the *pitṛs*, and the Viśvedevāḥ (all-gods), to take their places on *darbha* placed on betel leaves. The sixteen-fold *pūjā*, may be offered. Finally the *piṇḍas* are offered. The performer invites the father, grandfather, and great-grandfather to be seated, and declares his intention: *"Uttama loka prāpti artham*: For the attainment of the best *loka*". The performer then cuts the coconut-sized *piṇḍa* into three parts with silver wire, which the pandit provides. This has to be done with great care, holding the wire in a U

[45] Cf. Stevenson 1920:187-188.
[46] Joshi 1970:, Sharma 1964.

shape, with the help of the son-in law, or another close relative, so that it is cut into three equal pieces. As he does so the chief mourner should repeat the name of Viṣṇu three times. One third of this is mingled with the father's *piṇḍa*, saying, "*kāśyapa gotra nāmukadāsena vasu rūpeṇa*: So and so, from such and such *gotra*, is being mixed with the *piṇḍa* of such and such (naming the father), and becomes one with the Vasus."[47] One third is mixed next with the grandfather's, as Rudra. The third portion is mingled with the great-grandfather's, who now becomes one of the Adityas. The blending is done with the right hand, and has to be done to perfection so that there are no gaps. The *piṇḍas* are carefully replaced in their previous positions, and five-step *pūjā (pañcopachara),* is offered, with clothing represented by three pieces of thread, flowers, water offerings and other worship materials.

After the pūjā, *kumbha dāna* (gift of water pots) is offered, although according to one pandit this should be done prior to the cutting of the *piṇḍa.*[48] Twelve jars of water are offered to satisfy and quench the hunger and thirst of the *preta*, saying "May the *preta* be free from hunger and thirst". *Saṃ kalpa* is offered: "Whatever has been offered may it be not perishable, may it be permanent". The *āsanas* (seats) of the fathers are touched with *darbha* or fingers, submitting the rituals which have been performed to God. The *piṇḍas* are collected, and set aside for river disposal and the place sprinkled with Ganges water with *chandan* (sandalwood) and flowers placed where the *piṇḍas* had been sited. The CM apologises for omissions made through ignorance, pride, forgetfulness and illusion, and offers the final prayer beseeching God to bestow a son upon the family. Taking *darbha* by the roots, water is sprinkled on the seated divinities, and they are sent back.

At the end of the ritual, some Gujarati business communities perform the *gograsa pūjā*, making an offering to a cow. A live cow has been produced on at least one occasion in Britain, but usually the offering of water is made to a silver model of a cow, on the tail which is made in a spatulate form for the purpose. A new widow performs this. The sons perform the ritual for their deceased mother. Various coloured and scented substances such as sandalwood, alum, rose water

---

[47] 'Kāśyapa' is simply an example of a *gotra* name, equivalent to 'NN' in an English ceremony, and would be replaced by the actual *gotra* name of the family (Hemant Kanitkar, personal communication).

[48] Cf. Gold 1988:93.

and *kuṇkuṃ*, are placed on the to cow followed by sesame, *Ganges water* and flowers. The widow says, "My husband is my *gurū*, he is my god, he is my eternal *dharma*. He was my guide, give satisfaction to my sons and grandchildren." If a son performs the ritual for his mother he says, "*Pitā gurū*.." or "*Mātā gurū*..."; a brother says "*Bhrātā*.."; the husband says "*Patnī*..".

If there is no widow, all the gods and ancestors will be invoked with the oblations. The silver boat, ladder and sandals may also be offered *pūjā* for the sake of the journey of the soul. After this, offerings are again made outside to the ancestors to the crows, and if possible, to cows and dogs. If no birds come people get very upset. In one family offerings were put out for ten days and no birds came, and the family were really worried until the birds appeared on the eleventh day. Sometimes the mourners take the gift for the cows at Bhaktivedanta Manor. Gifts (*mokṣa dhenu dāna*) should now be offered to the Brahmin, including a cow or its equivalent value.

The thirteenth day ritual, the *śrāvanī śrāddha* (6.1), is rarely performed in Britain, although pandits may include a small part of the Lalitā *pūjā* in the combined ritual. The main feature of this day traditionally is the offering of gifts of all the necessities of life for the dead person to the priest, who acts as his surrogate. However these may be offered now on *barmū*, the twelfth day, particularly if this is a combined ritual.

If the deceased died during *pañcaka*, in addition to the performance of the *nārāyaṇa bali* a special *pañca-devata* (five god) *pūjā*[49] should be performed. One pandit tries to incorporate this rite into the combined ritual, but the Westmouth pandit is reluctant to do it at all and suggests that if the CM was not satisfied by the circumstances of the death it is advisable to have this done properly in India.

For many middle-class Hindus the rituals are seen more as a 'send-off' for the *preta* than in terms of begetting an ancestor, as Evison and Bayly have also noted in India. Bayly sees this as a change in the significance of the rites: "The concept of *shraddha* as a feast of commemoration rather than as the actual embodiment of the soul in a new body appears to have gained currency even amongst those who venerate all the gods of the Vedanta and exercise ritual purity."[50] In some Patel, Mistry and Lohana groups, the family does not follow the tradition of cutting the *piṇḍa* as described above. At one Lohana ritual I attended for an

---

[49] *Pañca-sūktas: Viṣṇu, Yama, Śiva, Satyeśa* and *Śāntī*.
[50] Evison 1989:106) Bayly 1981:183.

elderly man, twenty-six *piṇḍas* were made of boiled rice, plus one large one as the *preta piṇḍa*. After various *pūjās* the large *piṇḍa* was cut, but there was no blending. Although the preta is not regenerated formally with *piṇḍas*, the offerings of water and food, and planting a coconut in the garden, which Mochis and Mistrys do, are themselves symbolic of fertility and regeneration (cf.5.5):

> [The coconut] symbolises a womb, a very holy thing, and many people do it because it is religious, even if they don't understand its fertility aspect. At the same time it maintains the vegetable world in the same way that the release of the calf and cow maintains the animal world (GjPt).

This is an interesting acknowledgement of the connection between death and regeneration which is such a feature of the texts, and it echoes the themes of the pot as a womb and the *piṇḍa* as the body referred to by Parry.[51] Here there is also a connection between the regeneration of the individual and of both the animal and vegetable worlds, so that it is given a cosmic dimension. It remains to be seen how much of this tradition is retained in the absence, for example, of living cows, calves and bullocks as part of the everyday environment, as is the case in India.

The ambivalence of the priestly function in death rituals was reflected in attitudes concerning the pandit's fees during the period of impurity, since in India these would only be given to the *mahābrāhmaṇas*. The rituals up to the *sapiṇḍīkaraṇa* carried so much sin that the priest "has to do one thousand *japas* (repetition of *mantras*) to remove the sin", and no pure priest could accept gifts before the thirteenth day for this reason (KanPt). Some refuse; others take the gifts because it is essential for the well-being of the soul and the mourners, but they do extra penances and prayers to deal with the burden. All the pandits said they gave gifts away again, sometimes just retaining basic expenses, although several commented that their colleagues were greedy and demanded money.

In order to purify himself for the receipt of these gifts one Gujarati pandit did extra *pūjās*, often staying up all night: "Unless I do that there is no peace inside." He did not always understand the *mantras* but still had to pray. "I feel guilty because I must understand what I utter; because people will take my word for granted as good and correct." A former teacher and the son of a temple priest,

[51] Parry 1989:506-507. Cf. 5.3 above

with considerable knowledge of Sanskrit, he had found himself called upon to conduct various rituals, despite advice by fellow Brahmins not to perform funerals. Some Pushtimargis in the temple had argued that this would make him too impure to perform anything else, to which he had retorted, "How many of you came here without bathing?" They made the lame excuse that they did not go into the inner temple, but he said he would go to help anyone at a time of need. If he bathed and changed, after *tāra snān* (lit. 'star bath', when the stars appear), he would be pure enough to perform *pūjās*.

None of the pandits admitted to setting a fee, although they said that others did so. One pandit sometimes receives nothing, or gifts ranging from £11 to £50; few families offer much in the way of the other gifts mentioned in the texts. Those with some knowledge of the scriptural tradition may offer shirts, trousers or shoes, umbrella, footwear and a water pot as well as sesame, *pān* (betel), foodstuffs, milk, *ghī* and vegetables. The Leicester pandit did not originally wish to receive any gifts, because of the inauspiciousness and sin attached to them, but he realised that it was important for the welfare and merit of the soul for the families to give, as well as the merit and welfare of the givers. He also had to meet considerable personal expenses in the performance of his duty, with no other income. He gave away a proportion of everything he received. Many Westmouth informants were cynical about the Brahmins and preferred to give to charity.

Other rituals may be held after three, six and nine months which give peace to the soul and mark a stage in the lessening of mourning (see Chapter 8). The sixth month ritual, often now performed after three, is called *varṣi chhamāsi* (H. *varṣīy chamāhi*). If the family can afford it, the pandit conducts a small ceremony. The widow can now lead a normal life. The *varṣī samān* is performed at nine months or before the year is out; this and *varṣī chhamāsi* are sometimes done together when the morning period is abbreviated (GjSF57).

6.3. Stage IX. The annual śrāddha

The relationship between the ancestors and the living is not at an end after the post-mortem rituals. The new ancestor will, along with his father and grandfather, remain in a symbiotic relationship with his descendants, as seen above. They possess semi-divine status, but they are, in a sense, still mortal and trapped in the cycle of *saṃsāra*, rebirth and redeath, and are still connected in varying degrees to the places and relatives of their previous birth, depending on the *śrāddha* rituals to promote them from "the frontiers of dissolution to other life forms, where the doctrine of *saṃsāra*, however contrastive with purāṇic chronologies for an individual's sojourn in heavens and hells, seems not so disjunctive after all."[52] One way to ensure their final release (and the consequent need for descendants to perform the rituals) is to perform the *śrāddha* at Gaya. British Hindus who can afford it will go there as part of a pilgrimage to holy places

Honouring the *pitṛs,* one of the obligations incumbent on all Hindus, should be done daily, as has been seen.[53] In addition, individual ancestors for three generations should be honoured on the *tithi*, the anniversary of the death according to lunar reckoning, as well as during *pitṛ pakṣa*, the annual fortnight during the autumn month of Bhādrapada when all ancestors, known and unknown, are honoured.[54] The rites are often abbreviated and the ancestors are remembered as a group on the all-ancestors new moon, *sarvapitṛ amāvāsyā.*[55]

Many British Hindus remember both the *tithi* of the death of the deceased and the relevant day during the *pitṛ pakṣa*. Because of the difficulty in working out the correct anniversary according to the lunar calendar, the temple committee in Westmouth have recently made arrangements for families to honour their individual ancestors according to the nearest date on the Gregorian calendar, for which they pay £201 per year for each ancestor they wish to remember, plus any other anniversaries of importance. The names are written on a large wall chart. The pandit offers about fifteen minutes of prayers for that individual and family, and the family will then have the privilege of performing *ārtī* although sometimes the family do not actually attend for the prayer. Many families also make offerings at home and give gifts to Brahmins of their choice or to charity. In the pandit's opinion, some of those who do not even attend for their own family prayers would not do this at home either.

The *pitṛ pakṣa*, which occurs just before Navarātri,[56] is of importance not just for the remembered relatives, but for those souls which have not taken birth, who are born out of wedlock, and who have died without the proper rituals. Where

---

[52] Knipe IV 1977:118; cf. Gold 1988:99;. Evison 1989:132.

[53] Ch. 2.fn.10; 3.1; 3.2.3; cf. Stevenson 1920:229-230.

[54] Keith 1925:427; Kane IV 1973:333ff..

[55] Evison 1989:126- 128.

[56] Nine nights in honour of manifestations of Śaktī; cf.Knott 1986:305.

possible the dead should be named, as they are waiting during the fifteen days to see what their descendants will offer them. They want something to eat, so one or two pure Brahmins should be invited and offered water, sesame, dried rice and gifts of money according to ability - about £25 for someone earning up to £15,000. If someone has died childless and a son has not been adopted, a relative should do this on their behalf. The two Brahmins fast until they are offered a meal, which they eat first, and separately, before the performer, and then they bless him as he bows down to touch their feet.

Several pandits say they will perform the *śrāddha* in the home of other Brahmins, *kṣatriyas* and *vaiśyas*, but not *śūdras*. The latter might make an offering to charity and also give raw foods such as rice, coconuts, *ghī* and oil to the Brahmin, with the request that he prays for the soul of the deceased. Members of other castes might invite the Brahmin and his wife to their homes, requesting that the Brahmin's wife prepares the raw food which has been given.

In Westmouth, the recipient of the gifts is often a senior Gujarati Brahmin woman in the community, rather than the pandit. She seems to be willing to take food in the homes of many of her clients, and has served as a principal functionary when there was no pandit, so there is often some attachment to her. Frequently, however, informants used the expression to "invite Brahmins", even when the Brahmins would not eat in their home, and the "invitation" meant taking the gifts to their homes. This is seen as giving the family *puṇya*, merit, as well as making the departed "happy in heaven". A Gujarati Darji couple took the above-mentioned Brahmin a pound each of uncooked *chappātī* flour, rice and *dāl*, a bottle of *ghī* and a bottle of oil, an. d various spices and *ghur* (raw sugar) to honour the man's parents on their *tithi.* They also invited her to come and lead a *satsaṅg* (hymn singing) on the anniversary of his mother's death They felt they had been insulted when she had insisted on changing a sari they had given her for a more expensive one and expected them to pay the difference. Other members of the family were so disillusioned by the treatment they had received from Brahmins that they no longer made these gifts, but sent money to India to feed the poor.

The 20-year-old daughter explained that it was important to have a *satsaṅg* and read the Gītā for the deceased on the appropriate day during the *pitṛ pakṣa*:

> One chapter of the Gītā is supposed to give you merit. We haven't got *tulasī*,

> but you're supposed to water it and offer that chapter to the person who has died: you give them water through the *tulasī*, and that way you give the chapter of your reading to the one who has died. If you offer *prasād* to God he'll only accept it if you've got a *tulasī* on it, although nowadays he'll probably accept it because he knows there isn't any *tulasī* in England.

The above remarks reflect the confusion that can be created by the lack of specific resources in Britain, but also the pragmatism which concludes that God will accept inadequate offerings if they are made with the right intention.[57]

It is quite common to send money to India to feed the poor. Relatives in India may arrange a *satsaṅg* or a *śrāddha* ritual at or near their home or at the local temple. Sometimes money is sent for a specific purpose, such as offering sweet foods to an orphanage. A Punjabi woman said that for her father-in-law she and her husband arranged for his brother to feed 500 children in a school for handicapped in India with *pūṛīs*, two types of cooked vegetables, and sweets. Her husband also wanted to show them films, but he died before he could go there, so she hoped to do this on his behalf. She also sent money to the family pandit in Hardwar (5.8) with a request that he saw to it that "all the poor people are given something like a mango or a melon." A gift of money, a sari and *chunnī* (blouse) for the *mūrtis* (images of the gods) were also donated to the temple in Westmouth.

A Punjabi Brahmin and her husband paid for five anniversaries to be observed at the temple, including her guru's death anniversary, her marriage anniversary, each of her in-laws' *tithi*, and that of her baby daughter, who had died shortly after birth. She had recently had a vision of the baby as she was performing *tarpaṇa* for her father-in-law, "just as if she was sitting there opposite me, and I thought, why shouldn't I do it for her too?" and so it was arranged, although this was not commonly done. She said it had made her feel much better about the baby's death (cf. 6.1, 6.2.1). They do not make offerings for the baby in the *pitṛ pakṣa*, however, since there is "no *śrāddha* for little ones, since they had no life in this world". Even more important than feeding Brahmins is feeding a daughter's son, which reflects a sense of continuity, although the child is not part of his maternal grandparents' lineage.

If people forget the anniversary the ancestors come and remind their

[57] Cf. BG.9.2.6.

descendants by spilling milk, or some small misfortune, or in a dream. The Brahmin woman, above, was reminded by a small fire at the shrine which cracked "God's photo". She realised it was because she had forgotten it was *aṣṭamī*, the eighth day after the full moon, when she should have offered prayers for her guru. She also dreamed about the recently deceased husband of a friend, and rang her to ask if she had done anything for her husband. Her friend had forgotten it was his *tithi*, so she said, "It's all right, you can go on *amāvās* day, the dark night, you can go then, because that is the day you can do it for everyone, even though you have forgotten. If you have forgotten anybody it will go to him on that day.".

On the full moon day (*pūrṇimā*), offerings are made in memory of the "elderly dead", to repay the debt to them, received as a "credit from God". This also brings blessings to the giver. Ideally five to seven Brahmins should be invited and fed, but it is not always practical in this country, because it is not possible to obtain Brahmins willing to come and receive the gifts. The Brahmins who do receive the gifts have an obligation to give in turn, and the Gujarati woman who does so "donates money like anything to the temple, she takes one side and she gives it away. She gives more than she takes, and she is providing a service."(PjBrF45). This perception of the Gujarati woman who had received the gifts from other Brahmins gracefully, is in contrast to the Darji mother and daughter above, who felt that they had been insulted by the demand for a more expensive sari than they had given her.

Many Hindus do not perform the daily rituals to the ancestors, or offer them *tarpaṇa*, according to one pandit and some of my informants. One woman said that she acknowledged her husband, her parents and her guru by bowing to them daily, but made no offerings. Some older widows, however, make daily offerings on behalf of their husbands. Those who own a *tulasī* plant may offer water via the plant, others may go outside and offer it to a tree (GjLF70). One Gujarati widow began offering *tarpaṇa* to the *pitṛs* daily after her husband's death. She had been very distressed after her husband's death, and these regular rituals were very helpful. She recited a Sanskrit *mantra* obtained from the pandit, without knowing what it meant. Her husband died on the last day of the lunar month, *amās*, so on the last day of every month her daughter-in-law prepared a nice meal with sweets which was offered to him and then eaten by the family as *prasāda*. On the *tithi* of her husband's death fifty or sixty close family members are invited to come for a meal.

As the above accounts indicate, there is considerable variation in the way the deceased are remembered. The most common annual ritual is the offering of gifts to the Brahmins. A major change is the remembrance of the anniversary by the Gregorian calendar at the temple. In addition to prayers at the temple *satsaṅgs* may be arranged, sometimes lasting all night, and some people arrange for readings of holy books such as the *Rāmāyaṇa*. Arya Samajis, in addition to giving *dāna* in the name of the deceased, hold a *havan* or arrange for a reading of *Amṛta Varṣa*. Donations to charities such as Oxfam, or to organisations in India, are considered important, and feeding animals and birds is commonly mentioned. None of my informants omitted all forms of remembrance.

The post-funeral *śrāddha* rituals have several functions. By creating a new body for the deceased and promoting him to ancestor, they make him "safe" and give him a new place in the consciousness of the survivors. He is never completely safe, however, since the regular daily and annual rituals are required to propitiate him and ensure his continual interest in his descendants. The rituals also mirror the ritual and emotional state of the mourners, who have to adjust to his social death and their own reincorporation into a society in which he is missing. But as Bloch and Parry point out,[58] in contrast with Western individualism and the stress on the uniqueness of each person's biography, death is seen as "part of a cyclical process of renewal", so that he is not only reborn as an ancestor, but a descendant, possibly in the same family. The annual rituals are also straightforward acts of remembrance of known individuals and genuine concern for their well being, signifying a continuing link between the living and the dead and providing the satisfaction of knowing the debt has been honoured, as well as gaining merit for the performers.

[58] Bloch and Parry 1982:15.

PART III
Social and Psychological Dimensions of Death

Chapter 7
The British Context of Hindu Death

The model of the good death, which is still important to many Hindus, is often difficult to realise in practice in Britain, and problems often arise over various aspects of terminal care. After death the changes which have taken place with reference to the time and style of cremation, availability of priests and shifts in family structure also affect the way in which individuals and communities deal with bereavement. Part III explores some of the social and psychological aspects of the Hindu experience of death in Britain. Chapter 7 raises some general issues with reference to the care of elderly, sick and dying Asians. Two Case studies will be discussed in detail in order to throw light on the experience of hospital deaths.[1] Chapter 8 examines the social implications of death, including mourning traditions involving *sūtaka, śoka* and *aśauca*. Chapter 9 explores in greater depth the impact of death on a number of individuals and their families in the light of current studies of bereavement and grief, showing the importance of developing cross-cultural perspectives, concluding with a discussion of the way Hindus draw on their beliefs and rituals to find meaning in death. Chapter 10 reviews the preceding discussion noting areas of change and continuity, and practical considerations for professionals caring for dying and bereaved Hindus.

7.1. Caring for the dying

In Britain, while hospitals may be valued as a good place to be in order to obtain the best treatment, there may be concern about adequate emotional and spiritual support for the dying patients.[2] As a result, some patients wish to return to their country of origin to die. The ideal death at home rarely occurs in Britain because caring for the elderly or the sick in the extended family may not be realisable in

---

[1] Much of the material in this chapter appears in Firth 1993a, 1993b, 1993c. An abbreviated version of Case Study 1 appears without acknowledgement in Katz, Peberdy and Siddell, 1993. Comments by Sikh doctors and nurses are included since both care for Hindu patients and their comments are equally relevant.

[2] The growth of palliative care and the hospice movement in recent years has made home care easier than it was when my research began (cf. Katz 1993, Dickenson and Johnson 1993). At the time of writing, however, there appear to be few Asians taking advantage of the hospices, which may be due to lack of public awareness as well as anxiety about whether the needs of patients will be adequately met in the hospices.

practice. A Sikh doctor with many Hindu patients observed:

> [In India] the elderly in villages have more of a sense of preparation for death. Here there is a feeling that one can keep the old alive, without any preparation. Many people think, "Now we are wealthy, let's bring the old folks here." It is making a mistake because in Britain the elderly are sad and lonely, uprooted from their familiar environment where they had a role to play and a sense of continuity. There they were useful and accepted, with a full day. Here they are lost and lonely, and the [younger] women work, whereas there they did not. In India the older generation would keep old folks at home, because they would have had the experience of supporting the dying at home, but here people expect health care professionals to do it.[3]

Social mobility among British Hindus may mean that relatives do not live near each other, or even near their own communities. Small inner-city houses may make the extended family impractical, so if it exists at all it consists of three vertical generations. If both younger partners work, elderly people may feel isolated, bored, and lonely, instead of feeling they have a valuable role to play in the family and community. Donaldson and Johnson show that elderly immigrants also face the additional problems of age, racial discrimination, not having access to services and not speaking English.[4] Many families are unaware of the help that is available to them, especially if they are not part of a long established community. Even where there is an extended family to care for the elderly and/or dying patients, the women, who normally carry the burden of care, may find it difficult economically to give up work to care for the parent, or more commonly parent-in-law, or other relative. If they do, they may be left coping with a heavy burden of caring for the patient, dealing with housework, shopping and child care without the support of sisters-in-law and other relatives that they would have had in an extended family home in India. In one situation where a young Gujarati man had motor neurone disease, his wife had to do all the heavy lifting and caring, while his brothers, who lived in the house, did nothing to assist her. In other cases the social services may be expected to help, or, if finances permit, the patient may be sent to a private nursing home where probably no one speaks the patient's language. An elderly Gujarati Brahmin man had been sent home from hospital, confused, paralysed and incontinent. The relatives were told he could last for many years, so they arranged for him to go into a private nursing

---

3 Firth 1993a:28.

4 Donaldson and Johnson 1990:237ff..

home with a good local reputation. He developed bed sores, and the family often found him lying in wet sheets, and felt that the care workers did not bother to change him. The family took their own vegetarian food for him to eat, yet had no deductions for it. His wife spoke little English, and she felt ignored and often wept.

Hospices, which in theory could provide the ideal holistic type of care for Hindus, have a low take-up of places (10.2). Hospital care is often satisfactory when the patient and relatives manage to establish a good rapport with the doctors and nursing staff, when free visiting is permitted and the relatives can take food to the patient. The Hindu and Sikh doctors I interviewed, as well as other medical staff at the biggest hospital in Westmouth, recognised the problems which could arise with some communities unfamiliar with Western medical procedures, with large numbers of relatives turning up to see ill or dying patients.[5] This can be particularly disruptive at the point of death, when there may be chanting as well as weeping. These problems are alleviated to some degree when it is possible to move the dying patient to a single room where the last rites can be carried out with minimum disturbance.

However, there are also many reports of misunderstanding, due to poor communication, lack of understanding of cultural and religious traditions and differing expectations. Nursing staff, who do not know about the tradition of death on the floor, can be bewildered to find patients lying on the floor (7.1.1). Discussing such situations a Punjabi doctor observed, "I don't think that would be a problem if somebody had explained to the ward Sister that was the procedure. Obviously if you don't explain, the hospital are concerned for the safety of their patients."

Communication is often a problem when the patient and relatives do not speak English, or where it is assumed that they do not understand English because of a heavy accent, as was the case with Maya's parents (7.1.2). However, without adequate communication it is difficult to assess patients' needs and to make a correct diagnosis. Communication is also important for the patient. Rees, formerly a hospice director, points out that, "Next to pain, poor communication is the most important source of distress to the dying patient. Poor communication is often the result of haste, of being focussed on the next patient or visit instead of the present problem."[6]

---

[5] Firth 1993a, 1993b, 1993c.

[6] Rees 1990:306.

At issue here is not just difference of language, but different forms of non-verbal communication or of using English idiom. There may be different role expectations or goals, and there may also be stereotypes which preclude understanding.[7] Interpreters may not be readily available, or inadequate. In Westmouth there is a list of available volunteer interpreters, but they often live a long way from the hospital and cannot always drop everything to get to the hospital. Without proper training interpreters may condense or re-interpret or add information, rather than literally translate what is being said on both sides. The patient may be reluctant to discuss his or her real anxieties in front of a member of the community for fear of gossip. Sometimes Indian doctors, when available, are called upon to act as interpreters, which is satisfactory for explaining medical terminology, but not from the perspective of the doctors' own work. Sometimes the family have to depend on quite a young child to act as interpreter, particularly in the case of women patients. This practice, according to Rack, is "unethical, unprofessional, uncivilized and totally unacceptable".[8] The use of other relatives, particularly the husband, may also be problematic, as McNaught comments: "Reliance on family members tends to reduce the ability of the practitioner to act in his patient's best interest on issues where there is family conflict or misunderstanding."[9] This particularly affects women in patriarchal households, where either the husband or the mother-in-law makes decisions.

Impersonal treatment by some professionals, coupled perhaps with unfamiliar technology, which can be bewildering and alarming even to white Britons, may be more so to those who do not know what is being done to them, or have the concepts to cope with it. Informing patients or their families may involve trying to explain new concepts. A Sikh doctor had to try to explain to his sister-in-law that her five-year-old daughter, who had been hit by a car, was brain-dead:

> She was unable to accept she was brain-dead. As long as she was kept on a respirator she would be OK. Even a lot of the Asians who visited her found the concept of brain death difficult because she was warm, respirating and her heart was working. An educated English family would find it easier to accept the difference between coma, in which the brain was still active, and brain death. No one could accept the fact that we were keeping the body going, while there was no electrical activity showing. It took three days to talk it

7 McAvoy and Sayeed 1990; Donovan 1986:12.

8 Rack 1990:66.

9 McNaught 1990:35; cf. Rack 1990: 299; Firth 1993c.

through.[10]

Sometimes it is felt that lack of sensitivity on the part of doctors and nurses is racist, particularly when assumptions are made about the patient's or relative's intelligence, education and capacity to understand what is going on, as we shall see in Case Study II below. Generalisations and stereotypes about religion, cultural grouping, race or colour come into this category.[11] Patients or their relatives may be accused of "making a fuss" when they ask for more attention, or display emotion. Patients who are "difficult" or who cannot communicate may receive less attention than those who respond "normally"

Professionals who are unfamiliar with the patients' backgrounds and have little time to find out about their religious or social needs may also have problems with different attitudes to women, to modesty, to food, and to religious practices. Strict vegetarians have, for example, refused an egg salad, only to have the egg removed and the salad returned to them on the same plate, with no comprehension that the plate is impure. It is not always understood that diabetic Hindus will not want insulin made from animal products, or that dying Hindus may wish to fast to ensure greater spiritual strength and ensure minimum risk of excretion at the point of death. Remarks to the effect that "if they come here they should adapt to our ways" are not infrequently heard. On one such occasion the remark was made by a consultant, to whom I had passed on information about the anxiety and distress of a Hindu patient at being put into a mixed ward. A well-educated, cultured bank manager from Delhi, he had been hospitalised following a heart attack while attending his brother-in-law's funeral.

Another consultant refused permission for a Gujarati family to give Ganga water to a dying aunt (4.4.1):

> An aunt was dying, everybody knew she was dying. The doctors told the family, and the whole family was present at the death. But when the doctors switched off the life-support machine they wouldn't let the family give Ganga water or perform any last rites to this lady. The reason the doctor gave was that she would live a little longer, but there was no point, she was dying anyway, and they switched off the machine, and they said they must not give her anything that would give her a shock and kill her straight away, that would choke her. But it didn't matter anyway, because she was dying. Even today after ten years it still affects the family that they weren't able to do this. If they want to have a social occasion like a wedding in the family or

---

[10] Firth 1993a.

[11] Cf. Donovan 1986:129.

> something, they must do some penance before they can have any such occasion because they say she died without water, therefore her soul is still not free and her family is not free. They've got to keep performing all these rites that they weren't able to during the death, until the soul is free. Therefore all the children that are born into this family will have to keep on doing this for at least seven generations, just so this particular soul is freed. (GjKF30; cf. 5.3)

The husband of the above informant added that the soul of this aunt would be hanging around for one hundred years unless an expensive ritual called a *saptāha*[12] was performed. which the family was only able to afford after some years. His mother wondered whether the reason her son and daughter-in-law were childless was due to the unhappy ghost of the aunt. From the perspective of the doctors, who may have thought large quantities of water would be forced down the old lady's throat, the quiet and peace of the patient was paramount, and quiet explanations might have saved a great deal of stress on both sides.

The Hindus in this study do not have fixed positions about the difficult issue of switching off life-support machines, although the boundaries between active 'killing' and 'allowing to die' are acknowledged by Asian, as by other, doctors, to be hard to draw. Some doctors would always treat aggressively to prolong life, whereas others would support, in principle, switching off a life support machine when it is clear that death is imminent or the person is brain-dead. One Hindu doctor said that he would refer patients for termination of pregnancy, but would never want to take any action to shorten life:

> The attitude of Hindus would be to treat aggressively up to the last hilt. I can't dream of a Hindu considering euthanasia, partly because of attachment, partly guilt: the need to ensure [one has done] one's duty. If a father was ill and the mother was living with her son and daughter-in-law, neither would want to be blamed that not enough had been done. There can be massive outside pressures to make sure everything is being done properly. This doesn't allow you to do anything but treat aggressively. I can't imagine a Hindu signing something like the Living Will[13] - this is a very intellectual concept. Pain should be controllable, so termination should not be necessary,

---

[12] A *saptāha* consists of seven days of readings during which 100 sadhus are fed. In the UK this would be replaced by feasting Brahmins, friends and relatives. It is not the same as the *narāyaṇa bali* .

[13] The Living Will is a document which provides advance directives regarding terminal care (Dickenson 1993:73, 69ff.). Such wills are not legally valid in the UK but are in 40 US states and are the subject of fierce debate.

> but it only happens when there is a specialist centre. The average general practitioner has not got the expertise to deal with that. My own feeling is to continue treatment, even if for a very long time. I couldn't make a personal decision to turn off the machine without family involvement.

In the light of the Hindu concept of the willed death, such a view is interesting, and may reflect his own attitude to the treatment of his own, mainly white, patients' deaths, but may also reflect a possible conflict of interest between community and family pressure to maintain life as long as possible, and the desire of some patients to have control over their deaths.

According to several Asian doctors, there is a shift in attitude among many of their patients, from a fatalistic acceptance of illness and death which might be encountered in India, where death is more common and familiar, to a belief that modern medicine can fix everything. Khare observed that in India people in poorer lower-caste households faced more unexplained chronic diseases and deaths than other groups, which gave rise to "a sense of deep despair, helplessness and fatalism, bordering sometimes on indifference".[14]

The influence of Western views about disease as a cause of death has also blurred the distinction between natural and unnatural deaths in India, according to Bayly.[15] Wealthier households in India, and all members of the community in Britain, have access to medical care which increases the possibility of cure. This may lead to false expectations of what the hospital and doctors can achieve, and result in great disillusionment when death occurs. As Case Study 1 indicates, this can have unhappy consequences for the patients and/or relatives. A Punjabi doctor explained that Asians wanted their symptoms cleared, so that if a cold or fever disappeared they believed that they were cured. It was difficult to say the effects were of an underlying disorder. One of his relatives, aged 50, with motor neurone disease, could not accept that nothing could be done medically: "There is a feeling you should be able to keep people alive. Indians find it hard to accept that illness is terminal, they may feel that one says so out of malice. More and more people want to blame someone."

This, of course, has consequences for the good death, which implies acceptance that death is inevitable soon, and creates a tension between giving up and fighting, both for the medical staff and for the patient and his family. Yet knowing someone is dying has both religious and emotional implications. The

---

[14] Khare 1976:180-181.

[15] Bayly 1981:184.

medical staff need to disclose the imminence of death so that the family can set the last prayers and rituals in motion. Time and again the failure to be present and facilitate these was a source of grief to informants, and affected their mourning. A Punjabi Brahmin observed:

> The nurses and doctors won't do [the rituals], so obviously we must be told [death is imminent] rather than keeping this news away, and only being told after the death has happened. I know it's not easy to say, "Look, he is going to die." It's easier to say "He's all right, nothing to worry about", and then you are given a telephone call, "Sorry we couldn't save him", But there are rituals to be done before the person dies. Chanting the *Gāyatrī Mantra* is evergreen, giving you power, strength, satisfaction and peace.[16]

In practice disclosure is not so simple. The attachments between members of the nuclear family may be very intense, particularly between parents and the adult children who live near or with them. Several Indian doctors, while acknowledging the importance, from a religious angle, of knowing death was imminent, have described the dilemmas they face in having to inform relatives that a parent or other relative is dying, knowing the consequence might be emotional collapse or hysteria. Telling a person she or he has a terminal illness, needs to be done in a way which does not lead to the patient's loss of hope. Relatives might withhold information from a dying person in case they gave up, and not put up a fight in the way the medical staff and family would wish them to, particularly in the case of a premature death, where the belief that this is due to bad *karma* may make it even more difficult to come to terms with.[17]

The two following Case Studies illustrate the problems of disclosure of terminal illness. In Case Study 1, Ramesh does not wish to believe the judgement of his Hindu general practitioner that his father's illness is terminal, and prefers to believe the reassurances of the hospital staff. In Case Study 2, the mother and daughter are not told of Jaswant's terminal condition. It is possible that the consultants did not realise the conditions were terminal; it is equally possible that they did not wish to alarm the relatives or have to deal with embarrassing emotions.

---

[16] Firth 1993a; cf. 3.5.

[17] Neuberger 1987:25; Firth 1993a.

7.1.1. Case Study 1: Ramesh[18]

Ramesh's family left Uganda in the early seventies, having lost absolutely everything. By sheer hard work, they had built up a life for themselves in Britain. His father, Suresh, aged 73, began to lose weight and developed urinary and respiratory problems, which were eventually diagnosed as prostate cancer, and fluid on his lungs was drained. He was re-admitted for surgery in August, and the family were told that as much cancer as possible had been removed, that he was out of danger, and with medication he would not need a further operation.

When the reports came back from the hospital, the general practitioner, also a Hindu, sent for Ramesh and said he did not think his father would live for more than six months. Ramesh found this impossible to believe, particularly as the doctors at the hospital had been so reassuring. He wanted to believe them when they said there was nothing wrong: "Hospital doctors and surgeons maybe know more - I wanted to believe that. He was in a safe place, in hospital." He was really angry and broke down in the surgery. He wanted to get private treatment, but the general practitioner said the prognosis was now in God's hands.

In October Suresh was re-admitted to hospital following a fit which left him unconscious. He had more tests while in hospital which showed evidence of either pneumonia or TB. It was also clear the cancer was not responding to the drugs, so he was recalled for further surgery. He began to feel angry and depressed and said they were trying to kill him. Ramesh brought him fresh orange juice, and Suresh said, "Don't bring me this, I am dying." When TB was confirmed he was taken to an infectious diseases unit where he was kept in intensive care for four weeks, becoming very depressed. The family did not want to tell him he had TB, "in case he had more of a shock and acted like a mad person. We went in with masks. He asked us, 'Why are you like this?' but we didn't tell him about the TB in case he gave up."

He was found lying on the floor. Ramesh did not think (or want to believe) that his father assumed he was dying but thought he had fallen out of bed going to the toilet. Ramesh took two weeks off work, spending every day with his father, washing and dressing him. Suresh greatly appreciated this and told him, "When I see you, I see God." He seemed to recover and was released just before

[18] Names and some details have been changed to protect confidentiality. Case Study 1 was based on an interview. Case Study 2 was based on tape-recorded interviews and informal talks with Maya and Nalini over a period of five years. In both cases permission was given to use the material. Apart from Ramesh's own doctor, interviewed with Ramesh's permission, the medical staff concerned were not interviewed, and therefore their perspective has not been presented.

Christmas, with a six months course of drugs for the TB, which affected his appetite. In early February he was re-admitted following a severe pain in the chest, which was put down to the drugs. Although quite cheerful initially, by the end of four weeks, he again become depressed, saying to the nurse, "If I die today or after 2 years or after 5 years, what difference does it make, living a painful life?" The nurse told Ramesh that Suresh's condition was not serious - he was only talking like this because of depression. The specialist also told them there was no immediate problem - he would be all right if he started eating.

Suresh was discharged from the hospital in March and Ramesh and his brother began to feel confident he would recover. Ramesh had a three week lay-off from work and was able to care for his father. He and his brother carried him upstairs at night. Suresh was very embarrassed by the level of personal care he needed, but his son said, "I am your son, I will do this for you, I will never get fed up, this is my duty. I will give up my job, as my wife is working - we want you to get better."

In late March he coughed up some black material, which the visiting nurse and general practitioner thought indicated internal bleeding. Suresh was re-admitted immediately, but the doctor in the hospital told them it must be gas. Ramesh was reassured that there was nothing wrong so he went away for a couple of days. Suresh died of an internal haemorrhage while Ramesh was away. Ramesh said:

> My mistake was going away. I looked after him for eight months, and still feel guilty because I wasn't there.The only good thing is that he died peacefully. He could have lived three or four months longer and suffered. It is very hard to accept Hindu teaching that the time of death is predetermined. All my life I will feel guilty because I should have accepted the general practitioner's verdict rather than the hospital's. I should not have left my father. I never said goodbye, all my life these things will bug me. I have failed in my religious duties to my father. If someone comes to visit, or leaves the house, you go to the gates of the house to say good-bye. He died conscious, and I was not there.

Some of Suresh's remarks seemed to indicate that he had begun to feel his life was drawing to a close, even before he became seriously ill and depressed. He had seemed healthy and happy during his younger son's wedding, saying, "Let us enjoy Divali together, we can't see what will happen in the future." He felt he had finished his work and wanted to go to India, which he loved. He hated being ill and inactive, saying, "I don't want to live like this."Ramesh said:

> When he was alive he was often angry but he died with a smile on his face. He must have known because he told me to arrange his books or give them to the right people. He said, "I won't read them again... People are dying with millions. I have nothing." He changed at the end. He read everything and had religious talks. He said, "*Sannyās* means everything is yours, no matter what religion or colour. You are responsible for the whole world. Everybody has to go one day." and I said, "Why are you talking like this?" He had covered and numbered all his books. In the last month he said, "I have given up, I want to go." He had a gold chain and he said, "When my grand-daughter gets married, give this to her as a gift from her grandfather...Why are people afraid of death? I will die peacefully and happily."

Ramesh continued to feel intense remorse because neither he nor anyone else was present when his father died to say goodbye, perform the last rites or discharge his debt properly. He was not comforted by reassurance of his own doctor that he should take credit for the total dedication and devotion he showed his father during his last months. Their family doctor advised them that it would be harder for the father to become detached if they felt so bad, so the family arranged for the *Gītā Pāṭh* (non-stop reading of the BG) in the temple six weeks after Suresh's death' which combined both a meritorious action and a fitting memorial.

As the above Case Study illustrates, it is not a simple matter to assess when somebody is going to die, and it may be very difficult for family members to accept the disclosure of such information, even though, on another level, they need the information to assist the dying person to prepare for death. It is not always easy to tell the difference between premonitions of death and giving up hope, which is a feature of depression, yet unless such premonitions are recognised the dying person may not receive the help needed to have a good death. This case was complicated because of Suresh's multiple problems and periods of recovery, and because the hospital staff tried to maintain hope in the face of what seemed evidence of terminal illness, whereas the Hindu general practitioner was aware of the spiritual and emotional context of terminal illness for Hindus and was not afraid to tell the truth. Suresh's doctor, for his part, felt that the hospital had not supported his views, although he had known the patient for twelve years. He knew Suresh was dying, so it was important to acknowledge this, whereas Ramesh clung to the hope that he would recover.

7.1.2. Case Study 2: Maya and Nalini

Maya was fifteen years old when her father, Jaswant, died in hospital. Some time earlier in the year he had been admitted with a myocardial infarction (heart attack), with a history of diabetes mellitus and ischaemic heart disease. He had recovered from this, and a few months later was readmitted after he had a slight stroke with difficulty swallowing and vomiting.[19]

Maya's mother, Nalini, was a graduate. Both she and her husband spoke fluent English, but since his stroke he had difficulty speaking, and because she had a deep voice and accent, it seems to have been assumed that neither understood much English and Maya was asked to act as interpreter. It is also possible that Nalini was very distressed and anxious, which made communication more difficult. He was unable to obtain enough water for his ablutions, and either got up to get water for himself, or asked Nalini to fill Coke bottles for him so that he could wash himself. Maya and Nalini became increasingly worried during Jaswant's stay in hospital, as it seemed clear to them that his condition was deteriorating, but Nalini felt the staff either ignored their complaints about his condition or assured them he was going to recover. He had a tube inserted to help feed him, and he began hiccupping:

> They were strange sounding hiccups, so we told the nurse, and she just went up to him and she said he was making unnecessary noises and disturbing the other patients, and really, it was just because the tube was there, and it was not necessary for him to make this noise. She told us, "He only makes this noise when you are here."

Then on the day before he died he was very restless and had brought up a lot of black vomit which had not been cleaned up. When Nalini complained she was spoken to harshly, and had to clean up the vomit herself. The staff nurse said, "It is only when you people come that he gets excited. It would be better if you did not come so often." Later he put his blanket over his head, which alarmed Nalini, as that was a bad sign indicating that he thought he might be dying. Jaswant was very hot initially, and so Nalini opened the window, and then he became cold and started shivering, asking for a blanket. She had great difficulty getting hold of one, and a nurse told her, "Oh, when you people come he makes this kind of fuss, pretending he is not feeling well. The weather is changeable and he is feeling cold because of that." Half an hour later, after asking three times Nalini obtained a

---

[19] Details of the case were taken from a letter written by the hospital to the Commission for Racial Equality, in response to a complaint by the family. It is quoted by permission of the family and the then director of CRE.

blanket. By now she was so concerned by his appearance and behaviour that she went to the doctor, "and after a whole lot of persistence and persuading he came eventually... and half an hour later we were told he had pneumonia and they said they'd have to put him into intensive care." Maya and Nalini were now badly frightened, and then they saw what a friend described as another bad sign, flowers and wreaths from a funeral carried past the father's room

Once Jaswant was taken into intensive care Nalini and Maya waited for an hour and a half. Nalini was in tears, and a doctor and a nurse tried to reassure her. Maya kept on saying, "Is there anything to worry about?" and they said, "Nothing, we'll take care of him, pneumonia is nothing nowadays." She was asked to go into Jaswant's room and tell him that they were going to put an oxygen mask on, and that he should keep it on for his own good. She was then asked to wait outside while they catheterised him, which caused him to scream with pain. This upset Maya because her father was such a modest man. Nalini also went along to see him, but the nurse shut the door in her face without a word. Eventually the staff persuaded the two to go home. At 3:00 a.m. there was a phone call, and Maya, who answered it, was told, "Your father has passed away."

Maya and Nalini were stunned by the disaster. Jaswant had been a self-employed business man who had spoken of his death, but he did not seem to have been prepared for it and had not left a will, so their business affairs were in chaos. They had believed what they had been told about Jaswant's prognosis, and felt he had just given up and lost the will to live. Maya said:

> If he had known, he would have had everything done. He always told us, "I'm not scared of dying. I'm not worried at all, as long as I know what is happening." He would have prayed in his last time, but really he would have worried about us. He would have had a bit of strength, "at least my family's with me at my last time." We think he lost [hope], he couldn't just take it any longer, all these tubes around him, helpless, he was like a little child in jail. If we had the slightest idea, we would have sat in the waiting room all night. If we'd been with him, he would have been stronger and maybe he would have survived.

The most painful aspect of Jaswant's death was that neither of them were with him at the end, did not say goodbye and did not hear his last words. When they went to collect his belongings, which had been placed in a black rubbish bag, the staff showed no concern for them, or sensitivity to their feelings. Maya said:

> As we were coming out, this tall Sister ... looked at me side glance, and she was talking to the other nurses and she was laughing. I was crying ... and she just carried on laughing with the others. I said [to the Sister] "Did my father say anything at the end?" and she said, "Oh, do you expect people when they die to say things in your religion?"And I said, "I just want to know what his last words were", and she said, "Oh, I didn't know that you'd have expected him to say anything," as if it was something really strange and out of this world that a person dying would say anything. She said "I'll find out as much as I can and tell you", but the next day she went straight past me, not even looking me in the face, as if she had been told that if something has gone wrong, don't say anything. That raised another doubt that something went wrong that we're not told about. I mean, they're going to stick up for each other, they're not going to go against their colleagues, are they? But we should have a right to know.

Maya felt that the reason they were not being informed had a racist dimension: "They think we're all stupid. They think brown skins are idiots, they don't know a thing." Afterwards Maya and Nalini were told by a registrar that Jaswant had died from a massive heart attack, and they wanted to know why it had not been put on the death certificate. When they eventually saw the consultant, he said, "It wasn't exactly a heart attack, but at the end the heart had started pumping three hundred beats a minute..."

> He went on how everybody's got to die some time and diabetics die young, and he told us not what we wanted to know but what he wanted us to know. He kept shutting me up, and I was talking about how my father had high sugar levels, and he said, "You're obsessed about sugar levels," and that shut me up there and then. He's the one who assured us that nothing's wrong, always laughing.

When Jaswant's male relatives went to wash the body at the undertakers they found that all the tubes had been left in, and had become so hard they had to be cut. This caused so much upset that eventually, with all the other frustrations they had felt, Maya and Nalini went to the Commission for Racial Equality and asked to have the whole matter investigated. Maya said, "I just want to know what happened, why weren't we told? We wrote to the consultant to find out why my father died, and in his letter, he said that people like this usually deteriorate and die. That's another point that he's put against himself, so why didn't he tell us?"

In replying to the complaint, the hospital apologised for any discourtesy to Nalini, but did not feel there was any element of racism in their treatment there. The Ward Sister had spent a great deal of time with the family, especially at the end, trying to explain what was going on. There had been problems with the supply of blankets because of industrial action, although they did not respond to the complaint that they had taken a long time to attend to Jaswant. Although Nalini had complained that Jaswant had not been cleaned up after vomiting, the nursing notes stated that he had made it very clear that no one but Nalini should wash him. The letter explained the symptoms Jaswant had experienced, and said that the "final event ... was a cardiac arrest, but the actual cause of death was cerebral thrombosis and pneumonia." The hiccuping and swallowing difficulties were due to a further spread of the occlusion "with interference and interruption of the activity of other vital centres controlling breathing, blood pressure and cardiac rhythms... Medical treatment cannot be expected to control or stop every symptom from which a patient suffers with instant effect". The tubes had to be left in until after a post-mortem, and it was the technicians who would remove them with the approval of the pathologist. If there was no post-mortem, this was left to the funeral director. The funeral director, subsequently interviewed by me, thought that in this case the tubes, barring the catheter, should have been removed prior to sending the body to him. He left Asian bodies alone unless otherwise instructed, because he assumed Hindus, like Muslims, would not want bodies touched by non-believers.

Nalini and Maya were not happy with the reply, but felt it was pointless taking the matter further. Both had a deep sense of anger at the rudeness of the nurses and felt the apology was quite inadequate. Nalini was disturbed because Jaswant had died in pain and she had not been with him, or able to say goodbye.

About two weeks after her husband's death Nalini developed malaria, and was taken to the same ward where her husband died. She was so frightened that she would be killed or die that Maya and her aunt had to stay with her for the whole of the week she was there. They all felt particularly fearful at 3:00 a.m., the time that Jaswant died. For several months afterwards Nalini and Maya were afraid to sleep in their own house, and slept at friend's house.

The issues here were not overtly to do with the ideal type of good death, but the fundamental ones of adequate communication and disclosure, being with the dying person to the end, and hearing last words. But the good death involves dealing with 'unfinished business', seeing that the family are provided for, and saying goodbye, approaching death willingly and consciously, and dying in such a way that relatives can recount how the person died and what he said. Maya knew that her father would have wanted prayers, although he was not particularly orthodox. The overwhelming impression is of poor communication, different expectations and misunderstanding. Incorrect assumptions appear to have been made that neither Jaswant nor Nalini spoke or understood much English, which were perhaps explicable in view of his partial paralysis and her accent. It is possible that Nalini's level of distress made it difficult for staff to feel that they were properly understood, but it may also have been an irritant if the staff were not used to emotional relatives. Maya's accusation of racism was deeply upsetting to the staff. However, her reports suggest, at the very least, rudeness and a profound lack of sensitivity to individuals of a different cultural background, which would be perceived as racist.

The question of disclosure of terminal conditions is an issue which has been much discussed in recent literature.[20] It may well be the case that the staff did not wish to upset relatives who were already anxious. It is also possible that they did not, and could not, know the prognosis. However, the retrospective judgement of the consultant that the death was not surprising given Jaswant's condition, makes this difficult to assume. It is also possible that, as in the case of Ramesh, the two women did not wish to hear the prognosis, but if the staff were aware that Jaswant's condition was terminal, that would not explain why Nalini was prevented from seeing him in the intensive care unit, or why they were sent home. As in the Ramesh Study, both women were deeply disturbed at being absent at the time of death, and this continued to worry Nalini for several years. It was both a personal need to have remained with him, and a religious need to have prayers at the moment of death. This is fundamental to Hindus, both for the sake of the dying person and for the sake of the family.

In neither of the Case Studies was the dying man placed on the floor, nor was this perceived to be an issue. When Suresh was found on the floor Ramesh surmised, possibly correctly, that he had fallen. He did not believe, or want to believe, it had any other significance. Jaswant came from a less conservative background, but in neither situation was the primary expressed concern to perform any rituals. Had Ramesh been with Suresh he would have encouraged him to say "Rām, Rām", and would have given him Ganga water and *tulasī* had they been available. However, any concern about rituals at the moment of death was far outweighed by the grief at not being present, saying goodbye, and in Ramesh's case, his perceived failure to fulfil his debt to his father. He did have, however, a number of positive memories which emerged in the interview, which suggested in many ways that the father was indeed prepared to die, which might

[20] A number of articles in Dickenson and Johnson, 1993, deal with this issue.

in due course come to have significance for him. For Maya and Nalini, the death was unreservedly a bad one because it was so sudden, and because Jaswant had not been prepared for it.

7.2. After death

Because there are no taboos against women weeping, and fewer against men showing emotion than in Anglo-Saxon society, a great deal of distress may be shown on the death of a relative and this may disturb staff and other patients. According to a Sikh nurse, an Indian woman who had given birth to a still-born baby was criticised by the English nurses in the maternity unit for expressing her grief very loudly. A couple of her relatives and her mother-in-law were also wailing and "making a scene" in a way which would be regarded as quite normal and the "done thing" in a village setting at home, but was regarded as abnormal here. The nurses kept telling them to "keep your voices down," but the Sikh nurse said they needed to get it out of their system. Another Indian maternity nurse made the observation that white English patients would tend to blame either themselves or the medical staff, showing a lot of anger and guilt. Asian patients, once the first intensity of the grief was over, were able to accept the death as God's will much more readily (3.3; 8.3.1; 9.1).

Apart from Maya and Nalini, informants were generally appreciative of the help given after death by hospital and mortuary staff. Those who had experienced the sudden death of a relative also spoke of the courtesy and kindness of the police. In one Punjabi Khattri family, where only a daughter was available to go to the hospital to see her father's body, the policewoman who took her waited until she had had time to sit with the body and took her home again, visiting again the following day to see whether she could do anything to help.

Most Hindus will allow the nurses to help lay out the body and remove tubes, but there may be taboos against women touching men and *vice versa*, so men may prefer to deal with the body of a male member of the family and women with that of a woman. The family may wash and dress the body in the hospital, although it will have to be done again immediately before the funeral.

There are no formal religious objections against post-mortems among Hindus, such as there may be among Muslims. Nevertheless they may occasion great anxiety. According to one Hindu doctor, "Hindus are deadly against post-mortems." A Darji asked, "Does the post-mortem affect the *ātman?* It makes you really shake. I wouldn't want to make the body suffer after death." In view of the uncertainty about when the *ātman* really leaves the body, and the feeling that the body is in some sense holy and sacred, this anxiety is understandable. There are reports of doctors signing the death certificate of a frail elderly Hindu in circumstances where they would have insisted on a post-mortem for a non-Hindu. Some informants, however, have been glad of a post-mortem in order to understand the cause of death, although relatives may be disturbed by the sight of the body when they bathe it. Even a doctor who went to the mortuary to see his father's body after the post-mortem was shaken to find that the incisions, which had been crudely stitched up, had not been covered.

7.3. Professionalisation

The notion of professional people who are paid to arrange things for them is regarded by some Asians as a complete denial of the community aspect they are used to, and many people dislike the use of a coffin:

> Whoever heard of funeral directors in the Punjab? Here funerals are administered by third parties who take money for this purpose, whereas in the Punjab a funeral is very properly a community affair, where close relations and friends, when they had heard of a particular death, would inconspicuously go about the business of arranging for wood and other material with perfection .. the body is [even] put in a box with a name on it!

The speaker, a Sikh, expressed a common Indian view. He spoke of his shock, when his little boy died in England, of having to have professional funeral directors to conduct arrangements instead of the family and friends doing this, and of having a hearse to carry the little coffin, instead of carrying the child himself, as he would have done in India. He felt bereft because of this.

The director of the most commonly used undertaker in Westmouth tried to accommodate his multi-cultural clientele, but did not always know which community he was dealing with, unless, for example, Sikhs were wearing turbans. He did not seem to have found a means of distinguishing between different communities by their names. Bearing in mind the great sensitivity of many Asians, particularly Muslims, he tended to be wary of doing anything people might object to. As in the tube incident above, he might omit things which he would have done for a member of the host community. He noted that many young Hindus knew very little about their own customs, and felt that they had

> acquired the British habit of being afraid of death, of the body. They have to file past the open coffin in the house, but they have been brought up the

English way, and to have their own customs thrust upon them is a bit much. Little girls accept it. Many's the time I've been down to the chapel there and seen the little girls with their hands up on the table and their nose on the top of the table looking up at granny or whoever it is. You don't see boys doing that. Young lads stand off.

Several informants observed that the undertakers were more sympathetic to their religious requirements than the medical staff and other professionals, as noted above. This, of course, could be said to be good business practice, but one which, taking the Asian community as a whole, involves the undertakers themselves in a considerable amount of adaptation. They have to fit in large numbers of funerals at the crematorium in an efficient manner, sometimes four in an hour. Although the above-mentioned director tried to arrange for them to have 25 minutes, it was complicated by the huge numbers of mourners attending many Hindu funerals: "I've got to keep them happy, and I've got to keep the local authority happy, and the local authority isn't renowned for its willingness to bend." Often the young people made all the arrangements, and then older members of the community would turn up and try to arrange things differently, "pulling the family into line".

In some instances following a death at home, the body has remained at the undertakers' chapel of rest for a simple funeral instead of being taken to the family home, as seen above (5.5). A Brahmin from Fiji and his wife preferred this: "I don't think it is very nice to bring the coffin into the temple or house and open the face, and let everybody see it. It becomes a public display." The ambiguity of attitudes to the body is illustrated by cases of a sudden death at home. The undertaker has been asked to remove it as soon as possible, "because the women are in a very highly charged state, and the men are anxious to get rid of it" until the funeral. Some Punjabis believe it cannot then come back to the house again, reflecting anxiety about its impurity and inauspiciousness.

The disposal of the ashes in Britain (5.8) has created problems over the use of local rivers, with some local authorities forbidding any "poisonous, noxious or polluting matter" and "solid waste matter" to enter the rivers, although Poulter observes, "the definition of 'polluting matter' is unclear".[21] Water companies could refer bereaved Hindus and Sikhs to the relevant inspectors, indicating suitable areas for disposal after obtaining the relevant licences from the district fisheries inspectors. Severn, Trent and Thames Water authorities recommend

---

[21] Control of Pollution Act 1974; The Water Act 1989; Poulter 1990:125; 1989:83.

local boatmen who "could conduct a dignified and discreet ceremony on a commercial basis". One of my London pandit informants made use of this service at Southend. Seven water authorities were not aware whether such permission would be forthcoming, which Poulter comments is "unfortunate, since bereaved Asian families will be looking for a sympathetic and constructive response from their local water authorities rather than a negative dismissal of their pleas for cooperation and guidance".[22] A practical solution would be to provide printed information with constructive suggestions as to where ashes might be disposed of and about the correct procedures.

Facilities to enable dying Hindus to receive religious and emotional support that is needed should be improved. Medical staff may have problems coping with such needs within existing structures, or with recognising unconscious prejudice or ignorance. A Punjabi doctor commented, "Carers don't [need to know] about cultural diversity - but they only need to listen for a few minutes, to be sensitive." Where the staff are aware of cultural needs, the care is frequently excellent, as a Punjabi Brahmin said, when his mother was hospitalised following a stroke:

> I have no criticism. She couldn't speak and they asked us to go any time, take food or anything, and there were no restrictions. At first she was in a ward and then in a room by herself. ... We took some *gangajal* and some *tulasī* leaf, and the hospital asked us if we wanted to do various religious rites and ceremonies, anything to do with religion, and that is why they didn't remove her or touch her or do anything, until we went there. They asked me if I wanted to do anything before they took the body.

This sensitivity needs to be manifested from the outset - over the details of nursing care, respect for different beliefs, and finally, over openness and willingness to communicate with patients and relatives so that mutual compromises can be made and no one dies alone.[23] Sensitivity is also needed over the arrangements for the timing of funerals, preparation of the body, and dealing with the ashes. Bureaucracy can often take priority over human needs.

---

[22] Poulter 1989:84.
[23] Firth 1993c.

Chapter 8
The Mourning Period in Britain

Since the death of an individual often deeply affects those around him or her, it is important to explore the social effects of a death on members of the family and wider community. The first section of this chapter discusses the importance and value of the mourning period, drawing in particular on Hertz and Van Gennep. The following sections examine the experience of British Hindus, the concepts of *sūtaka* and *śoka*, food restrictions, community support and the public expression of grief up to the end of the mourning period. Finally the the position of Hindu widows is discussed.

8. 1. The importance of the mourning period

Following a death, various emotional reactions are normally channelled into socially constructed and acceptable behaviour, often for a prescribed period.[1] As indicated in Chapter One, Van Gennep, following and expanding on Hertz, postulated three stages in post-mortem rites which mirrored the bereavement process: separation from the deceased; the liminal or transitional period, during which the mourners are set apart and may be regarded as being in a state of impurity; and reincorporation.[2] This has the dual function of incorporating the deceased into the realms of ancestors, and the living back into normal social life.

Mourning rituals give shape and meaning to bereavement, providing 'milestones' which allow the bereaved a gradual time to let go of the deceased and adjust to the changes in their lives psychologically.[3] According to Rosenblatt, both the final ceremonies and the knowledge that they are coming at a certain time help the bereaved to 'work through' their grief more effectively so that afterwards they can make the transition back to some sort of normality and adapt to changes of status socially, such as that of a widow, or an eldest son who has to take on the father's role.[4]

---

[1] The disappearance of a prescribed period of mourning in much of Western secular society is thought by some writers to cause difficulties with dealing with grief (Gorer 1965; Kubler-Ross 1969; Ariès 1976, 1981,1985; Walter 1990, 1993; Peberdy 1993:3.2ff.; Siddell 1993). Hockey (1996a) warns against romanticizing mourning rituals in other cultures, since they may reflect not only the ethnocentric view of the writer but also a culture's belief system, without meeting the survivors' psychological needs.

[2] Van Gennep 1960:11ff.; Hertz 1960.

[3] Hertz 1960:81-82.

[4] Rosenblatt *et al.* 1976:8.

From a psychological perspective a period of withdrawal and isolation following the intense activity associated with the funeral, may be a natural reaction of individuals and families to a death, as they may not feel able to engage in normal social interactions even when there is no associated belief in contagious impurity or inauspiciousness as in Hindu and other cultures. A structured mourning period, as is also found in Jewish, Sikh, and Muslim communities, legitimises a period of withdrawal with clear guidelines as to how mourners and community members should behave, strengthening social and religious bonds. It allows for times of talking about the deceased, periods of weeping and times for prayer or scripture reading which help direct the attention of the bereaved away from their own feelings towards God or "some transcendent and sacred core of social and moral value"[5].

Death is not just the physical loss of a person but the social death of an individual, which affects both the immediate family and the wider community, depending on the age and status of the person. Thus Hertz suggested that the death of a very old person who had ceased to play a significant social role, and the death of an infant, receive less attention than that of a person who had a significant social and economic part to play in society.[6] The social death of the individual is closely connected to beliefs about the way the soul gradually separates from its earthly ties and acquires "a final and pacified character in the consciousness of the survivors". That is why the idea of an "intermediary state between death and resurrection imposes itself, a state in which the soul is thought to free itself from the impurity of death or from the sin attaching to it." This requires a liminal or transitional period, "because the double mental process of disintegration and of synthesis that the integration of an individual into a new world supposes ... requires time".[7]

The Hindu pattern of mourning seems to be a classic example of Hertz' and Van Gennep's theses, with rites of separation (4.3-4.4.1; 5), a liminal period during which the family remain impure and inauspicious (6.1-2), and rites of reintegration (6.2.1). The latter have the dual function of providing the dangerous *preta* with a new body so that he becomes an ancestor "with a final and pacified character in the consciousness of the survivors",[8] and allowing the mourners to

[5] Huntington and Metcalf 1979:11; cf. Turner 1967:94.

[6] Hertz 1960:76: Rosenblatt et al. 1976:8; Huntington and Metcalf 1979:142; Bloch and Parry 1982:5; Prior 1993:251-252.

[7] Hertz 1960:82.

[8] Hertz 1906:83.

end their period of extreme grief and resume normal life. Even when the *śrāddha* rites are not seen or understood as creating a new body, they are understood quite clearly as giving the person a 'send-off' to his ancestors or wherever the family believes he has gone, and removing him, and themselves, from the dangerous liminal state.

In India the rites of separation begin before death, in the case of a good death, or at the moment of death, with a cremation almost immediately (Ch. 5). This enables the mourners to enter the liminal or mourning period from the time of death in a highly structured manner which lasts until the *śrāddha* (rites of reincorporation) on the twelfth day and thirteenth days.

In Britain, the pattern has shifted because of the change in the timing of the funeral. The liminal period begins *before* any rites of separation, particularly in the case of a sudden or hospital death where there may have been no rituals at the point of death. There may be a period of eight or more days until the funeral and a consequent shortening of the gap between the funeral and the rites of re-incorporation, the combined *śrāddha*. The rites of separation thus occur in the middle of the period of mourning, rather than at the beginning, causing a shift in the whole structure of the mourning period.

8.2. *Sūtaka* and *śoka*

Sūtaka, the period of impurity following death, is associated with the inauspiciousness of death (5.1). According to a Kumhar man:

> *Sūtak* is for sixteen days from the day a person has died, when close family, relatives and friends come and pay condolences, and *śok* [sadness, sorrow] is where the close family stay with you and reminisce. During *sūtak* you cannot do any good things like going to the temple, eating out or touching the *mandir*. *Sūtak* in India came about because the person had died at home, and we keep ourselves at home for sixteen days, according to the Veds [Vedas], to allow the air to clear. It has nothing to do with the *pret*, because if it is a good death, it goes straight to God. In India, living in one house as one family, it's a symbolic gesture. For a widow, *śok* is for six months to a year. She can't go to special functions, only to work or to funerals. If a very young male has died, his family members will wear black until everything is done. *Śok* affects the whole family, even unmarried sisters.

Sūtaka affects family members as soon as they hear of a death, no matter how far away, so they bathe and change because "it's not very nice", although "it is nothing to do with ghosts, *bhūta preta*, as we don't believe in that"(GjDF).

Until they have bathed many Hindus do not eat or drink. Many Hindus also bathe after condolence visits. *Sūtaka* is most severe on the day of the funeral, when the body is usually brought back to the house. Those who touch the body or coffin are especially impure, and they and the other mourners bathe and change as soon as they return home, before they eat or drink, to "create a change of mood". Friends and relatives returning to the house of the deceased after the funeral wash their faces and hands and sprinkle themselves from a large bowl or bucket of water outside the front door before entering. After the funeral of an immediate relative, some strict Gujaratis bathe in a friend's house, placing polluted clothes into cold water to soak before returning home. A young Patel said he would have felt anxious if he had not done this, for fear of harm, but if it was impossible it would not bring bad luck.

Sūtaka is often spoken of as if it is interchangeable with the term *śoka* (sorrow), in the sense of this being a period of formal mourning, although the latter lasts much longer - for four to five weeks, particularly in the case of a young man's death, and up to a year for a widow. It also seems to mean the actual feelings of sorrow or sadness (*duḥkha*). According to a Gujarati pandit,

> *Śoka* is best described by the term 'mourning', grief, or a general state of dejection, whereas *sūtaka* is a period of impurity brought in to enable people to think properly, to keep the mind, *man*, pure and working properly, to keep a good balance and develop the religious side.

For those mourning someone who has had a good death in old age the restrictions are less severe, just as grief is expected to be less severe. While mourners do not normally prepare food at home or offer it to visitors during *sūtaka* a Patel man commented, "An old person can prepare food at home if necessary, because in old age you have to die and the person has had a fulfilled life. Therefore *sūtak* has no sense." The implication is that there is less need for grief (*śoka*) and less inauspiciousness for those who have died in old age, and thus less need to observe the rules of *sūtaka*.[9] A Patel woman went to her mother's funeral in another city. She was offered food at her brother's house, which had worried her initially because it went against the rules of *sūtaka*, but she decided that it was legitimate to eat because it was the funeral of her own mother who had died in old age. This seems to suggest that the concern to

---

[9] See Raheja 1988:58 ff.

observe *sūtaka* is related to danger, to fear of the ghost, which in this case was perceived to be benign. It is the unfulfilled desires and attachments of the deceased which are perceived to be threatening (3.2.2); hence the observance will be stricter for a premature or sudden death.

During *sūtaka* the mourners adopt an abstemious life style. The chief mourner and other immediate male kin often do not shave their beards; heads are rarely shaved in Britain. Some families sleep on the floor; others have abandoned this "because the houses are too cold" (KhM50). The son of a Punjabi pandit from Fiji understood these traditions to have arisen out of ordinary thoughtfulness, but added:

> I don't see why everyday food and things like that have anything to do with death. I did these things out of respect for my father, but what are thirteen days? My sister-in-law was told to sacrifice a bit of comfort for her husband by sleeping on the floor, but what is the sense? If they said don't sleep at all, that would be different, but if you are going to sleep what difference does a bed or a floor make?

The chief mourner, siblings, other sons, daughters and the widow try to get as much time off work as possible, sometimes claiming sick leave if employers do not permit more than three days of compassionate leave. It can be difficult to get leave for a relative who is not a parent or a spouse. A Gujarati woman who had taken compassionate leave after her father's death asked for further leave within the year following an uncle's death. Her employers could not understand why anyone would wish to take more than a day off for an uncle - yet he had lived in the same household and had been like a father to her. A young doctor felt obliged to return to part-time work four days after his father's death. After his morning calls he returned to the house, changed and sat all afternoon with his mother, and returned to his surgery in the evening. This pattern was quite helpful at the time, as he was so devastated. Subsequently he felt guilty that he had gone back to work less than a week after the death, and wondered how good a doctor he had been during that period.

There should be no TV, no music tapes except religious *bhajans*, or radio played during this time. Sexual relations are forbidden. The family shrine or *mandir* cannot be used. It may either be covered or removed by a friend with all the *mūrtis* and the pictures of the gods.

Up to the twelfth day there may be readings from various books, depending on the sectarian affiliation of the family, or their particular attachments. These may be done by the pandit, who will come for a couple of hours daily, or by members of the family, community or *satsaṅg* group. The *Bhagavad Gītā* is very popular. Some Gujaratis read the *Bhāgavata Rāhasya* or the *Bhāgavata Purāṇa*, others prefer the *Garuḍa Purāṇa*, although one young widow was horrified by this: "Does my husband really have to go through all that?" Some Punjabi and Sindhi families have readings from the Sikh scripture, the *Gurū Granth Sāhib*.[10] This may be read over a period of ten days until the *pagrī* on the eight or tenth day (*sādhāraṇ pāṭh*), or non-stop for forty-eight hours at the end of the period (*akhaṇḍ pāṭh*), after which there are prayers (*ardās*), followed by the giving of the *pagrī* (turban).[11] In Westmouth Arya Samajis read from an anthology called *Amṛta Varṣa*[12] which takes two hours. Often everyone participates. It contains poems by Tulsi Das and Kabir in addition to those of the writers. The reader is told always to remember God and death. Kabir says:

> Death is inevitable. We should remember this and do nothing wrong.
> The world is illusory. Someone makes a house and calls it his own but it is no-one's. It is just an inn [*serai*, temporary resting place].
> The world is foolish; some say, 'He is my brother, she is my sister, he is my husband, this is my son.' This is all temporary. At death all will go.
> O God, have mercy, don't see my bad deeds. I have committed many sins, but now I am at your threshold. Don't mind my misdeeds. You are the only one who can give me solace. (*Amrta Varṣa* p.21)

In addition to the readings, songs may be sung, reflecting the ephemeral nature of existence. One such song often sung by Gujaratis in Westmouth is said to have been composed by a Gujarati saint, Narasingh Mehta:

> We ascend old age,
> In old age the sons grow old,
> Their wives kick you out,
> Your children and their wives abuse you.
> The girls are taken away by their husbands.
> You can't eat,
> Because your system can't digest.

---

[10] Several Sindhi informants from the Amil caste, who regard themselves as Hindus, said they have Hindu marriages but Sikh funerals. Some Punjabi Hindus also attend the Sikh *gurdwara*. An elderly and much loved Punjabi woman had both Hindu and Sikh funerals (5.5).

[11] Cf. Cole and Sambhi 1978:120.

[12] *Amṛta Varṣa* was written and compiled in Nairobi by Shanti Devi Puri, Pashpavati Handa, and Sahagvanti Ghai; hitherto unpublished translation by Ram Krishan Prashar.

You're deaf.
Your legs give way,
So you can't go to the temple to pray.
It's best to pray to God now. (GjPM30)

The humour of the above song reflects both a realistic attitude to the decrepitude of old age, and the need to detach oneself from both the body and human relationships which ultimately let one down. Such readings and songs draw those present together, giving religious meaning to the bereavement and placing the loss in a wider perspective (cf. 9.5).

8.2.1. Food restrictions

As soon as death has occurred, some families throw out all food in the house, barring *ghī* for the body, as is done in India. In other households this is done on the day of the funeral which is especially polluted (GPM30). In India, the family normally fast until the funeral is over (5.3), but that is clearly impossible in Britain where the funeral may be seven or more days away. Many mourners fast on the day of the funeral until it is over. Ideally, the family do not cook during this time, certainly for the first few days after the death, although it is sometimes necessary to do so if there is not enough support from relatives and friends. In many communities the son's wife's family provide food for relatives and friends after the funeral. Surya's daughters decided to resume cooking themselves after three days because they needed something to do (9.2.4). Before this, a Sikh neighbour and caste friends helped. In a Gujarati household where the deceased had been murdered, the family were considered so inauspicious that no one would help them so they had to cook for themselves.

Most Punjabi informants reported fewer restrictions regarding food than Gujaratis, some of whom will not even go into the kitchen until the *sapiṇḍīkaraṇa* on the twelfth day is over (6.2.1). Any food eaten is very simple. In one Punjabi Brahmin *jāti* no fried foods such as *pūris* or sweets are prepared, just rice, *rotī* (*chapattis*) and *dāl*. Gujaratis eat 'hotchpotch' or *khichṛī*, a mixture of rice and *dāl*, and buttermilk, sometimes for up to forty days, which was "very boring" (GDF20). No sweets are prepared, although a Lohana woman prepared some for the pandit following the funeral of her husband's brother-in-law. She did not say whether he actually ate them. Hindus who normally eat meat abstain.

While many people, especially Pushtimargis, prefer not to accept food or drink in a house in *sūtaka*, relatives and friends travelling long distances often accept tea, coffee and food, like the Patel woman (8.2.1), who accepted food at her brother's house after her mother's funeral. However, when a Gujarati girl, Rohini, offered visitors tea or coffee as a matter of courtesy, she was told that it was the wrong thing to do:

> In the Hindu Punjabi religion you can eat at the mourner's house, but in the Hindu religion[13] if people come to your house you do not say hello or goodbye to friends, they just come in. You don't offer them any drink. I didn't know anything about how to conduct mourning. When people came I said hello and invited them in, and said, "Please sit down. Do you want anything to eat or drink?" and they said, "No, if you don't mind, we won't have anything." Then my Mum or Dad said, "Look, you don't offer drink or food when people come; it's just not right, you don't say hello, you don't say goodbye." It puts you in an awkward position because it just seems to me that you're not welcoming them in. You just open the doors, look straight faced and don't even smile at them, and let them come in. I felt a bit silly that people were sitting there conversing, talking philosophically about death and everything, and yet I couldn't offer them any entertainment. But Punjabis are different. Whenever I was at my friend's house after the death of her father, I don't know whether it was because she didn't know or they don't have the same thing as us, but she did offer me coffee, and I had a cup at her house, because I don't mind taking a cup of coffee when a person is dead. I think the reason for not offering tea or coffee is showing that they've come to mourn. They think drinking coffee, tea, eating something is being happy. It would show you were being normal and that's not allowed.

She had no idea, until her parents explained the custom to her, that this had anything to do with impurity. The experience of death is not a common one in Britain, and it is often only at such times of crisis that younger community members begin to understand their own traditions.

8.3. Community support and the expression of grief

The mourning period is a time of social support and bonding and provides opportunities for the proper expression of grief (8.1). As soon as a death has occurred friends and relatives will rally around to help. Even if the deceased died abroad, mourning procedures are set in motion in Britain for the requisite period, and relatives and friends come to offer their condolences. The narratives of the

---

[13] Some Gujaratis make the assumption that all Punjabis are Arya Samajis, which they regard as a different religion to Sanatana Dharma, seen here as 'Hinduism'. Cf.Bharati 1967:303 and Nye 1992a:129.

death help to make sense of the death and of the person who has died, and in the case of a good death, provide a lasting source of inspiration and a shared experience with those who have also been bereaved.[14]

In the house a *ghī* lamp (*dīvā*) is lit immediately after the death and placed in front of a photo of the deceased, and kept burning until the funeral, when it will be replaced by another one (4.4). Furniture is removed from the living room or rooms, white sheets are spread on the floor, and the chief mourner and the widow, if there is one, receive condolence visits. If the house is big enough, one room will be used by the men and another by the women, although men may also greet the widow.

Friends offer to help with practical arrangements, such as taking the mourners to the registry and undertaker, fetching relatives from the airport or the station, or offering accommodation. No one is ever left alone in the house, especially at night, and if members of the family are not available, others will go. A Brahmin from Fiji immediately went to help two of his Sikh friends:

> They didn't know what to do. When K's father died, I told him I would register the death, get the certificate and deal with the undertaker. That is one worry off their minds. The most unpleasant worry is going to the hospital and sorting things out. It is a pleasure for me to do things like that for people. What is half an hour, an hour, to do a good deed for somebody? I've been through that and I know what distress it is. Half the time you can't think straight, or go to the loo, even.

Many informants have found this period helpful, provided there were opportunities for the family to have a break from the stream of visitors. One widow told me that in East Africa it was the custom to leave the family alone during meals and in the afternoon, whereas here people kept arriving all day. One of Nesbitt's Gujarati informants told her that visitors did not come on Tuesday, Wednesday, Sunday or after 6.00 p.m, except for close relatives and those bringing food (personal communication). A Punjabi Soni family were helped by a neighbour, whom they had known since they were in Kenya. He took control when there were too many visitors in the evening, saying "That's enough now, let's give them a break."

The large number of visitors coming from long distances for condolences, and even more for the funeral, can be quite stressful, both in financial and

[14] Cf. Hockey 1996b; Walter 1996.

emotional terms. Small houses do not always have enough space, even for people willing to sleep on the floor. It can be expensive to feed many visitors if they remain for several days, or, as in the case of a Patel family, for three weeks.

During the mourning period in a Punjabi family, whom I visited regularly, visitors would arrive and sit on the floor which was covered with white sheets. The widow sat huddled in a corner, with a white sari pulled over her face, occasionally weeping quietly. Her sister sat next to her, patting her and consoling her. The visitors - mainly women during the day and both men and women in the evening - talked about her husband, saying what a fine person he had been and how he was greatly respected and loved. The suddenness of the death was sad, but it was God's will, and he had died a good death because he had said "Rām Rām" at the point of death. They also shared their own experiences of bereavement, weeping as they remembered the son, brother or parent who had died. A Punjabi-speaking Muslim thought she wasn't showing enough grief and said "*Ronā*" (cry), but if she showed too much grief or for too long, the women would murmur "*bas, bas*" (enough, enough), obviously seeking a balance. During the day the women recited *Amṛta Varṣa* together for about two hours. After this an elderly Punjabi lady known as Māta-jī gave a little homily in Punjabi, about God being in control and everything being in His hands. God was in everything; cats, dogs and people all had the same *ātman*. This man was a good man and would go straight to God or be reborn into a good life. In the afternoon the widow sat before her husband's photograph, which had a lighted *dīvā* in front of it, and read two chapters of the BG so that she could complete it before the funeral.

She found it helpful to be reminded that death was universal, and she was not alone in her experience of grief. She was consoled by reminders that the death was a good one, and that it was God's will (9.5). At the same time, the visits were quite exhausting, as she felt numb and bewildered, and had little time for rest. Although I had initially hesitated to intrude into a home after a death, I found that condolence visits from English friends and colleagues were immensely appreciated:

> When people help you they are like God, they visit you and do things for you. God hasn't got a body, only strength, and He comes into people and gets them to help. Many people come and cook food and bring flowers, and that is all God inside people. If I was in a happy state I could go out and ask for help but when I was in *duḥkh* [suffering] I couldn't go out and ask for people for help and you came and offered to put people up. (PjKF60)

Another Punjabi valued the visits made after his loss of his father:

> Visitors give us courage. It hasn't happened just with you, it happens with everybody. You are not alone in losing your father. They share your grief with you. They tell you of people who won't cry and get mentally sick, and try to make you cry. When someone is sharing your sadness you cool down, they help you. They don't share money or the cost. You cry, "Oh, I lost my father", and it reminds them of their own loss, and they treat you like a son or a brother, and you remember him and feel relaxed. (PkhM45)

8.3.1. Weeping and wailing

Wailing, which Hindu, Sikh and Muslim teaching discourages,[15] nevertheless persists in many South Asian village areas (4.4) and in a few communities in Britain, although there was no evidence of this at the funerals I attended. Ritualised wailing seems to have several functions. It reinforces social bonds, but it also forces the female mourners who are in a state of shock to begin expressing their grief, or if they are hysterical, to channel it into a controlled form. It also enables the mourners to experience the proper sentiments which they might otherwise not feel (9.1).[16]

A number of informants commented that although it was against religious teaching to weep, tears had therapeutic value. While it is no disgrace for a man to show emotion, particularly when saying farewell to a parent or child at the funeral, it is the women for whom emotion is not only permitted, but expected as an indication of their attachment to the deceased.[17] One of the most distraught women I saw at any of the funerals I attended was the daughter-in-law of a deceased woman. Some of the other mourners commented approvingly on her attachment, but a number of younger informants felt there was often an element of public display in such situations.

Rohini described the period of *śoka* following the death of her grandmother in India. Her uncles in India and Dar es Salaam had performed their own rituals:

> We had it here. People came from all over London, Leicester, everywhere, not because they knew my grandmother, but because they knew my parents, and to mourn for the fact that my father's mother had died. It seems wrong that it's expected of them. It made my father feel better, but he didn't have

[15] Hindu: BG.2.11, 26; Kane 1973 IV:218; Sikh: *Ādi Granth* 1410; Cole and Sambhi 1978:121-122; Prickett 1980:121; and Muslim: Rahman 1989:168.

[16] Rosenblatt 1976:7; Huntington and Metcalf 1979:24-26.

[17] Cf. Parry 1991:19ff.; Madan 1987:130ff.

> time to mourn in private. My mum had to remain in the room. She was very close to her mother-in-law, with whom she lived since she was married at the age of sixteen, and she did feel grief for her. I only knew my grandmother until I was six or seven. That feeling of attachment wasn't there. So you have this guilty consciousness that everyone is feeling bad, while you, the granddaughter, can't feel anything. I did feel bad that my grandmother had died, for my father's and mother's sake, but I hardly knew her, so I couldn't grieve. It's strange to cry for someone you don't know, because the tears won't come out.

As the above example illustrates, second or third generation Hindus can feel alienated from the more traditional aspects of their communities, and be disorientated at the time of a death if they do not know what should be done. They may be taken aback at the restrictions and rituals associated with death and bereavement. Rohini spent some time consoling a Punjabi friend after her father's death. Rohini observed that she had many relatives who came

> who during her father's life had been enemies, and suddenly they were crying about him, and she just thought they were being very hypocritical, and she couldn't handle it. She even told one old woman to stop being such a hypocrite - when he was alive she was really nasty to the family. She just felt that people who had really felt for her father should have come and no-one else. Her mother had to cry with them or they would get the wrong idea, and they were upsetting her more and more. The *Bhagavad Gītā* was helpful to her.

The therapeutic value of the visits was recognised, but they also aroused ambiguous feelings:

> Every time somebody comes you start the whole story again. It is flickering in front of your eyes. When visitors come you offer tea because you don't know whether they have come from Manchester or the other side of London - that's 45 minutes to one hour for every person who comes to sympathise and as soon as they've gone you get five minutes peace and somebody else walks in. The first two to three days are the worst. First of all it's so real, then it just becomes a habit - you tell the same old story like a tape recorder. Although you're still bereaved, you don't feel as much as you did the first couple of days. Sometimes I felt my mum was forced to cry, and it was artificial. You can't tell people, 'Look, don't make them cry'. They are there to sympathise and that is the way they do things. Probably in the long term it is valuable, because you've talked about it so much that you're fed up with it, you're really talking about it and feeling it. (GjDM35)

Even though there is general acceptance of the twelfth day for the combined *śrāddha* (cf 6.2; 6.2.1), there is a tradition that the sixteenth day (*Gj. Solmū, Pj. Solavah)* is the final day for *sūtaka* for some business castes and even for some Brahmins. If it has not already been done, the sons are presented with a *pagrī* (turban), and there is a feast. A Gujarati Patel said that this was the day when the soul finally separated, and all sin was removed. Others said that *sūtaka* lasted for 40 days ending on an inauspicious day (PKhM45; GjDM50), others emphasised that this is when *śoka* (PKhF60; GLF45) ends. If this is a common belief, then it is not clear what function the *sapiṇḍīkaraṇa* actually has, but it does suggest that in the minds of some Hindus, the ending of impurity and the departure of the soul are regarded as simultaneous.

After the twelfth (*barmu*) or the thirteenth (*termu, terama*) day, or, for some castes, such as Vanyas, Lohanas and some Khattris, the sixteenth day (*solmu, solah*), women once again wash and oil their hair and wear the *bindī*, although some close relatives will not wear ornaments until the fortieth day, or even three or six months later. On the twenty-fifth day there is a ritual called *māsi so,* and after thirty or forty days many communities have a *satsaṅg* at home or in the temple if they can afford it, inviting Brahmins, friends and family to come for a meal. Prayers are said for *ātma śānti ke liye* (for the peace of the soul). Gifts, such as an engraved dish or glasses, may be given to all the guests in memory of the deceased."The feast is to break the mourning, to say '*jay śrī kṛṣṇa*', when you feed the Brahmins and give sweets to children. Four or five families often bring Yamuna water in a sealed pot, and it is distributed after six months or one year." (GjLM70). On each occasion marking a shift in the mourning, gifts of uncooked food, money, and clothes may be offered to Brahmins, or money sent to charities. Some send the latter to India, others prefer to send it to Oxfam (6.2.1). The house will be purified with *gangajal* or milk and water. It is now possible to go to the temple and religious festivals, although weddings will not be attended for some weeks or months, dependent on when the elders decide mourning should end.

The period of mourning (*śoka*), as we have seen, depends to some extent on the age of the deceased; for a younger person it may be for weeks or months. A Darji family observed *śoka* for twenty-one days for a forty-year-old nephew, but another such family in Westmouth kept it for two-and-a-half months for a nephew who had died in Mombasa, where *śoka* is often kept for up to six months. This was seen by their friends as somewhat excessive, implying that the uncle had felt guilty at not returning to East Africa after the death. When the nineteen-year-old brother of a Punjabi Khattri woman died many years ago in India the family observed *śoka* for one year, but now "everything was more realistic because people were more educated and wanted greater simplicity because life was so busy." For widows it may continue for a year, but may be shortened by family elders to allow for auspicious rituals and out of sensitivity to her needs.

8.4. Widows: Indian perspectives[18]

Widows in any community have to face massive social changes in terms of their status and roles. For Hindu widows there have also been considerable changes in attitudes to marriage and widowhood in recent times. Most widows in Britain are older women who grew up in India or East Africa. With their contemporaries they are still influenced by traditional Hindu values, while living in a society in which different concepts of marriage and divorce, women's rights and sexuality are constantly made evident through the media, the social milieu, education and contacts at work. This is having an influence on the attitudes of younger Hindus towards relationships, marriage and the family. The effects of migration to Britain and changing attitudes need to be understood against the background of the traditional Hindu views of marriage and widowhood in the context of the particular history of widowhood in India.

In India the ideal of womanhood in higher castes was based on the concept of *satī-strī*, the good woman or the perfect wife, who dedicated herself (*vratā*, vow) to the well-being and long life of her husband (*patī*). She was thus a *pativratā*, committed to the *dharma*, or moral obligation of ensuring her husband's health and welfare, so that his premature death was an indication of her failure to live up to this model. Her most honourable option historically was to follow him onto the pyre, which gave rise to the anglicised term 'suttee' for the act of widow burning.[19] She *became* Satī the goddess with miraculous powers, which gave the act additional religious (and popular) sanction. She was never a widow: the true widow was a woman who did not to go along with her husband on the pyre, whether from choice or coercion. While the emphasis on suttee is

---

[18] Material for this section is appearing as 'Hindu widows in Britain: continuity and change', in Bradley, Fenton and Barot, 1996/7.

[19] For convenience the term 'suttee' is used for the act of widow-burning, whether voluntary or involuntary. '*Satī*' refers to the woman who ascends the pyre and is declared to be possessed by the goddess. Not all widows who were immolated were regarded as *satīs*. Dubois 1906:361; Kane 1973 IV:604.

disproportionate to its actual numbers, the ideology of the *satī-strī* remains significant, as was evident in the furore following the 1987 suttee of Roop Kanwar in Rajasthan (below). The continued emphasis on arranged marriages indicates the importance of traditional religious, social and economic values, in spite of increasing education and social change.

The *satī-strī* embodied Sanskritic "ideals of unselfishness and self-sacrifice" among the upper classes.[20] She would have internalised the view that a virtuous and auspicious wife died before her husband, and that his premature death indicated both her own bad *karma* and failure to fulfil her vow of ensuring his well-being. Her most usual option was the life of the widow ascetic following a yogic discipline in order to expiate her sins and those of her husband. A young widow was particularly vulnerable in her husband's extended family household, especially if there was property. In earlier times, in a common form of levirate[21] liaison, *niyoga,* a childless widow bore a child by a brother-in-law or male relative of her husband's, to ensure sons who would inherit the deceased man's property and perform the essential ancestral sacrifices.[22] Remarriage has always been a possibility in lower castes, often to a younger brother.

The status of a widow in contemporary India depends on her age, whether she has children, particularly adult sons who can protect her, her relationship with her husband's family, and whether she has property rights. A young widow is often scorned and blamed for her husband's death. Highly inauspicious, she cannot participate in auspicious rituals. Bayly suggests that she is "perceived almost literally to be part of her husband's body [so that] her presence in a household raised questions of pollution; she is in effect, in a 'liminal' and dangerous state". As "another man's physical leavings" she is unsuitable for remarriage.[23]

Her loss of status is emphasised immediately after her husband's death with a ritual reversing those of her marriage. Stevenson's description in 1920 is still relevant today. The new widow was dressed in her marriage finery and then stripped of her *maṅgala-sūtra*, the marriage necklace, and other jewellery, and

---

[20] Leslie, 1987/1988:8; Kakar 1978:73-79, 88; Evison 1989:31; Bṛ.Up.1.5.17; GP II 4:91ff..

[21] A levirate relationship was an ancient Jewish tradition in which a woman married her deceased husband's brother or near relative to bear sons in the husband's name.

[22] Saraswati 1988:71; Altekar 1959:143ff.. *Niyoga* was condemned by Manu (9.64-44) and its existence justified by later authorities by saying it was permitted then but forbidden in the Kali age. Its relevance lies in the continuing practice, especially among lower castes, of marriage to a younger brother.

[23] Bayly 1981:175.

the red marks of marriage removed. Her bangles were broken on her husband's bier and placed on it, or at the river and then thrown into the water. A Brahmin widow until recently wore only a single coarse garment and had her head shaved monthly, which Stevenson describes as "...the widow's scarlet letter, which, together with her terrible name Rāṇḍīrāṇḍa (one who has been a prostitute) testifies that she is now penalised for the sins of a previous life".[24]

This ritual still continues in parts of India. While tonsuring is rare older women may choose it, at least temporarily, partly because of fear of offending public opinion. The widow is expected to lead a simple ascetic life, which may be difficult if she has to feed, educate and arrange marriages for her children. Many widows gravitate to Varanasi where they can "expiate the bad karma to which the prior death of their husband testifies" often driven away by in-laws.[25] The deliberate choice of sannyāsa, however, allows the widow to recover her lost honour.[26] Gandhi thought that adult widows should adopt 'satīhood'. For him, the "real Hindu widow is a treasure...."

> who should cling to her suffering, thus proving herself not by mounting the funeral pyre at her husband's death, she would prove it with every breath that she breathes...She would shun creature comforts and delights of the sense... Knowing that the soul of him whom she married is not dead but still lives, she will never think of remarrying.[27]

It is not surprising that some widows chose to mount the pyre in view of the religious sanctions associated with suttee and the dismal alternatives to it, although others were coerced, especially in Rajasthan and Bengal.[28] Suttee was officially outlawed in 1829, but the huge popular response to Roop Kanwar's suttee reveals the continual influence of the ideology of the *satī-strī*.[29] Roop Kanwar, aged eighteen, died on her husband's pyre, apparently willingly, "showering blessings and benedictions on the crowds while chanting the Gayatri mantra...even when 'the fire consumed her torso and flames enveloped her neck'".[30] The huge crowds flocking to her shrine regarded this as a religious phenomenon, but Indian feminists have seen this as a revival of a traditional view

---

[24] Stevenson 1920:204; cf. Padfield 1908:205; cf. Dubois 1906:353; Leslie 1991b:8-9.
[25] Parry 1994:51; cf. Eck 1983:329.
[26] Ojha 1981:278.
[27] Gandhi 1958: 81-81, cited in Singh and Singh, 1989:57.
[28] Altekar, 1959:137.
[29] Leslie 1991b:2; 1987/88:18-19; 1991b:6.
[30] 'A pagan sacrifice', *India Today,* 31 October, 1987, cited in Leslie, 1987/1988:10; cf Mishra 1989:51-52.

of womanhood and marriage in a move to restore the concept of the *pati-bhaktā*, the woman who worships her husband as God, in a patriarchal system which connives at murder.[31]

The third alternative, remarriage, was encouraged by reformers, including Gandhi, if they were 'virgin widows'. This aroused much opposition, since many upper castes forbade the remarriage of any widows on the grounds that once a chaste daughter is given in marriage (*kanyā dāna*), she can never be given to any one else.[32] Some castes permit marriage to a younger brother, "to keep the same blood" or honour in the family, but also to retain control of the dowry or inherited property; this is one of the first practices they give up if they wish to Sanskritise themselves to improve their status. Among educated families nowadays remarriage is taking place more frequently, even among Brahmins, as registered civil marriages become more acceptable. Educated working widows can be independent and are an economic asset to a potential partner.

A religious ceremony cannot be repeated, but the second marriage is based on caste traditions, often reinforced by a civil contract. Legally it has to be a publicly recognised ritual according to 'the customary rites and ceremonies of either party', in which the widow is recognised as the wife of the new husband, and their children are recognised as legitimate.[33]

Men have always been able to remarry, and are often encouraged to do so. if they have young children. If a man intends to remarry he might not even attend his wife's cremation, but tears a piece of cloth off her red garment and hangs it over the door when the corpse departs, to signal his intention.[34]

8.5. Hindu widows in Britain

There were five Punjabi and seven Gujarati widows in my sample. Six of the Gujarati widows and two of the Punjabis were 'twice migrants', having grown up in India and gone to East Africa on their marriages at the age of fifteen or sixteen. Many had lived in an extended family until they came to Britain, where they often moved into nuclear households, which has some bearing on their adjustment. The Punjabis were Brahmins, Sonis and Khattris. The latter were Arya Samajis, the others were from Sanatan Dharmi families. The Gujaratis were Brahmin, Patel, and Kumhar, and included followers of Sanatan Dharm,

---

[31] Shekhawat 1989:47.

[32] Stevenson 1920:206; Pandey 1969: 214-215; Chadha 1978:155.

[33] Menski 1985:15.

[34] Cf. Madan 1987:129ff..

Pushtimarg and Swaminarayan. There were considerable variations in their levels of education, ability to speak English, and employment experience. Few had their own kin in Britain, and only the Gujaratis belonged to local caste associations. Other variables were the size and the extent of their local caste groups and extended families, especially the absence or presence of their natal kin in Britain. All of them had children, one of the crucial elements influencing the status of widows.

While I got to know many widows, such as Surya and Nalini, very well, one or two others were nervous about saying too much in case the information upset adult children, mothers-in-law or daughters-in-law who were present. I did not meet any remarried widows, some of whom are second (polygamous) wives.[35] I did not meet any childless widows.

The situation of a widow in Britain depends on her social position, her economic resources and whether she has her own sons and/or kin who will ensure her welfare. Older women are more likely to keep to a longer period of mourning and to internalise beliefs about the inauspiciousness of the widow. Gujaratis from East Africa belonging to strong caste groups tended to be more conservative than Punjabis, although one Brahmin woman with a leading ritual role in the community retained many of her functions in the home and temple.

An elderly Kumhari woman, on the other hand, felt so impure and inauspicious that she did not go out for ten years. She had loved bright colours: "I wore the biggest *bindī* in town." Once this red marriage mark was removed, she felt that "this was it".She was a bad omen to be shunned. She wore only white, and adopted an ascetic life style, praying and making offerings to her husband. As a Kismat widow commented, "You have to cover your face at festivities in case you are thought of as bad luck. You can't be there when the bride and groom come or do *ārtī* (prayer before the gods with a lamp) for the new couple."

Whether or not the marriage has been happy, her position and status change drastically, emphasised by the stripping of jewellery and marks of marriage described above. She has to dress up in her wedding finery. Her glass or plastic bangles are removed, often by older widows, when the body is brought in, and smashed on the coffin. One Gujarati pandit finds this is so painful that he will not watch it, so he tells her to remove them herself and place them in the coffin.

---

[35] In Britain second wives who were married abroad are considered legally married, but since 1986 they have been prohibited entry; cf. HC 395, paras. 278-280.

When she married she carried a coconut, so she may be asked to take a coconut around the coffin to return it (5.5). Her red marriage marks are rubbed off by the older widows. Her *maṅgala-sūtra* (marriage necklace) may be broken, with a piece of the gold used for the mouth of the deceased. She is not supposed to go the to the cremation because it would be too emotional, and "if she went she would sacrifice herself" (GjPt65).

One young Gujarati was unprepared for the shock of the ritual. Her bangles were forced off by a senior widow and placed in the coffin. She had to remove her nose ring. When the body had gone she was made to sit in the bath while the widows poured water over her. Wearing a white sari she had to carry a *dīva* into the living room to place before her husband's photo. As a sign that she was bad luck, all the married women turned their backs on her so they didn't have to see her face. She would never be allowed to wear make up or a *bindī* again, although she could wear gold bangles. She could wear light colours because she was young, but never red, green or yellow. According to a recently widowed Lohana woman, such rituals only take place if the mother-in-law is still alive, suggesting a punitive element legitimised by custom. The practice of married women turning their backs on the new widow when she first appears in her widow's clothes, reflects the traditional view of the inauspiciousness of the woman whose husband predeceases her, and indicates the pressure on her to conform and adopt these views when she is at her most vulnerable.

A widow is expected to show appropriate grief and may be criticised if she does not show enough sorrow. Several of the Punjabi widows felt less constrained by public opinion than the Gujaratis, partly because of a more liberal Arya Samaj tradition, and partly because they were not members of such large, closely-knit caste groups. Nalini refused to wear white or pale colours as she felt it was hypocritical, and continued to wear the same clothes as before, although she always chose dark or muted colours. She secluded herself because she was so devastated by her husband's unexpected death, not because it was expected of her, and lost all interest in social and religious activities. Several older women wear white or pale colours because, as a Gujarati Brahmin said, "In our hearts we don't want to wear bright colours. I have lost a husband and a son." A widow who does not conform can encounter severe criticism, even from her own family. Speaking of her Punjabi friend's mother, Rohini commented:

> Her grandmother is there at the moment, and her mother is just back to normal. She wears bright colours. A widow is supposed to wear white, but

> she doesn't believe in that, she wears lipstick and make-up and colours. Her mother really tells her off, she goes, "You didn't care for him", that's coming from her own mother. She says, "Look, grieving isn't just what you see physically, it's what you feel inside that matters". I suppose because her mother is old she is finding it hard to believe that anyone could grieve inside when they look so colourful outside.

Widows without relatives or children in Britain may feel particularly isolated. An older woman with sons has at least fulfilled one of her main functions. A young widow living with her in-laws may be blamed for the son's death. She is vulnerable to gossip, and blamed if she has unwelcome advances from men. A working woman can find the restrictions particularly irksome, and some women return to their families if they will receive her.

Other roles in the family also change when a father dies. The sons, or occasionally a daughter, have to take responsibility for the widow and any younger siblings. Even when people are not living under one roof, the dynamics of the extended family are likely to alter far more after the death of a parent than in the more fragmented nuclear family system where adult members are expected to be independent. An older widow not already living with one of her children, may move in with her son's family and find satisfaction in caring for her grandchildren or the family business; others prefer to live independently, without interference from their children. There may be little room or welcome in a small nuclear household especially if the two women are not accustomed to living together. When his father died, a professional man felt he ought to have his mother live with him. However, she and his wife came from very different educational backgrounds and did not get along very well, so she remained alone in her old home for much of the time. The young man's problems were compounded by anxiety that people would talk about them and criticise him: "That is not the accepted Indian culture. They'd say to her, why are you living alone? I keep an eye on her...and do everything for her, but when she dies there will be a lot more guilt, because I'm her only son here."

While widows should not perform any auspicious rituals, such as the *havan*, a number participate in the weekly *havan* in the *mandir*. Many of the these are from Arya Samaj backgrounds, which place less stress on death impurity than those following Sanatan Dharm, and this may come to have an influence on more conservative women. According to a Sanatani Brahmin, this was "not religiously right because while they are not impure, they are not complete, not part of a unit" (PBrM55).

Many widows adopt a more ascetic lifestyle out of dedication to the husband and a desire to find meaning in the bereavement. Surya had already adopted a religious life style before her husband died, participating in the weekly *havans*, and regularly discussing religious issues with her friends. This became more profound in the years following his death.

Attitudes to remarriage are similar to those in India among similar class and caste groups. Brahmin widows are normally not allowed to remarry, but other castes, such as the Lohanas, Prajapati Kumhars and Darjis are allowed to remarry if they are young. Many of these marriage are to younger brothers "because the woman might wish to remain in the family"; there may also be pressure from both sets of parents if there are children and property considerations.

Śāstric (scriptural) marriages can only occur once but second marriages can be legitimised by a civil registry wedding as well as caste rituals. For a Lohana marriage the groom's sister-in-law placed a *thālī* in front of the bride and groom, filled it with water, and told them to look into it. She then pushed their heads together as a symbol of their union. A Kumhar widow married someone outside the deceased husband's family. Following the registry marriage, the groom's parents left an empty pot outside their house, which the bride had to fill and carry into the house, where the pandit said some prayers.

Older women who were widowed before the marriage was consummated are still considered married because of the hand clasp at the ceremony. Those who have led an ascetic lifestyle, are revered as 'virgin widows'. A Punjabi Khattri woman who was widowed at thirteen was called 'Rani' (princess), and honoured as leader of the clan because she had been clean and pure all her life.

While there is evident continuity of traditional attitudes to marriage and widowhood, young women (and men) study and work alongside British young people with different concepts about the family, individuality and choice of partners. Many younger educated women are also reacting against a patriarchal view of women whose primarily role is to ensure their husbands' spiritual welfare both by their piety and by producing sons, a view reinforced by Hindu society, literature and myth.[36] His premature death thus becomes her failure to fulfil the role and a source of blame and guilt. On the positive side, many women view marriage as a religious and spiritual union in which they have invested all their emotional and spiritual resources, which is not surprising for those who were

---

[36] Kakar 1981:56ff..

raised with this end in view and married very young. If the husband dies the only satisfactory option is 'satihood' in the Gandhian sense.

It can be seen that the traditional Hindu mourning period follows the pattern described by Hertz and Van Gennep, of rites of separation, an intermediate or liminal period, and rites of reincorporation. In Britain, because the cremation is delayed, the liminal period of mourning is set in motion first. This time legitimises social withdrawal and the expression of grief, which most informants said they found helpful and therapeutic, with structured periods of talking, readings or singing *bhajans*, and for the women in particular. There is normally a great deal of social support following a death, which reinforces the bonds between family and caste members. Roger Ballard points out that the mourning period provides

> a structural, verbal and conceptual framework within which everyone can express all the many dimensions of their grief, in which deep sorrow at the loss of a beloved person is only the first. Beyond this elaborate mourning - the whole process of *afsus* (giving regrets) - gives both the immediately bereaved and their entire kinship network an opportunity to review and comment on the fullness of the deceased person's life (personal communication).

These comments are set within a "framework of meaning by constant reference to the inscrutable powers of the Ultimate", which has its own logic. Life has a purpose, and the deceased has manifestly fulfilled this. The narratives about the death perform an important function in maintaining and teaching about the tradition, as a source of inspiration and meaning, and as a way of retaining the deceased as a member of the family (9.40).

Chapter 9
Loss, Grief, and Adjustment

In Chapter 1 the appropriateness of using Western psychological categories in cross-cultural perspectives was questioned. Because there appears to be no literature on Hindu bereavement as such, the work of Western psychologists will be referred to as a framework for exploring and understanding the experience of grief in British Hindu individuals.[1] It seems useful to take what is said basically at face value, but to be constantly alert to different nuances, use of metaphor, and cultural and social expectations which might influence the way in which grief and suffering are perceived and described (cf. 1.2 above). The relationship between adjustment and religious belief and practice, is of fundamental importance to this study as a whole and will be explored in the last part of the chapter.

9.1. Grief in a cross-cultural perspective

Rosenblatt concluded that despite cultural, psychological and biological influences, "people everywhere experience grief, that people everywhere experience the death of close kin as a loss and mourn for that loss".[2] It is difficult to assess grief in those cultures where social constraints prevent its outward expression, or to judge how genuine and deeply felt it is when people are coerced into weeping:

> Rather than saying there is a single human response to loss, it is more appropriate to say there is a substantial range of responses, each of which authentically express feelings of loss when supported by a cultural context that defines those responses as expressions of loss.[3]

People are basically the same and go through similar grieving processes, but with "a unique constellation of culture, social context and connections to the object of grief".[4] While anthropological and sociological studies suggest that the public expression of grief is socially constructed, the concern here is to try to elicit factors relating to the private emotions of the bereaved which cannot be

---

[1] Kübler-Ross 1969; Raphael 1983; Parkes 1986; Worden 1991; Stroebe and Stroebe; 1993 and Stroebe 1994.

[2] Rosenblatt *et al.* 1976:124.

[3] Rosenblatt 1988:69-70; cf. Rosenblatt 1993:104, 110-111.

[4] Rosenblatt 1993:110-111; see also Eisenbruch 1994 I:286; Bowlby 1980:42; Peberdy *et al* 1993:13.

understood in isolation from cultural influences.[5]

Rosenblatt recommends that in referring to the suffering of those from other cultures we "put quotation marks around the terms we use from our own culture". Terms describing emotions, such as 'grief', 'depression' and 'anxiety' should be suspect, as are terms such as 'hypertension', since these are particularly American (or Western) ways of categorising and understanding emotional and somatic conditions. He points to different ways grief is responded to, from an emphasis on calm in Bali, to extreme grief in Egypt, and anger and aggression among the Kaluli of Papua New Guinea. One difference he notes, citing Kleinman, is that grief in the United States is psychologised, whereas in many cultures such as China it is somatised, in other words, it manifests itself in physical complaints.[6] To try to transpose, for example, a theory of denial onto a Chinese patient who is unaware of his psychological pain is, according to Kleinman, to commit a category fallacy.[7]

Krause, in a study of the use of a specific expression, 'the sinking heart', used by Punjabis in Bedford to reflect a range of psychological and somatic conditions, rejects the notion of relativism, since it is possible to make sense of what people in other cultures are saying or doing, at least in some respects. Even if Western psychiatry seems inappropriate in a non-Western context,

> It would be premature for us to claim that psychopathological findings from western cultures have no application whatsoever in any non-western culture ... Many key western psychiatric symptoms refer to conceptual constructs which are influenced by western philosophical traditions. These symptoms may either be absent or nonsensical or have entirely different meanings in cultures where other philosophical traditions are influential.[8]

As an example of the different ways in which psychological states may be interpreted, Krause shows that the "generalised hopelessness" which characterises depressive disorders in London women would not be regarded as abnormal among Hindu, Muslim and Buddhist women who would regard hopelessness as an aspect of life which can only be overcome on the path to salvation. The "sinking heart" can only be understood fully within the Punjabi cultural context, yet can be understood by non-Punjabis, provided a direct translation into a

---

[5] cf. Prior 1989:133ff; Huntington and Metcalf 1979:23ff.

[6] Rosenblatt 1993:13-14, 16; Kleinman 1986.

[7] Kleinman 1977, cited in Eisenbruch 1984 II:324.

[8] Krause 1989:563-4.

"western illness category" is not attempted, but it is seen rather in the context of "cultural and social aspects of stress and suffering".[9]

In Chapter 1.2 reference was made to the concepts of grief work and grief process. These have often been seen in terms of stages, phases or tasks of grief, although there has been considerable debate about what these are, how many, and the usefulness of such categories, particularly where they have been viewed as prescriptive and fixed.[10] However, a simplified use of the concept of three broad stages, which may overlap in time, seems helpful in exploring grief, and will be used in the following discussion.[11] The first of these includes shock, denial and disbelief, characterised by "Bewilderment, disorientation and a loss of perspective ... as well as a lack of energy and motivation".[12]

The second stage is one of great pain, when the bereaved person begins to face the reality of the loss. This is a period of social withdrawal which coincides with Hertz' intermediary period and Van Gennep's liminal period.[13] There may be pining and searching, and feelings such as guilt, anger, disorganisation and despair may be experienced.[14] Parkes and others believe that the bereaved need to focus on the loss and weep, as well as recognise and deal with anger and anxiety, so that "anything that continually allows the person to avoid or suppress this pain can be expected to prolong the course of mourning".[15] However, as has been seen (1.2), in some cultures the expression of emotion is not encouraged, and theories of grief work need to take this into account. It is not just the expression of feelings and weeping, but talking and remembering, keeping a place for the deceased in a new form.

The final stage is one of reorganisation and recovery when the bereaved person begins to adjust to the new situation and functions again with some semblance of normality.[16] Freud's view[17] that this is achieved successfully when the emotional energy is reinvested in a new object or interests, may be

---

[9] Krause 1989:574.

[10] Worden (1991:10ff.) thought the 'tasks' of grief work were more appropriate than stages. For discussion of stages, cf. Kübler-Ross 1969:38ff.; Parkes 1986:26ff.; Shuchter and Zisook 1993:23ff.; Walter 1994:70ff.; Stroebe 1994.

[11] Siddell 193:13; Raphael 1983.

[12] Raphael 1983; Worden 1991; Siddell 1993:13.

[13] Hertz 1960:129ff.; Van Gennep 1960:147ff.; cf.Shuchter and Zisook 1993:23-24.

[14] Parkes 1986:27.

[15] Parkes 1972:173; cf. Worden 1991:46-47.

[16] Parkes 1986:27, 107.

[17] Freud 1917:253; Parkes 1993:95.

inappropriate in a South Asian context where ancestors are worshipped, particularly for widows who may never let the deceased go in Freud's sense (cf. 8.4-5 above). The conventional view that one must 'let go' of, or become detached from the deceased has been challenged by Walter, Stroebe and others (1.2 above), who acknowledge the important place the deceased continues to have in many cultures. The concept of 'recovery' needs to be used with caution. Shuchter and Zisook show that many people maintain a "timeless" emotional involvement with the deceased, so that "aspects of grief work may never end for otherwise normal bereaved individuals".[18] Worden sees one of the tasks of grief as adjusting to "an environment in which the deceased is missing", and "relocating of the deceased" which is, in the Hindu context, a more useful concept as it is precisely what the *śrāddha* rituals do.[19]

There is some debate as to what can be thought of as 'normal' and 'pathological' forms of grief.[20] In Western psychiatry this is judged by what appears to be inhibited, chronic or prolonged grief, so that the bereaved person gets 'stuck' in a particular stage such as denial, anger or chronic weeping, and fails to work through the process.[21] A classic example is that of Queen Victoria, who had her deceased husband's clothes laid out for him daily for the rest of her life. Yet her behaviour might have been considered normal in another culture, and her continued obsession with Albert legitimised by rites of ancestor worship, as we have seen with Hindu widows. Eisenbruch warns against imposing Western schemata on to non-Westerners as "normative".[22] Rosenblatt cites a Brazilian study in which infant and child deaths were only mourned for a few days, as they were regarded as inevitable and a "function of the individual child's will to live. However, they continued to be thought of as family members who would be joined again in heaven". He contrasts this with an Egyptian study showing that prolonged depression and suffering for years after the death of a child is seen as quite normal, encouraged and supported by the community.[23]

---

[18] Shuchter and Zisook 1993:25.

[19] Worden 1991:15-18. Walter (1996) suggests that much of the 'clinical lore' about the purpose and process of bereavement misunderstands the complexity of Freud, Parkes and Bowlby since they all recognise the need to retain a connection rather than argue that there should be a separation from the deceased.

[20] Raphael 1983:59ff.; Parkes 1986:124ff.; Worden 1991:21ff., 65ff.; Middleton *et al.* 1993:44ff..

[21] Raphael 1983:59-60; Wortman and Silver 1989:352; Siddell 1993:29ff..

[22] Eisenbruch 1984 II:324.

[23] Rosenblatt 1993:14-5.

Bereavement can be complicated by sudden death, especially suicide. Earlier losses also affect bereavement. Migrants, especially, may have already experienced multiple losses, including homeland and close kin. Many Hindus in Britain have had one or more experiences of loss of country. Some older Punjabis and Sindhis were forced to leave their homes in what became Pakistan, at the time of partition.[24] Those Hindus who migrated to East Africa again had to leave their homes. The loss of homeland in itself is made up of many losses. Eisenbruch believes that the "massive social losses" resulting from uprooting, which may be undetected, need to be taken into account in any studies of bereavement. Such groups and individuals may lack the emotional and social support needed to enable them to cope with these and other losses,[25] because the death is not just of an individual - it may also be the death of a way of life. Kakar notes the traumatic effect on a Hindu who is separated from the extended family:

> The psychological identification with the extended family group is so strong that even the loosening of the family bond ... may be a source of psychic stress and heightened inner conflict. A separation from the family, whatever the necessity or reason for such a step, not only brings a sense of insecurity in a worldly social sense, it also means the loss of 'significant others' who guarantee the sense of sameness and affirm the inner continuity of the self.[26]

This suggests that those who have separated from the extended family prior to a bereavement will be particularly vulnerable when a death occurs, but also throws light on the grief felt by individuals such as Ramesh and Ashok (7.1.1) when their fathers died. Thus the closely knit mutual dependency of the extended family, arranged marriages and the need for sons in the Hindu context affects the dynamics of family relationships which will influence the nature of bereavement. Western society regards the independence of adult children and the nuclear family as the norm, whereas Indian society would, in theory at any rate, regard this as an anomaly which does not fit into the traditional Hindu social, religious and ethical code, although values in urban India are changing as well as for British Hindus. There can be difficulties for those who are caught between the two cultures, when the "bereavement codes of the immigrant and the host society

---

[24] Singh, Kushwant 1989.
[25] Eisenbruch 1984 I:228, 296ff.; cf. 1984 II:325.
[26] Kakar 1978:121; cf. 36, 73-77, 89-91, 133ff..

do not mesh".[27]

The way the dying person and the relatives are treated by professionals and the level of social support before and after the death are also important factors in adjustment, as the case studies (Ch. 7) have shown. The absence of appropriate religious rituals or badly handled rituals can also affect the way in which the bereaved cope with the death.[28]

It is important not to see the stages as prescriptive, as is sometimes the case in counselling practice, but as useful but flexible guidelines. Siddell wonders whether the stage theory has taken the place of mourning rituals in Western culture, "guiding the bereaved from shock and disbelief through acute grief to full recovery and reintegration into the life of the community," and warns of the danger of them becoming reified.[29] As Eisenbruch shows, the stages vary between individuals, between groups within any given culture, and to a greater extent cross-culturally, and the timing also varies greatly from culture to culture.[30] The stages of psychological adjustment seem to have parallels in Van Gennep's three stages. The pre-liminal period, with the rites of separation, coincides with the time of shock, denial and outburst. The liminal or transitional period is the time for experiencing the grief and often isolation from the world when there may be, as in Hindu society, formal mourning. The final period is when many cultures observe rites of reincorporation which give the deceased a place in history, ritual and the unseen world with God, the ancestors or is reborn. This is the time of adjustment to everyday life in a new set of relationships and situations which have some continuity with the past, but are also different.

9.2. The three stages of the mourning process

9.2.1. Stage one: immediate loss

The initial response to a death is often shock, numbness and disbelief.[31] Although Hindu informants gave examples of this, a common reaction immediately on death was said to be an outburst of emotion, often bordering on hysteria, particularly where women were concerned (cf.4.4; 7.2). There may also be social expectations that strong emotion be expressed (8.3-8.32). Close relatives who are sent for after a death are told that the deceased is very ill rather than dead for fear

---

27 Eisenbruch 1984 II:330; cf. Rosenblatt 1993:105.
28 Gorer 1965:110ff.; Parkes 1986: 171ff.; Walter 1993:36.
29 Siddell 1993:14.
30 Eisenbruch 1984 I:287ff..
31 Parkes 1986:82.

they will collapse when no one is there to support them. There may also be denial and disbelief that death is impending or has occurred, which can lead to prolonged and inappropriate mourning afterwards. It was seen how Ramesh (7.1.1) found it difficult to accept his father's illness as terminal and preferred the hopeful prognosis given by the hospital doctors to the more realistic one given by his own general practitioner, continuing to deny the various indications that his father himself was aware, at some level, of his impending death.

Maya, after the phone call from the doctor announcing her father's death, "just stood there, not believing, not knowing what he had said, I mean, those words have changed our lives"(7.1.2). Nalini, the widow, collapsed totally. When I visited her the following day, she was prostrate and semi-conscious on her bed, while another friend massaged her legs, quietly murmuring to her. Now and then she vomited. I visited frequently for five months after the death. Nalini kept saying, "I can't believe he's gone." She was deeply disorientated, with no energy or initiative, and was anxious about their financial position as there was no will. Maya, on the other hand, had to be the strong one and kept calm initially because she had taken so much responsibility, but she had a delayed reaction some weeks later, hiding herself in the lavatory to cry so as not to upset her mother.

Other informants described an immediate emotional outburst, sometimes with uncontrollable weeping throughout the mourning period, as well as a sense of disbelief that the death has occurred. One woman "screamed and screamed" on hearing the news of her father's death, and fainted at the mortuary. Her husband was very supportive. He let her cry as much as she needed to, which was a great deal, and tried to calm her down, talking to her about death: "He said everyone has to go. That bond is there, but you have to move on."

Ashok, after his father died of a heart attack, went to see the body:

> I went alone and touched his feet as a sign of respect. I sat down and sat still and held his feet and I did some prayers, absolutely not believing that this had actually taken place. Later I brought my brothers to see him, and they were very distressed, but the most distressing experience was my younger sister. I had to keep my cool and comfort somebody else. When she came from her own home we didn't tell her that my father had died, but that he had had a heart attack. I had to tell her when she arrived at our house, and she went absolutely hysterical. I am sure it's a healthy thing.

He did not know how people could keep such emotions in check. He also had emotional outbursts without warning, and had to be comforted by his mother. "You couldn't control it, so you left that particular room and whoever was available came and comforted you and then you went back and comforted somebody else. It was fairly traumatic but I am sure it has positive value." The custom of sitting on the floor was very difficult, but he valued the way people came in to pay their respects and give comforting advice, although it was so draining: "But the thing of chatting about your father and how good he was, and he's no longer with you - you know, I've never had so many emotional outbursts, but in that week I had so many I couldn't cope. It was personally distressful, although it was a boost that people you trusted came."

Prema found it very difficult to deal with the death of her father in Bombay, as she had not been with him. A Brahmin graduate, she had never integrated into the community in Westmouth, so she had no social support, nor did she have the advantage of rituals or a structured mourning period and had to deal with her grief on her own. Her husband became very irritated by her emotional outbursts. A month after the death I visited her shop, and found her in tears, which she said were hard to control:

> It is over a month but I cry every day. My husband says, "Why do you sit and cry in the shop? You shouldn't cry in front of customers." My husband couldn't cry at first but he cried the next day. His father died when he was only 2½ years old, and he didn't even remember him, so my dad was his father, and he really respected him. We left all his letters lying all over the house, just as they were before he died. I thought my parents would never die. He had cancer, but that wasn't bad, he had a good death, and his face was shining. I have no friends here at all except you. I didn't take much time off work because my husband said, "You had better not take time off because you will go mad, you will cry and cry, you had better come in the shop", and he took half days from his job to help me.

Because her father had a good death, her relatives in India felt that she should not be so distressed. Her brothers kept phoning up, two or three times a week, giving her as much support as they could from a distance.

Violent outbursts of emotion can be disturbing to other people in situations such as the hospital setting (7.1) and one Hindu doctor felt that it was often exhibitionism. He was no happier about the British way of dealing with grief, which was too detached, with inadequate social support. He was concerned about the influence of this on the Hindu community. According to the Vadodara group (1.2), Westernisation and urbanisation were also influencing the way people responded to grief in India, with an unhealthy move away from natural spontaneity which could store up trouble for the future:

> Grief should be expressed. In cities and urban life the expression of grief is unfashionable - we laugh quite openly, we don't cry, it's just not done. We don't seem to mind shouting at people when we get angry, we don't seem inhibited about that. But we do seem to be inhibited with our tears and sorrow. In the village where my in-laws live it's not the case. People are very open about expressing grief (GjBF35).

Many younger British Hindus felt that weeping was healthy and its suppression was unhealthy. Emotion should be expressed in a natural way, for both sexes, but weeping because of social expectations could be artificial and divorced from genuine feeling. The frequency with which violent outbursts were reported among Hindus, however, in contrast to reports of numbness and shock in Western studies, seems to validate the view that the expression of grief is socially constructed.[32] Whether social permission to express such violent emotions at the time of the death eased the subsequent grief of the mourners was not something I was able to prove, although this was often claimed. This would be a fruitful area for further research. Once this first reaction has worn off, there is still the problem of adjusting to the changed state.

9.2.2. Stage two: Facing the reality of the loss

The second stage is concerned with facing the reality of the loss, which may be a time of pining and yearning, great sorrow, and often anger, sometimes in the form of blame, guilt and despair.

Anger seems to be a common aspect of the early stages of grief, and it is often displaced on to other people, such as the medical staff. In the Indian context, however, it is difficult to acknowledge blame towards a husband or, in particular, a parent, since honouring them is a sacred duty (2.1). Gough notes that in India sons are taught from early childhood

> that aggressive thoughts, let alone acts towards parents are gravely sinful and to be shunned. The parents are highly idealised and enveloped in an aura of

[32] Cf. Hertz 1960:51, 83; Block and Parry 1982:3ff.; Huntington and Metcalfe 1979:24ff.; Prior 1989:138ff..

sanctity. Children are taught that the father and mother are the first gods to be worshipped. Among individual Brahmins, the expression of any form of aggression towards the father appears to be attended by deep guilt. Neither should a son permit himself the thought that his father is punitive towards him.[33]

In her view, the repressed aggression reappears in the horrifying portrayal of hell, and in the anxiety that failure to perform the proper rituals may put at risk the souls of the ancestors. It may also be reflected in the taboos and anxieties around pollution and fear of the potentially dangerous ghost, which may be functioning as metaphors for anger. There are also expectations about required behaviour towards older brothers and other relatives. An extract from a recorded discussion with the Vadodara Group illustrates this. I had described a Punjabi woman in Westmouth who had collapsed at her mother-in-law's funeral, but it was not clear whether this was due to grief or because it was expected of her.

Dr. B: Probably you [i.e. the daughter-in-law] unconsciously wish her dead, but don't want to think it. You hate yourself for having wished ill because your upbringing doesn't allow this, so you can't face it, but you continue to have it in the background of your mind. We are not strong enough to acknowledge to ourselves, yes, I dislike my son, or my mother-in-law. You must love your son or your father or your mother.
Dr. C: If, as a child, you don't love your parents you can't show it, you are made to feel guilty. How can I possibly not love my parents? Children are made to feel they've got to love their parents. People don't acknowledge anger and dislike, it's not that it's not present.

One lecturer recognised the barely repressed anger and resentment her own mother had displayed towards other members of the family following the death of a fourteen-year-old son, although she was less able to acknowledge her own resentment towards her mother, firstly for preferring her brother, and later, for her treatment of her. Other members of the Vadodara group recognised resentments arising from sibling jealousy which could affect the way subsequent grief was handled if the sibling died, giving rise to guilt if the brother or sister had subconsciously wished the other dead.

Anger towards a husband is also taboo, as he is expected to be thought of as a god (8.4). None of my Westmouth informants, in fact, referred to any feelings of anger or resentment against either parents or a spouse. Even Maya and Nalini,

---

[33] Gough 1958:458-9; cf. Kakar 1978:118ff..

whose circumstances were made very difficult by Jaswant's failure to make a will, never showed resentment or blame towards him. Blame was very rarely expressed towards anyone, especially towards God. Only one Indian informant reported this, although it was far more common among British informants to question divine action (9.6). Interestingly, although death is personified as Yama in popular mythology, there was no suggestion in any of the interviews in India or Britain that anger or blame could be directed at him.

Among the Westmouth Hindus, the most obvious examples of anger and blame were shown by Maya and Nalini. Their main anger was directed towards the medical staff, and the nurses in particular, for the way the three of them were treated, particularly the rudeness of the nurses both before and after Jaswant's death. It was at Maya's insistence that the case was taken to the Commission for Racial Equality. Maya's energy kept her going for some months, until there was a reply from the hospital, but still this was not satisfactory, either in terms of an explanation or an apology. Eventually she gave up the fight, but decided to work hard and study law. Nalini continued to be depressed and anxious for many months. When she was at home alone she went over and over details of his death, worrying about whether he had died in a lot of pain, and feeling guilty that she had not been there to say goodbye.

Another widow, Madhuben, felt angry because when her husband became desperately ill the receptionist at the surgery would not accept the seriousness of the illness, even though the previous day the doctor had tried to get him into hospital without success. The receptionist refused to arrange for the doctor to call, or for an ambulance to come, and the latter would not come without a letter from the surgery. Eventually the son went to the surgery and sat there until a doctor agreed to visit. When the doctor came he was shocked at the husband's condition and got him into hospital straight away. He died the following day, before his wife and son had time to see him. She sometimes felt angry with God, and very angry because the receptionist had been so unhelpful. For several months she had brooded over this, but eventually realised that "people come and go. It is luck (*nasīb*) and not everyone's luck is the same." Reading the *Rāmāyaṇa* and the BG helped a lot, as well as seeing religious films (9.4).

Sonal felt very angry at the way her brother's death in Westmouth was handled by his wife and her family and friends. Their father had been a Sikh and their mother had been a Hindu. Sonal said her brother had considered himself to be a Hindu, and his wife was a staunch Hindu. Following the death Sonal's husband made all the initial arrangements. Subsequently, close Sikh friends and the widow's relatives took over, arranging a Sikh funeral followed by an *Akhaṇḍ Pāṭh*, which Sonal felt was inappropriate. She and her husband were also angry and distressed by the coffin going into the house and being opened,

> because you live there and would always picture it. It is also not fair on the kids. He should have had a private ceremony in the Chapel of Rest, like his mother had. They should have asked what we wanted as well. I am his sister, I had a right to say. Our Sikh friend said that he was pretty sure that was what he wanted. I said no, he was very, very Hindu. I didn't like the idea of opening the coffin, he didn't look so good and that is what really got me. I felt people were hypocrites. I heard what they said. They could have gone to the Chapel of Rest to see him if they had wanted to.

According to Menski, Gujarati families are more likely to consult the wishes of a married sister or daughter of the deceased in making funeral arrangements, whereas Punjabis would take the view that because she now belongs to a different lineage, her wishes are of less importance (personal communication). This situation was complicated by the fact that there were no other relatives of the husband in Britain, and the widow was so prostrate that she was unable to make decisions about procedures.

In all these examples, the distress felt during this stage was compounded by the sense of helplessness in the face of misunderstandings, confusion and muddle. The problems faced by Maya and Nalini in the hospital were very real ones; Madhuben's husband's condition was ignored by the doctor's receptionist, although the illness was terminal; and Sonal felt marginalised by her brother's friends and in-laws who had failed to involve her in the funeral arrangements. Their anger thus had legitimate targets. In other cases, such as Ramesh, the anger was turned against himself in terms of intense guilt, instead of expressing any resentment against the hospital staff who had reassured him, in the face of the evidence, that his father's condition was improving.

While the term 'guilt' has its own peculiar meaning in a Western Christian context, in everyday use Hindus and English people use the word in a similar way to express remorse or self-reproach at having failed in love or care, or in one's duty to a parent, which for a Hindu can have profound consequences. The main references to guilt concerned things which had been neglected or omitted for dying relatives. This may be compounded by the anxiety that the dying person whose desires are not satisfied may also be troublesome for the family after death, and the person who has failed to perform his duty towards the deceased also acquires bad *karma.*[34] It is the complexity of these emotions that makes it so important for Hindus to be present with the dying person.

Ashok, whose brother died in an accident in the United States, did not know what the right rituals should have been and allowed the undertaker to give his brother a Westernised funeral. He did not see the body until the day of the funeral. Only later, following another family funeral, did he discover what should have been done, and felt bitter regret that he had not realised he could have sprinkled the body and said some prayers. This illustrates the extent to which Hindus, at a psychological level, need to feel involved in the funerals of family members, to have the rituals they want, and to feel empowered to act as they think fit, if they are not to experience guilt at failing in their duty.

Following the death of Ashok's brother, his mother fell out of bed and became blind for two days. "Her whole world became black to her, because he was her eldest son, and she could feel his vibrations." She experienced another of the common reactions of bereavement, depression, which Parkes describes as the "loss of aggressiveness, which seems to occur along with feelings of apathy and despair once the intense pangs of grief are past their peak".[35] This was marked to some degree in all the bereaved I visited, particularly in Ramesh who was taking medication for it, and in Nalini and the other widows.

One of the difficulties of a sudden or unexpected death can be unresolved arguments and 'unfinished business' between the deceased and bereaved, as there has not been a chance to deal with the issues. Eisenbruch points to the risk of atypical grief resulting when someone has not been able to complete his relationship with the deceased.[36] The sense of "if only I had done or said so and so" is common after any death, but particularly after an untimely one. We have seen that Maya, Nalini and Ramesh had a lot of problems with this. A Punjabi teenager had nightmares following her father's unexpected death because they had had an argument the day before and had not spoken to each other. She felt obsessed with guilt because of this.

There may be ambivalence in the relationship, particularly in marriage. In an

---

[34] Cf. Gough 1958:459.

[35] Parkes 1986:104.

[36] Eisenbruch 1984 II:374-5; cf. Parkes 1986:102, 148ff..

arranged marriage in a joint household where there is little privacy, the marital bond may not be the primary emotional bond.[37] On the other hand, as in the examples of Nalini and Surya (9.2.3), there may be great attachment and dependency. The closeness of family ties in the extended family, particularly between parents and adult children and between siblings, may also make for difficulty in accepting the bereavement when a death occurs, as Ramesh found.[38] Even some years after his father's death, Ashok said, "At times I feel lost. My own personal life is such that I need to discuss things with somebody I can trust. I have very few people like that, very few friends... My father, with his maturity, would have given me a bit more guidance."

A sense of the presence, or even the sight of the deceased is a common phenomenon. Freud referred to this as a "hallucinatory wishful psychosis" and Parkes refers to 'hallucinations' or 'illusions', remarking that these are a normal reaction to bereavement.[39] Rosenblatt is critical of this kind of terminology, since experiences of the "spiritual nearness" of the deceased are culturally legitimate in many cultures; "they are neither normatively nor statistically abnormal".[40] Worden, in commenting on the frequency and normality of these experiences wonders whether "these really are hallucinations or possibly some other kind of metaphysical phenomena".[41] These experiences are of particular interest in the Hindu context, since there is such a strong bias towards a fear of the spirit of the dead as dangerous. However, a number of informants in India and in Westmouth reported that they had felt the presence of the deceased shortly after death in a very comforting and non-threatening way. One Punjabi woman in Westmouth said of her father, "I used to feel he was all around me, he was here. I felt comforted that he was there, guiding me. Even now I feel he is guiding our destiny. In dreams he gives positive advice." Susheela, whose father had died suddenly, said that when she went to the hospital to see him she had a tremendous sense of his presence in the room with her, which was a great comfort. Prema, whose father died in Bombay also reported a sense of his presence for a week. This was also felt by her family in India, when her brother was given a wage rise and her sister and sister-in-law both got new jobs.

Many informants reported that the deceased had appeared to them in dreams,

---

[37] Kakar 1978:126ff., 133ff..
[38] Kakar 1978:56ff., 120ff..
[39] Freud 1917:253; Parkes 1986:70.
[40] Rosenblatt 1993:110.
[41] Worden 1991:26.

some of which had great symbolic significance. Nalini expressed great frustration that her friends had had important dreams of Jaswant while she had not (7.1.2). After Jaswant's death Nalini's friend dreamed three times that Jaswant appeared, had a cup of tea and told her that he was very happy. Another friend also had a dream, in which he appeared very happy, and said:

> "Oh, she [Nalini] has got plenty of money with her, I've done so much", and he showed me a list in my dream. I realised it was *śrāddh* in those days, so I rang her and said, "Have you done [*śrāddh* rituals] for him?" It was a reminder for her, (PBF45; cf. 9.3.1)

Nalini immediately phoned her sister in Delhi and asked her to hold a *śrāddha* ritual in her husband's name and feed 50 poor boys outside the Hindu temple, and she gave a sari and blouse and a gift of £9 to the temple in Westmouth.

A third friend dreamed about Jaswant just after the mourning ceremonies were over. She saw him in her bedroom, sleeping, but he awoke and said, "I want some blankets, I am very cold." She had not known that Jaswant had asked for blankets in the hospital. She went straight to Nalini's house and told her she had to give some blankets to the priest, but Nalini phoned her brother-in-law in Delhi to arrange to give some blankets to the poor. Nalini wondered why he didn't appear in her own dreams:

> We have so much trouble - why doesn't he come in my dreams, or Maya's? I want him to come in my dream and say something. We remember him every day and night and cry for him, and always pray for him, and read the *Gītā* for him. Why does he not give a message to me?

Clearly, for Nalini, the need was to have any kind of dream of Jaswant. Although such dreams are often taken to be a negative sign that the deceased is dissatisfied and requires gifts, in practice they are often welcomed by the bereaved person as a reminder of the lost one.

9.2.3. Stage three: Reorganisation and recovery

The third broad stage in the bereavement process involves adjustment to a life in which the deceased is missing, and to move on. To do this involves 'relocating' the deceased, so that the bereaved have a relationship with the thoughts and memories of the deceased which allows them to function effectively in their lives.

Within the European Catholic tradition, part of this relocation involves prayers for the dead and gives a sense of continuity which may be absent in Western Protestant and secular society.[42] Hindus regenerate the dead as ancestors with whom it is possible to have a new and different relationship, receiving blessings in return for offerings and prayers, although, as has been seen, there is also an element of risk if they are neglected.

Rituals help this process. They provide milestones in the grieving process, giving permission to move on to a different stage as well as giving meaning. As Eisenbruch points out, the stress of bereavement among ethnic minorities is complicated by the failure to provide traditional rituals which give comfort and meaning for a community, making grief work for the individual more difficult.[43] Hindu culture, as we have seen, provides beliefs and *śrāddha* rituals which help to facilitate and legitimise this process,[44] and the failure to do so causes great anxiety and great distress.

Adjustment and recovery depend on the individual's own personality and past history of stability, previous losses, the degree of attachment and dependency, and the level of social and family support.[45] Cultural expectations may make widows' adjustment more difficult, and as has been seen (8.4-8.4), they may be expected *not* to recover according to the concept of the *satī-strī.* Shuchter and Zizook point out that many normal people maintain a timeless emotional involvement with the deceased: "...aspects of grief may never end for a significant proportion of otherwise normal bereaved individuals."[46] Resolution can be made more complicated by people trying to grieve like the host community rather than following their own traditions. Rosenblatt also points to the complications which may occur in mixed marriages at the time of a death, since each partner is likely to have different expectations.[47] Even within the Hindu community, a marriage between individuals of markedly different caste and regional backgrounds can cause misunderstandings and difficulties when death occurs, as was found by Sonal, above, and a Punjabi Arya Samaji woman when her Gujarati Sanatani husband's relatives died.

For Maya (7.1.2), recovery began with the recognition that the pursuit of the

---

[42] Peberdy 1993:23; cf. Walter 1990:27, 92ff..
[43] Eisenbruch 1984 II.330.
[44] Huntington and Metcalfe 1979:44.
[45] Worden 1991:31ff.; Parkes 1986:208ff.; Eisenbruch 1984 I & II.
[46] Shuchter and Zizook 1993:25.
[47] Rosenblatt 1993:105.

complaints against the hospital were not going to be fruitful, and she began to direct her energies into helping her mother sort out their financial affairs and working hard at her studies. After seeing a film about the goddess Santoṣīmātā, she made a secret vow and fasted one day a week in her honour. Nalini gradually began to gain confidence. She used to read the *Hanumān Chālīsā* regularly from the beginning, when she could not cope with anything else, but later began to read the BG and other books. By the following year she no longer wanted to keep talking about the loss, because "After all, the past is the past. It's all over now." She found that what helped her the most was becoming independent and no longer depending on her friends or relatives for help: "My attitudes have changed. I don't believe in tomorrow. Today is all right." Maya, for a time, rejected her religion because she had prayed to God to take her and save her father. Because he had died she felt abandoned by God, but she gradually returned to her religious practice.

Parkes observes that the bereaved often identify with aspects of the deceased.[48] Eisenbruch notes that apart from new social obligations, the loss of a parent for individuals in ethnic groups, forces them to declare their ethnicity in the public rituals. They may also find their sense of identity is threatened, which forces them to re-establish their links with the parents' culture.[49] A bereaved individual may take on his parent's beliefs and behaviour. Ashok began to take more of an interest in the temple, which he had bothered little with previously, and had also begun to visit bereaved members of the community. Since his father's death:

> I have taken a lot more interest in my own self and religion and praying myself now, which I never previously used to do. He used to do this every day, so now I have a nice little *mandir* and I try to pray and make sure my sons pray as well. My wife doesn't believe in this sort of thing but she makes the lamps for us. You look at life a bit more deeply, although for some it doesn't last. It gave me a jolt, with long lasting effects.

The following case study of a close family is described at length because it provides an interesting contrast to the cases of Maya and Nalini and Ramesh. It illustrates a relatively good death, the value of dreams and signs, and the way in

---

48 Parkes 1986:107ff..

49 Eisenbruch 1984 II:325; cf. Kakar 1978:121; cf. 9.1 above.

which individuals and the family derived support from the community and from the readings of *Amṛta Varṣa* and the BG, integrated the teachings into their own belief-systems and found great solace from them.

9.3. Case Study 3: Lila, Surya, and Susheela

Surya, then in her 60s, is a follower of Arya Samaj. When an elderly Punjabi lady in the community died, I took Surya and her daughter Susheela to the funeral. Returning to the house, Susheela said, "I wasn't sure I wanted to go but as I've never been to one before, I thought it was about time I went."

A few days later her father, a quiet amiable man, went to the surgery to collect a prescription for Surya. Susheela saw him leave as she stood in the window, and felt that he ought to have turned and said something. While in the surgery he had a heart attack, characterised by breathing difficulties but no pain. Their doctor, a Hindu, tried to help him without success, and then, as he died, told him to say "Rām, Rām." He was taken to the hospital in an ambulance. The doctor rang Susheela, telling her he had had a heart attack and she should go at once to the hospital after getting someone to stay with her mother. When she got there she found he had died. The nursing Sister was extremely kind and asked her if she wanted to sit with him for a while. She sat there holding his hand, which was still warm, unable to believe that he was lying there dead, looking so peaceful. "I wish I had been there ten minutes earlier, so I could have said something, I could have heard his last words." She became aware of his presence, which was immensely comforting.

She waited at the hospital until another sister, Meena, arrived. As it had been a sudden death, they then had the ordeal of the police questioning them. They were told this was just a formality, and the police were very kind and sensitive. Because Meena was so upset, a policewoman offered to take them home and another offered to drive their car back. The same policewoman turned up the next day offering to help in any way she could.

By the time I heard of the death, the following day, all the children who lived in Britain had arrived, and those who lived abroad were on their way. Visitors began to pour in with their condolences, sitting on the floor around Surya (8.3). The daily readings of *Amṛta Varṣa* with relatives and friends, and Surya's reading of a chapter of the BG every day gave a structure to the pattern of the day. A Sikh neighbour prepared food, and other friends also brought food.

Susheela found this period a terrible strain. It was only six weeks later that she felt she had some time to get on with her own grieving. As the only daughter living at home she had seen a lot of her father. She took the brunt, initially, of all the domestic arrangements.

Her sister, Lila, a student at the time, had felt uneasy before her father's death, because he had asked whether she was coming down for the May Bank Holiday, and she had told him she would stay in London to complete an essay. Rather than saying she should get on with her work, or saying she should come, he became very quiet, which she felt was strange, as he was so easy-going normally: "it made me feel as if he really wanted me to come down but didn't want to pressurise me." She also dreamed that he had died:

> I saw him lying there surrounded by flowers, and when I got up, I reassured myself that there is a Hindu belief to say that if you dream somebody is dying, it actually makes them live longer... I wasn't actually seeing myself; I was the onlooker. Then on Monday morning, when I went to college I heard the 10 0'clock chime [the time of the death]. I was walking along with my friend who said, "Look, there is a magpie, let's look for another one quickly". I said, "Why?" and she said, "It's 'one for sorrow, and two for joy', so if you see one you should look for another." I don't go in for these things. I don't even know what a magpie looks like. We didn't see another.

At her lodgings her landlord gently broke the news to her. Bewildered, she went upstairs to change out of her pink trousers and socks into a more appropriate colour, and then her landlord walked her to the tube station. While she was waiting on a bench, tears rolling down her cheeks, an Indian man came up and asked what the matter was. She told him what had happened, and he said, "Don't cry, think of God and of his spirit going to God." He sat on the train with her, trying to console her: "Even now I remember his kindness. Then all I can remember is a blur, just uncontrollable crying." At home she found the house changed around with the relatives there and her father's picture displayed with a lamp before it.

She and her mother did not see the body until just before the funeral, when they all went to the undertaker's, which was difficult. An Arya Samaj priest from London performed the rituals. At the house he made her brothers walk around the coffin. She felt excluded: "I don't agree with that sort of distinction, because he is our father just as much as the boys' father." The women all went to the crematorium, and were glad they could do something which would have been frowned on in Kenya. Afterwards they had *havan* at their home.

For Lila, both the rituals at home and in the crematorium were of equal importance. Some Punjabi friends told her that if her father had died at home his body would not have been returned to the house for the funeral, so she was glad that he had not died at home. She did not feel guilty for not being in Westmouth when her father died because she could not have done anything to help him. He died in the one place where he might have been saved and the doctor had done everything possible. It was impossible to see the future:

> Although it was a shock for the family, in a sense it was good for him to go like that. He wasn't bed-ridden or ill. He had a shower and got dressed and was chatting to people on the way to the surgery. When Dad died the doctor took him in his arms and said "Are you in pain," and Dad said "No", then he said "Rām, Rām" as he died, like Gandhiji. That is a great consolation. I like to know he was so good, that's what he deserved, and if that has integrated him into God, that is even more of a good thing for us. He wasn't into scandal or slagging anyone off or criticising. He disliked disharmony. He was very true, he never harmed anyone, and was never vicious. You have to be pure of spirit to have a release like that, to be really detached from material things and relationships. At the time of death you think about the things that you are most attached to; to think about God is a sign that you are attached to God. My father is still there somewhere, reborn or integrated with God. He still exists.

Lila continued to be puzzled about the signs such as the magpies and dreams, and the mysterious appearance of a photograph of her father taken two weeks before his death which had been pushed through the letter box. He had picked it up and placed it on the heater in the hall "as if it was ready there for what was to come". Her dreams showed her how her bereavement was progressing:

> Though we had the funeral and we had seen the coffin, I don't think I accepted it for a long time because I used to dream a lot about him. I was staying with a lady who was studying Jungian psychoanalysis, and used to do dream analysis. I told her about this dream I had about my Mum and me watching my Dad burning in lots of flames, and then all of a sudden there was a skeleton which was pulled out of the flames. She said, "That's when you accepted when he had died. That's a sign of the spirit when you see the bone. The spirit is there but the body has gone." After this I dreamed less about him being alive.

The daughters valued the visitors coming, but were concerned about their mother's welfare, as she was ill and very fatigued and never seemed to have a break. They wanted some space and time to be together as a family. They joined in the readings occasionally which gave them inner strength, but because relatives were staying there, the sisters had to look after them. Although some people offered accommodation, and a Sikh neighbour was immensely helpful, they managed as well as they could on their own.

Surya was clearly depressed a long time after her husband's death, but never complained about her situation, nor was there any sense of 'unfinished business'. There were enough elements of a good death in the way her husband died to provide deep consolation, and her religious beliefs provided great sustenance in coping with the subsequent losses (9.5). Sad and negative thoughts sometimes "came up like milk", so she had to remind herself of religious truths by her practice of *bhakti* and reading the scriptures (9.5).

It is difficult to judge anyone's level of recovery, especially of a widow whose entire world alters to the degree that Surya's did. Following her husband's death her eldest son died after a prolonged illness, and a close brother shortly afterwards. These multiple bereavements took a toll on her health, but she maintained a cheerful and serene outlook and continued to be actively involved in the weekly *havan* at the temple. Adjustment is a slow process. The individual will continue to have periods of grief or sadness, and miss the lost person, but can begin functioning again in a different world.

9.4. The loss of children

Recovery from the loss of children is particularly difficult. Bereavement studies show that even still births and neo-natal deaths can cause long term grieving. Klass suggests that for a parent the loss of a child represents a loss of part of one's self, since the "process of parenting is one of identification with the child".[50] This is never fully recovered from, since there is a loss of the future, "the empty historical track". Vimala (below), whose teenaged daughter died suddenly, was mourning the loss of her hopes and anticipation as well as the girl. There is also a loss of competence, since parenting is part of a sacred obligation involving protecting the child and keeping him or her from harm, so that when a child dies there is a deep sense of failure. There were three women in Westmouth who described the deaths of their babies, three girls and one also lost

---

[50] Klass 1988, cited in Siddell 1993:58.

a son, which they still remembered for years afterwards. The fourth woman, Vimala, lost an adult daughter, and was visited a few days after the death. As we shall see in the brief accounts below the pain of the loss continues throughout their lives. Had the losses described been of sons they would have been exacerbated by the expectations laid on Hindu women to produce healthy sons. The fact that the three who lost infant daughters all went on to produce sons, and that Vimala already had sons, would have given some consolation and also redeemed them in the eyes of their families, but did not mitigate their sorrow for the lost daughters who were never replaced.

Hertz and others note that the deaths of infants in many societies are treated in a fairly cursory fashion as they are not yet seen as social beings.[51] In developing countries the infant mortality rate is very high, and if many babies die in one family, a casual or fatalistic attitude may be psychologically protective. However, the fact that the rituals may be less elaborate does not mean that the child is missed any less by his or her parents. Kakar points out that according to the *Dharmaśāstra,* a Hindu child is newborn until he reaches the age of the sacred thread ceremony at around the age of eight, when he becomes twice-born,[52] although after the first tonsure at around two he begins to develop social relationships. In India a child who dies before the first teeth appear is buried, not cremated as the infant is too pure to need the purification of a fire.[53] Kakar suggests that perhaps this difference of emphasis regarding infant deaths is also because the rituals are male-dominated. While they have little social significance that is not to say they do not have personal significance, and women have their own way of dealing with the grief (personal interview). If an older child dies it is a much more serious matter, especially if it is a son, since so much is invested emotionally, socially and ritually in him. Informants whose relatives lost sons spoke of prolonged mourning with heavy constraints on the rest of the family.

Prema had a still-born baby girl in Bombay. She had felt uneasy whenever she visited her sister-in-law's house, as she felt there was jealousy of her pregnancy. When she gave birth in hospital she was alone, as her mother had left and the doctor had not arrived. She managed to get hold of the baby until the nurse came in. "I can still see her face. When something is beautiful you lose it. She was so

---

[51] Hertz 1960:76-77; cf. Block and Parry 1982:4; Eisenbruch, 1984 I:294.

[52] Kakar 1978:16.

[53] In India the dead baby may be wrapped in a white sheet, like a pillow case, with sugar and salt to help it dissolve quickly. There may be a few prayers said. The impurity lasts for three days except for a mother who is still undergoing the birth impurity.

beautiful." She felt that the baby was not hers - ultimately she was God's daughter, and was taken by Him because of her (the baby's) *karma*. At the same time she attributed the death to her sister-in-law's malice (3.3 above). After this loss she prayed to have twins, and three months afterwards became pregnant with twin sons who were born in an English hospital.

Prema's apparently inconsistent explanations of the child's death in terms of *karma*, malice, and also God's desire to take his daughter reflect both the need to blame and to find an emotionally and cognitively satisfying explanation (9.4). Kakar mentions the tensions and jealousy which can exist between a young bride and her husband's sisters[54] and in this family the bond between brothers and sisters was particularly strong (9.2.1).

Chandra was eighteen when her eight month old baby daughter died suddenly while being prepared for a bath. Two days beforehand she had dreamed that the baby had died, but was reassured that this meant she would have a long life (see Lila's dream, above). After this she stopped believing in dreams. "It was really hard. Why are you still living? You are still eating and drinking but that is all. But after a few days you have to come back and face life. I was expecting another baby and began to worry about the new one."

She had two more babies, and then lost her fourth, a boy, at birth, just after arriving in England, when there were few Hindus in Westmouth:

> That did not hurt so much as the first. You are tempted not to have any more when the loss of the first one hurts so much. The mother carries him for nine months and then comes home empty handed. There was no ceremony. We didn't know much. They took me to the hospital mortuary and I held him for about ten minutes. He was perfect. I looked at all his fingers. He weighed seven pounds. At home people themselves deal with it in our own way with our prayers, but we were new and couldn't ask for what we wanted. We don't know where they buried him. If we had done it with our own hands we would know where he is. Maybe he is in a common grave. I had no one to help me when I got home, and as we didn't know people here there was no support. If you can't talk to anyone it gets very heavy. After the baby died I was in hospital for a week, but when I got home and saw my two older kids, they gave me so much love I realised that if I don't love them no one else will. At that stage there is no comfort and you don't feel like doing anything. You have to cook and clean and get busy. However, I recovered after six months.

---

[54] Kakar 1981:73, 75, 195.

Now, after more than thirty years I wonder what they would be like if they were still alive.

She had another son, born a year after the boy she lost who looked exactly like the lost child. She thought he had come back. Even after more than thirty years it was very painful to discuss these deaths, and she had never stopped thinking about either baby. The sense of helplessness which Chandra and her husband felt in the hospital was very commonly reported by Hindu informants (as well as by Sikhs and Muslims), but is also a common experience of the indigenous white community after the death of an infant or child, since the parents are particularly vulnerable at this time.[55] The lack of a local Hindu community to provide support and advice exacerbated a painful situation.

Padma lost her first baby, a girl, in Delhi, when she was nine days old, from tetanus as a result of an infected umbilicus. The baby became more and more ill, so her husband Ram wrapped her in a towel and took her to the doctor, who said, "I don't think she will survive, I am afraid that the mother is going to lose her first child." They got into a taxi, and went first to one hospital, where they gave her injections, and then to others, but to no avail. Padma could barely walk as she had septic stitches, so she stayed behind. She had a sort of waking dream, in which she heard her husband saying, "Give me the child, I will take her home. She can die in front of her mother so she won't suffer afterwards." The doctor said, "That's your responsibility. If you want to take her we won't accept her again."

> He brought her home and she was just in and out of the door, like that (sigh) and she was gone. They didn't tell me. but I knew she was dead because they were crying. They just took me out of that room. Maybe I shouted. I never saw her again. I couldn't see, even if they had wanted me to see her because when you have had a baby everything is loose. The eyes are not strong, the muscles, so they kept me out of there. You mustn't move for 20 days, or read or do needlework. In some families, such as my own, women go into their parents' house for the first baby, but I had to stay with my in-laws. I don't know if my husband went with her when they buried her. There is a place where they bury children, and they do special ceremonies, put something special there, yoghurt and a red cloth. He has a very good heart, but he was very upset. I had lost my child. I didn't feel I should be there, that I should go

[55] It is only very recently that organisations like FSID (The Foundation for the Study of Infant Deaths) and SANDS (Stillbirth and Neonatal Death Society) have encouraged a more humane approach to the experience of stillbirth and neo-natal deaths.Cf. Siddell 1993:60ff..

> with her. It might have been worse. If I had burst too much over that I could have damaged my heart.[56]

Padma's perception of her physical state is interesting. Because "everything is loose" after childbirth it would have been dangerous for her to witness the child's burial. She accepted that she should be protected from any further grief. She was inconsolable, but had a great deal of support from her husband's family, especially her sister-in-law who tried to look after Padma, but kept returning to see the baby, who was "a very beautiful girl, like a statue, really beautiful with long curly hair, like the god Kṛṣṇa".

Shortly after the infant's death, Padma's sister-in-law had a dream in which the baby appeared and said she would return if she was offered bananas, which the family offered to Mātā-jī (3.2.5). Three months later Padma became pregnant with her first son, who was born a year after the baby's death. She felt extra protective towards this child who she was convinced was the spirit of the baby girl. She and her husband had several significant dreams to do with their son's arrival, which confirmed their belief that the daughter had been reborn. About the time of conception she dreamed that her guru, Swami Dayanand Saraswati, had filled the space under her bed with *vibhūti* (sacred ash), which she and her nephew tried to put into a very large box. The guru produced an enormous piece of *barfī* (a sweet). Cutting it in half, he gave her half and offered the rest to people sitting around her bed. This was seen as a good omen, and she became pregnant shortly afterwards.

Subsequently, she and her husband felt anxious about the safe arrival of the child. While Padma was staying at her mother's home just before the second birth, her husband dreamed that the guru had walked in through the gate in a very happy mood. The husband said, "Don't leave us", and the guru said, "Don't worry, I am still here, you will soon have good news. Don't be scared." Padma added:

> Two days after this I had a big chubby boy, he was all red. The nurses used to love him and take him away and play with him. But I still miss her. Sometimes I think she is still here, just to soothe myself. My husband never ever talked to me about her, because he didn't want me to remember bad things that happened. He was upset inside but he never ever showed it. After

[56] At the time of writing Padma is recovering from heart surgery.

> the third day he went sick, he had a very sore pain in his back because he had got soaked when they went to look for a doctor. He said, "I am going to die like the baby. I've got the same disease she had." I still remember that, tears come in my eyes. I was really upset.[57]

Unlike many of the other deaths under discussion it was felt that in this situation reticence was the best way of protecting the mother rather than talking about the deceased.

Vimala found her seventeen-year old daughter hanging half out of her bed, apparently dead from what was later described as a brain haemorrhage. She phoned for an ambulance but the line was busy, so she dialled 999 and called the police, who were very helpful. When the ambulance came, neither parent was allowed to go with the daughter because they were so upset. The police waited with the family, and a phone call came from the ambulance staff to the police, confirming that the girl was dead. Vimala did not know whether she had died at home or in the ambulance, and did not feel she could handle the truth

The girl had had a very good relationship with her mother, and helped a great deal in the family shop. The parents were beginning to think of her marriage when she had finished her studies. Vimala said that if only she had known her daughter was going to die she would have talked to her, told her things, and let her have what she wanted. The neighbours who came in to commiserate with her told her she had to endure it, as it was God's will, but this was not very helpful. Her husband would not let her go to the sea with the ashes as she was crying too much but she wanted to throw cakes and flowers in the water: "I can't sleep, I can't forget, I want us all to be together at night, the whole family."

While all four women recovered enough to get on with life, and three of them went on to bear sons, they all continued to mourn their daughters. Padma, more than twenty years afterwards, found herself seeing her daughter as a grown-up woman as she performed a memorial ritual for her guru, and decided to offer prayers once a year in the temple for her, too (6.3.1). She found some compensation for the loss of her daughter by adopting a niece in India as her daughter. The girl never lived with her, but Padma and her husband took responsibility for her marriage arrangements. For Vimala, the loss of the future was particularly acute since the marriage of the daughter was being planned. The daughter had fulfilled all her parents' expectations by working hard at school, whilst the sons had been a big disappointment, showing little interest in the

---

[57] He did not die but lived to be an most helpful informant!

family's religion or their business. What seemed to grieve her most, however, was the loss of a sympathetic and beloved companion.

9.5. Finding meaning

Adjustment seems to be related to the extent to which the bereaved find cognitive and emotional satisfaction in the way they understand their loss. This does not mean that there will be no more pain or sorrow, but the assumption of normal or nearly normal functioning seems to depend, to some degree, upon the extent to which meaning is found in the death. For the Hindu, this depends not only on the explanatory system of the bereaved with regard to the nature of suffering and the after-life, but also on the extent to which the deceased has had a good death. However, little research seems to have been done exploring the relationship of various types of religious belief to adjustment to bereavement. Yet, as O'Dea points out, religious beliefs and practices provide meaning in the 'limit situations' or 'breaking points' of powerlessness, uncertainty and scarcity, particularly in the face of death

> by providing a grounding for the beliefs and orientation of men in a view of reality that transcends the empirical here-and-now of daily experience. Thus not only is cognitive frustration overcome, which is involved in the problem of meaning, but the emotional adjustments to frustrations and deprivations inherent in human life and human society are facilitated.[58]

Geertz also takes the view that religion enables people to formulate "by means of symbols ... an image of such a genuine order of the world which will account for and even celebrate the perceived ambiguities, puzzles and paradoxes in human experience."[59] According to Peberdy it is likely to be more difficult to contemplate death for those who have no sense of immortality or a belief in an after-life: "The experience of loss and grief may be equally strong for both, but for the unbeliever and the agnostic there may be the extra burden of searching for meaning, and perhaps finding none at all."[60]

It would seem that a fairly perfunctory religiosity does not provide a deep enough understanding of the religious dimension of life and death to make sense

58 O'Dea 1966:6-7.

59 Geertz 1966, cited in Sharma 1978a:22; cf. Berger and Luckman 1966:119.

60 Peberdy *et al.* 1993:19; Parkes 1986:177-178; Shuchter and Zisook 1993:32.

of it. For Jung, finding a religious meaning in life and accepting the possibility of death was a fundamental aspect of the second half of life, without which individuation could not take place:

> As a physician I am convinced that it is hygienic ... to discover in death a goal towards which one can strive; and that shrinking away from it is something unhealthy and abnormal which robs the second half of life of its purpose. I therefore consider the religious teaching of a life hereafter consonant with the standpoint of psychic hygiene... From the standpoint of psychotherapy it would therefore be desirable to think of death as only a transition - one part of a life-process whose extent and duration escape our knowledge.[61]

Jung also observed that those approaching death were often aware of it at the psychic level, and suggested that it was neurotic in old age *not* to focus on death. The psyche, he thought, made little of death, but "the unconscious is all the more interested in *how* one does; that is, whether the attitude of consciousness is adjusted to dying or not".[62] This is particularly interesting in view of the Hindu concept of the good death which is prepared for and entered willingly. Grof and Halifax stress the importance of beliefs in approaching death:

> Different concepts of death and associated beliefs have a deep influence not only on the psychological state of dying people but also on the specific circumstances under which they leave this world and on the attitudes of their survivors... Most non-Western cultures have religious and philosophical systems, cosmologies, ritual practices, and certain elements of social organization that make it easier for their members to accept and experience death.[63]

For Hindus, their symbolic universe contains the concepts of the cycle of birth, death and rebirth, of creation and destruction, *saṃsāra*. That which is Real lies beyond this ever-changing manifestation, and for many the whole of their spiritual lives is geared towards the realisation of this.[64] It can be apprehended in this life if one follows suitable disciplines, and so the boundary dividing this world and the next is a very fine one and life has to be lived with this constantly in view. The rituals and the social context of death provide a framework for

---

[61] Jung 1961:129.
[62] Jung 1965:10.
[63] Grof and Halifax 1977:2; Badham and Badham 1987:6-7; Bowker 1991:3ff., 209ff.
[64] Cf. Kaushik 1976:266.

finding meaning, with the constant reiteration of teaching about the ephemeral nature of this life and the eternal nature of the soul, not just in general terms but about *this* particular individual who has gone to God or has been, or will be, reborn. Williams points out that the rituals are informed by definite premises, and if the premises change so does the meaning. This is difficult to maintain in a different or changing cultural setting when it is not shared by others, as it becomes "mere performance of a script" or play-acting.[65] In the diaspora context these premises are changing and it is still necessary to make sense of personal suffering. Weber's concept of theodicy, of justifying and making sense of suffering and inequalities, is also useful in understanding the importance to Hindus of finding meaning in what they experience in relation to personal suffering. Talcott Parsons, writing of Weber's emphasis on the problem of meaning, suggests that there may be discrepancies between

> expectation systems which are institutionalized in normative orders and the actual experiences people undergo...what the people interpret to be the consequences *for them* and for the aspects of the human condition to which they are attached, of conformity or nonconformity with an established normative order".[66]

A rational explanation is needed which minimises the tensions between normative expectations and actual experiences, which, as Eisenbruch points out, eases the suffering of grief by enabling the person to "explain to himself the 'cause' and 'consequences for his system of values' of his loss".[67] Nevertheless discrepancies are inevitable, particularly in explaining apparently meaningless suffering. The drive to find meaning has led, in the Indian context, to the doctrine of *karma* (3.3.1), which Weber describes as "The most complete formal solution of the problem of theodicy".[68] In principle, if the *karma* theory is held then no suffering is ever unjust because it is always the result of past sins. Madan comments that "Even the unbearable is never really undeserved" and reflects the moral ordering of the universe.[69] Many informants seemed satisfied with the explanation that the time of death was fixed, either by God or by one's previous

---

[65] Williams 1981:4-5.

[66] Parsons, 1965, cited in Weber 1965:xlvi.

[67] Eisenbruch 1984:287.

[68] Weber 1965:145, 146-147, 155, 266-268; see Sharma 1978a:24ff..

[69] Madan 1987:127; 4.2 above . Cf. Sharma 1978a:24.

karma, or both (3.3). However, such an explanation, as Weber commented, may not be emotionally satisfying. Some informants, shattered by premature or unexpected deaths asked, "Why did this have to happen?" or "Why did God let this happen?" Nalini (7.1.2) could not understand why God had done this to her:

> Why did God have to take him away when he was so young? Why doesn't God come and help when the person wants to live, when he is doing so many good things [for others] in his life?... My husband was so religious, he prayed every day, not in temple or shrine, but a few minutes at bed time. He sat in silence and prayed with his heart... He was always helping people, always right, always happy with his family, with the children. I miss him in the kitchen, around the house. God helps people - why didn't he help us? Bad characters do well, why do good people die?

Karma alone was not a sufficient answer at the outset, although constant reminders, both of *karma* and God's will, seemed to make an impact eventually. A young Gujarati widow asked of her husband's death, "Was it his bad *karma* that he should have to suffer like that?" (GjBrF30). Ramesh also had great difficulty with the notion that his father's death was predestined because of previous *karma*. The concept of a God who intervenes to prevent suffering seems to be contrary to the doctrine of *karma*, yet this was a theme which recurred frequently when informants were struggling to understand their suffering. Sharma comments that Weber's theodicy of justifying the goodness of God in the face of suffering, is not a problem in the Hindu context, but it is certainly an issue for a number of British Hindus.[70] This may reflect inconsistencies in the individual's belief system, or the influence of Christian concepts (and problems) about the nature of God and suffering. For the *bhakta*, God is seen in personal and loving terms, and might be expected to help or save his devotees, thus outweighing *karma*,[71] but raises the perennial question in Western philosophy of why a good God would allow suffering:

> If two babies were born at the same time and one suffered, why? If we are all children of God, why doesn't He help both equally? A loving father would treat them equally. If God were good He would have no right to treat people differently (GjLF55).

---

[70] Sharma 1978a:24.
[71] BG 18.30; cf. Ch. 3 above.

A Hindu doctor thought there was no answer when trying to rationalise the death of a child:

> When a child dies both the child and the parents suffer. We may say everything that happens is good from God, as if God wanted it that way. It is very difficult to rationalise, and as a doctor you're always looking for justification. Is this what God has written down? If a young husband and father dies, what is the justification for that? Maybe he did naughty things, but other people suffer.

However, as Sharma indicates, there may be alternative levels of explanation.[72] We have seen this operate in the examples of infant deaths where the death was explained both in terms of *karma* and as a gift of God which is subsequently withdrawn. Chandra, who lost two babies at different times, tried to understand her suffering in terms of her own *karma*, because,

> God gave them to me and God took them back. In the end you have to accept it, that it is in God's hands. No matter what you do, you make some programme, but God's programme is different, and can't be changed. Whatever happens is ultimately said to be for good, but I can't see good, as I didn't have another daughter, I never got my girl back.

Referring to her daughter's neo-natal death, Padma used a similar expression: "It was God's gift that He gave me, and He took it back. I didn't ask why, it didn't occur in my heart why He took it from me." For all these women the losses were still very profound. Attempts to understand them in terms of God's will were not wholly successful, as in the example of Prema (9.3) who also tried to explain her baby's still birth in terms of *karma* and her sister-in-law's ill-wishing.

Surya found *karma* a useful concept to understand what she had been through, but also felt that God (Bhagvan, Paramatma) was actively involved in the world. Life was "*sukh-duḥkh*", happiness and sadness together, and sometimes one was sick or short of money. God set *karma* in motion, and ultimately death was in God's hands, so there was no point fighting it:

> If you are a *bhakta*, then everything that comes to you, you accept, as God's *icchā* (wish). When people die you are cut up with crying, your head is in

[72] Sharma 1978a:35ff..

pain, your eyes hurt, and then you think this is not in my hands, it is in God's hands. If He wants to take your son or your husband, what can you do? If you believe in God then you have to recognise everything comes from God, He is powerful over us all. After birth is death, everyone dies. God gives us a body and *ātma*, and when the body is dead and burned the *ātma* remains eternal. Once you know this, why do you want to fight or be angry?

Sometimes when I am alone, I think, "Oh God, what is going on? What is my life now, the children have gone and now I am alone, what about me?" Then I think, he has gone and my turn is coming. I pray to God, "My body is yours, my husband's body was yours, my children's bodies". Who is dead? Nobody is dead if you believe the *ātma* is eternal. People come and go, come and go, and you think, my parents have died, others have died, then [the people who come to visit] say, "My son has died, my daughter has died", and share with you. In every house death has come. When I cried, I reminded myself of this and then I had *śānti*, peace. Everyone's turn will come, and when my turn comes my children will miss me, as we miss our parents, but in *saṃsār* there is birth and death.

People have free will *(buddhi)*, but there is also a sense of God being in overall control of events, intervening to assist people through others: "God sends people when you suffer. He hasn't got *rūp* [a body] like you, only *śaktī*, [strength], and He comes into people and gets them to go and help others. I can't go out when I am in *duḥkh* [sorrow], and people like you come and offer to help."

Surya told the story of a woman who had lost her husband and went to the guru to help her, and he told her to go to a house in which nobody had died and fetch some water, but in every house somebody had died. [73]. "When you understand that death is universal you gain *gyān* (knowledge)." Her sister-in-law had never understood this, and after her own husband died got into a terrible state of prolonged grieving. Her hair went white, she lost weight, and was always crying "Oh, oh, oh". Eventually, despite some very strong resistance, she accepted help from the Brahma Kumaris who convinced her that all this came from God. She changed completely, from being depressed, aggressive and jealous to having understanding, and in turn consoled Surya.

For the devout *bhakta,* God's hand is seen in whatever happens, although

---

[73] This seems to be a version of the Buddhist story of Kisagotami, a young woman who approached the Buddha for help when her child died. He told her to go to every house and bring back a grain of mustard seed from every house in which there had been no deaths, but she found no such houses, and he used this to teach her about the impermanent nature of *saṃsāra*. (Humphreys, 1970::83-5; Rimpoche 1993:28-9).

karma is also a factor in understanding premature deaths. A Punjabi man "stood like a rock" when he learned of his son's accidental death while saving the life of a child: "Never say that God has done a bad thing to me. If You want to give this to me, I'll take it with happy hands. You took my son; this is what You are offering to me. I'll take it with open hands." Training in detachment through meditation and reading is an important factor, not just in facing death, but in learning not to cling to those who have died.

The belief in rebirth is also very important as a way of coming to terms with death, as was seen in Chapter 3, and frequently manifests itself in observations about a baby born shortly after a death. The teaching of the BG in particular, as informants like Surya and Lila found, also provides reassurance at a cognitive level that the soul is eternal, shedding the outworn body like a caterpillar. Surya said:

> My husband's body died, but he is not dead, he has taken another birth in another life. Then you pray that God gives him a nice place, in a nice *janam* (life), and that he lives always with a happy *ātma*. Then he will want to be born, he will come and somebody will become pregnant. It is birth and death.

Concepts of rebirth were particularly consoling to the women whose babies had died (9.3). Precognitions, dreams and signs of a good death came to have a great deal of meaning. Ashok felt that his uncle's presence, when his father died, might be some sort of message that the father's death was meant to happen. Lila and Susheela wondered whether the unusual coincidences occurring around the time of their father's death, such as Lila's dreams, indicated a sense of destiny, which would make the event more manageable. A Patel widow had long readings after her husband's death, explaining Swaminarayan teachings which greatly comforted her sons and answered many of their questions; they also felt that as Pramukh Swami knew about the death it was God's will (4.1). Surya's family also shared the readings and rituals with her when they could. This helped Lila find meaning:

> I have thought about reincarnation because that is what one is brought up to believe. The Indian cinema also has a great effect on you because it doesn't impose any different kind of thinking, it just takes religion for granted. In Britain you become aware of different people's beliefs - that they don't believe in reincarnation. But I believe in it. After my father died, I

> remembered that part of the *Gītā* which says you are foolish to grieve for a body when the spirit is not there. The spirit has a change of clothes. Really you are just grieving for material things. But it is still a personal loss for the family. However you try to console yourself, you still feel sad.

A Punjabi Brahmin had felt despair at the age of sixteen when his little nephew died in India. He had cried all the time, and had found no comfort. Now that he was more mature he had found great consolation from the BG when his mother died: "Religion teaches that God who gives you this grief also gives you the power and energy to bear it. One is more attached to the old, which is to do with the relationship."

A number of younger Hindus described turning back to Hindu belief and practice following a death, as Ashok reported (9.2.3). Mohan found that he had become more religious since the death of his brother:

> I have come closer to the spiritual side. I was a non-practising Hindu but since my father and brother died I get these periods when I do [religious practice] and then I do it too much. The *Gāyatrī Mantra* has really helped me, as it pulled me through bronchitis when I thought I was a goner, and it has really helped me and made me more whole. With that I can detach myself from anything, any trouble, whether domestic or work.

From the evidence it seems legitimate to view the psychological processes of bereaved British Hindus as sufficiently similar to those of indigenous British individuals to be used as a basis for discussion, and the three broad stages of bereavement, are a useful way of exploring this. It is important, however, not to impose them, but to remain aware of cultural differences in the ways in which emotional states are described and demonstrated when belief systems, rituals and social and mourning patterns are very different. The first stage of shock and denial at the initial separation is common, and intense emotional outbursts, noted above, are also common to many cultures.[74] It is interesting to speculate whether the taboos on the expression of emotion in British culture contribute to the psychological problems which may follow a death. As we have seen (8.3-8.3.1) some Hindus are critical of such outbursts, believing them at times to be a response to social expectations, but they do give permission to feel and express grief.

The second stage, of pining, yearning and feeling sorrow also seems to be a

---

[74] Eisenbruch 1994: II:335.

common experience, and parallels van Gennep's liminal period, although the psychological process can take much longer. Anger is often a feature of this period, but only a few of my British Hindu informants acknowledged it. It was directed principally towards professionals who were seen to have failed in their duty to the dying. A few initially expressed anger towards God, but none against a parent, husband or older sibling. Aunts and sisters-in-law were the only relatives to receive negative comments. More common was guilt, such as was expressed by Ramesh, for having failed in one's duty, possibly exacerbated by anxiety that the newly deceased would be unsatisfied and cause problems for the mourners. It was therefore interesting to find a number of informants reporting that they had felt the presence of the spirit of the deceased as entirely benevolent and caring.

Many Westmouth informants derived a great sense of satisfaction from indications that the deceased had been appreciated by the community and they valued its support. Ballard observes that "it is the healing power of mourning - and the sharing, and hence the dissipation, of grief within the entire *sangat*, as I once heard a *gyani* very beautifully put it - that really does the trick, providing there is space and time for that to happen"[75] (personal communication). The saddest informants were those who had no such support, no shared memories of the one who had died, and no reinforcement of the framework of meaning which the individual might be struggling with.

The third stage, reorganisation and adaptation, begins when the mourners begin to restructure their lives and redirect their emotional energy into a renewed ability to function. For Maya, adjustment meant dropping her fight with the hospital and channelling her fight for justice into a determination to study law. Her mother, Nalini, gradually found satisfaction in learning to be independent and running her own life. Both recovered their religious beliefs and practices. Surya did not have to deal with this level of anger, or with the guilt felt by Ramesh, and despite her further losses, found meaning in her children and grandchildren and an important role in the temple. Some widows, however, never recover in this sense, and continue to channel their energy into devotion to the deceased husband, as well as to the gods or their guru.

The insights of Stroebe, Rosenblatt, Eisenbruch and Walter, are important as

---

[75] *Sangat*: assembly, gathering, here the Sikh congregation. The *gyani* is someone who is well-read in the Sikh scriptures. The remarks are equally applicable to Hindus.

reminders of major cultural variations as to what constitutes recovery, and the importance, to Hindus, of the on-going, symbiotic relationship with the dead (1.2). The belief that the ancestor, in whatever form, *is* actually in existence somewhere is very real for my Westmouth informants. A large photograph of the deceased is garlanded and given a prominent place in the living room and/or in the family shrine, with flowers and a *dīvā*. Prayers and offerings are made, if not daily, on anniversaries, the *pitṛpakṣa* and other festivals. The annual *śrāddha* not only keeps the memory of the deceased alive, but functions to maintain him as an eternal being. Such an expression of a continuous relationship with the dead, even if reduced to the annual *śrāddha* after the first year, affects the nature of the bereavement process. Whether this aids greatly in coming to terms with the death, or whether it prevents what some Westerners might perceive to be a necessary and healthy separation, is something only further psychological research can ascertain. It seems likely that a sense of a continuous relationship with the deceased helps to lessen a feeling of the finality of the loss and blurs the distinction between life and death, thus enabling people to face their own and others' deaths with greater equilibrium than if the deceased has ceased to have any kind of existence. This is a problem in Western post-Protestant culture in which there are no rites of reincorporation to give a place for the dead or to reintegrate the bereaved into their new roles in society. It allows no legitimated sense of continuity with the dead, truncates mourning rituals and provides little or no social support or framework of meaning.

Recovery or adaptation thus obviously depend on such factors as family structures and dynamics, as well as the influence of the caste and religious community to which the bereaved belong. The few Hindus in Westmouth, like Prema, who had little support following the death of a close relative found it difficult to cope with the early days of the bereavement. Eisenbruch stresses the problems the absence of such support creates in ethnic minority groups generally, since they have often had to cope with other separations and losses.[76] Such support validates the withdrawal and grieving, provides reassurance and assistance, and is often accompanied by reminders of religious teaching. It is thus important to keep in touch with the bearers of the tradition. The constant repeating, over and over, of the story of the death helps to force onto the mind the reality of the loss, and in the context of formal and informal rituals helps the bereaved to find a new place for the deceased, to reconstruct their world, and find

---

[76] Eisenbruch 1984 II:330.

religious and philosophical meaning in it.[77]

However, it was a struggle for Hindus who had experienced the premature or bad death of a partner, parent or child to make sense of the death in terms of the familiar teaching about *karma* and God's will. Nalini, Maya and most of the mothers described above found themselves questioning God's will and the nature of *karma*. The concept of rebirth was particularly helpful to the mothers, several of whom saw the dead child returning in a later infant. Regular religious practice, reading from the BG or other texts seemed of particular help when their beliefs and confidence failed them. Even Surya, whose husband died a relatively good death, had to think through the implications of religious teaching to make sense of her loss. She found the BG in particular helped to direct her thinking in a positive way, recognising that death comes to everyone, but the soul never dies.

[77] Cf. Jackson 1965:220-225.

Chapter 10
Good deaths? Prospects for the future

At a time when there is a good deal of discussion about contemporary representations of death, the value or otherwise of the concept of a good death (or a "good enough death"), and ways of enabling the dying to explore their own spirituality and search for meaning, it is useful to be reminded of a community attempting to maintain a model of a good death in a Western secular context. The problem for Hindus in the diaspora is how to maintain the model in the context of medicalised hospital deaths and state bureacracy. This chapter reviews the issues confronting dying and bereaved Hindus in Britain and points to practical implications for the future.

10.1. Death in Britain

Good deaths for Hindus do not occur in isolation. They are located in the heart of the family in a ritual framework which encapsulates a belief that death is merely a transition to another life and not an ending. This requires advance preparation and willing participation and control. Many elderly people withdraw mentally into the forest while remaining at home - a symbolic *vānaprastha* - to develop their spiritual lives and religious practices.[1] Despite all the changes occurring in the diaspora, this is still a fundamental aspect of British Hindus' world view which underlies moral and religious motivation. Nor is the death itself seen as an instantaneous event. It is a process taking at least thirteen days, involving both the mourners and the Brahmin priests who regenerate the newly released *ātman* and relocate him in heaven or earth, or enable him to be liberated. They are thus involved in 'giving birth' to the one who has gone, and the sense of the importance of this involvement has been retained in Britain, even if the mourners do not understand the full meaning of the rituals. The good death, then, is more than the events at the death bed, and the knowledge of and narratives about it have a positive term impact on the relatives and wider community. Bad deaths are anomic deaths, in the wrong time and place, without preparation or the appropriate rituals, and, as the studies of Ramesh, Maya and Nalini demonstrate, make adjustment more difficult.

Terminally ill Hindus need, in principle, to know of the diagnosis, so that they

---

[1] Cf. Blakemore and Boneham 1994:77 ff. for a discussion of the experience of ageing Asians in Britain; Vatuk 1980.

can prepare spiritually and fulfil their obligations to their families, although, as shown above, this can create problems of disclosure. Yet without this knowledge the appropriate preparations cannot be made and the dying person may be alone at the point of death. It important to be conscious to remember God if possible, which has implications for drugs and pain relief, discussed below. To have relatives present, therefore, is extremely important for the dying as well as for the survivors who will not only have to deal with the normal aspects of bereavement, but any additional stress of failure in their sacred duty and anxiety over the fate of the deceased.

After the death Hindus face immense changes because of the professionalisation of death. The loss of control of the body and post-mortem and funeral procedures can make people feel anxious, insecure and marginalised. By breaking up the continuity of ritual action, the fundamental *process* of death is actually altered. My pandit informants in India believed the soul would not be released properly in these circumstances, but would continue to wander around in a distressed state. British pandits are also concerned about delays, but feel that as long as the mourners and the pandits perform appropriate rituals in the spirit of faith, they will still be effective. However, this may be making the best of a bad job, since traditionally the cremation plays such a fundamental role in the release of the *ātman.* Beliefs about the nature of the soul and the way it departs and moves on are most likely to be challenged by the shift in the ritual pattern, and the Vedic and Purāṇic origins of the funeral and cremation rituals may become diluted or lost. This process is evident in the NCHT service (Appendix), which includes portions of the BG and the Upaniṣads but bears little relation to the traditional texts used in the death rituals in India.

The major part of the funeral takes place in the home, incorporating aspects of the ritual appropriate to the pyre and the procession, which have both disappeared. This may contribute to a growing shift in the role of women, since they are able to be present and sometimes participate in the rituals. Even Gujarati women, who have tended to be more conservative than other groups, are beginning to go to the crematorium, which is much less traumatic than the open pyre. Significantly, some pandits permit daughters to act as chief mourners at the funeral and the *śrāddha,* which marks a major change in attitudes to the role of women in British Hindu society. The cremation has altered radically, with no circumambulations, *piṇḍa-dāna* or *kapāla kryā.* If there is no pandit, the NCHT service may be used, or one devised by a caste leader or a local Brahmin. The homily, the arrangement of the mourners sitting in rows in the chapel facing the priest or chosen leader, and the lack of movement or ritual actions in relation to the body, make the cremation service very similar to one in the host community, except that there is no music. Despite the efforts of the pandits, the purpose of the service at the crematorium may be shifting towards the consolation of the mourners in this world, rather than being concerned solely with the progression of the deceased to the unseen world. Both the cremation and the *śrāddha* may thus become more of a memorial and a "send-off" than acts of separation and regeneration and reincorporation. However, a growing focus on the survivors may provide new ways of coping with bereavement as long as there is no accompanying anxiety about the deceased.

In Britain, in sharp contrast to India, the mourning procedures are set in motion *before* the funeral, so the original pattern of a liminal period following the rites of separation has been altered. The need to return to work before the mourning period is over curtails many of the mourning customs, and may prevent families from receiving as much support as is desired or needed. However, the delay before the funeral allows relatives to arrive from all over the world, and parts of Britain. Because they have to be fed, given drinks and may have to be accommodated, the restrictions associated with *sūtaka* are being eased.

The daily offering to the deceased and ancestors is largely maintained by older women, and by widows in particular. The *pitṛpakṣa* is still observed, but the temple makes provision for special prayers to be said on the date of the death by the Gregorian calendar. This alters the astrological significance of the *tithi* based on the lunar calendar, but it constitutes an effort to maintain the traditional ancestral links in an institutionalised form, and provides revenue for the temple.

Since many pandits function as both temple pandits and family *purohitas* they have to perform funeral rituals. As Killingley points out:

> The priest or pandit is also taking on a pastoral role, providing advice on ritual and moral matters for Hindus living in an undefined area surrounding the temple, who are as it were his parishioners... In these circumstances, the priest is both agent and regulator of change, negotiating with his clients, particularly the older women of the family.[2]

---

[2] Killingley 1991:4.

While in theory the pandit who has to take funerals, and thus acts as the ritual scapegoat for the sins of the deceased person, has diminished status in comparison with 'pure Brahmins', in Britain such distinctions may become less clear, since the same pandit normally also has to conduct auspicious ceremonies such as marriages. This may also subtly alter perceptions of inauspicioussness and imppurity. Pandits play a major role in determining the ritual processes that have been developing in Britain. Despite the claims of some pandits that there is only one way to perform a particular ritual, the content of the rituals is constantly being renegotiated and developed according to need. Menski shows "that classical Hindu law favoured continuous ritual innovation and flexibility", in which there is "a complex conglomerate of sanskritic and local/caste customary practices that show quite considerable flexibility".[3] The pandit

> ... does not just sit there expounding scripture; rather he guides almost imperceptibly, so that the crucial adjustment processes that have to take place in a new environment cause minimal imbalance and tension... Typically for anything Hindu, there is no central regulation here, so the priests are helping to build modified traditions that may or may not stand the test of time and may become peculiar to their own clientele.[4]

Some younger Hindus seem to be less than satisfied with their priests and want to know what is being said and done, and why; the ensuing dialogue provides a valuable opportunity for priests and clients to examine the significance of different aspects of the rituals. Several pandits have expressed a desire to write their own service appropriate to British circumstances, to replace the NCHT service but Menski shows that rituals are differently structured for different client groups and adjusted to their respective caste status and area of origin. As long as there are trained and experienced pandits who are used to such negotiations, it is unlikely that a standardised service will be produced for general use, although there may be a place for one in situations with no pandit, containing some of the main readings, *mantras* and prayers. Killingley comments: "Change in Britain is continuous with,

---

3 Menski 1991:44; cf. Bayly 1981:182.
4 Menski 1991:48.

and facilitated by, the change and variety in the South Asian past, both ancient and modern; it need not mean getting more like the British and less like Indians".[5]

In view of the considerable change and modification of Hindu death rituals in Britain, continuity of religious belief is likely to be maintained through texts such as the BG which have become part of Hindu consciousness, reinforced by shared readings teachings and narratives, by films and videos and by visits to India. These have a universal application and are not dependent upon religious functionaries to provide meaning. If, in time, the umbilical link with India is loosened and the second and third generations no longer go back to take the ashes or perform the *śrāddha*, the significance of the rituals may become diluted but this need not diminish their emotional and social importance. Despite Huntington's and Metcalfe's doubts about the efficacy of rituals in enabling the bereaved to perform "psychological work",[6] and the fact that the rituals which are performed in Westmouth are simplified, they have significance for the participants: "Rituals have the function of diverting people's minds and keeping them busy. They were invented by the sages as a game with divinity, and give people time to cool down and start facing life" (GjPlM50). But they also give a deeper meaning to the death, particularly if it is a good death, as they conform and reinforce beliefs and facilitate the progress of the deceased. If the rituals are not performed adequately, or missed out altogether, as in the case of the old lady who did not receive Ganga water at the point of death (4.4.1), the emotional cost to members of the family may be very high, since they have not only failed in their duty but their future security is threatened. Thus, both the formal rituals and the informal directing of the bereaved towards spiritual realities provide religious meaning to death, comforting and reassuring the mourners by helping to make sense of what O'Dea calls "the limit situations" or "breaking points" in life.[7] As Bloch and Parry observe, "the rebirth which occurs at death is not only a denial of individual extinction but also a reassertion of society and a renewal of life and creative power".[8] The mourners have an active role in the process of transforming the 'unknown' into a manageable ancestor with whom it is possible to have a relationship, and the activity is important in moving from a situation of

[5] Killingley 1991:3.
[6] Huntington and Metcalfe 1979:44.
[7] O'Dea 1983; cf. Berger and Luckman 1966:118.
[8] Bloch and Parry 1981:5.

powerlessness to one in which there is a sense of control.

The mourning traditions are still strong in established caste groups, and provide a framework for shared grief and mutual support and help. While some younger Hindus are critical of the social expectations associated with this period they recognise the value of community support, and those who do not have such a support system are particularly vulnerable. Widows in Britain still have particular difficulties, especially if they have no adult children to protect and care for them, but the safety net provided by the welfare services, and work opportunities for younger ones enable them to live independently if they wish or need to.

When exploring the ways in which Hindus grieve, a broad pattern of three stages was adopted to provide a basis for discussion, and this seems to be useful as long as it is flexible and not prescriptive. However, as in many cultures, the first stage often includes violent outbursts of emotion, which was criticised by some Hindus in this study, but regarded as therapeutic by most. There appear to be no long-term studies comparing the adjustment of those who express grief openly and those who do not, although it is often assumed in current counselling situations that the open expression of grief is vitally important to the ultimate adjustment and recovery of the individual. However, the concept of recovery as commonly understood is also questionable in the Hindu context, especially for widows who are expected to continue mourning the dead husband. In the context of *śrāddha* it is better to speak of relocating the deceased, bearing in mind that informants have a very real belief that the deceased is somewhere, whether with God or reborn, perhaps in the same family. This is reinforced by scripture readings, the regular offerings to the deceased, memorials on the anniversary and the annual *pitṛ pakṣa,* and gives solace to the dying as well as to the bereaved. While the bereaved have to adjust to a new day-to-day world without the deceased and restructure their lives accordingly, any concept of recovery has to take into account the on-going place of the deceased in the lives of the living and the symbiotic relationship between them,.

Even for those with a deep faith, the struggle to find meaning and purpose in death is not straightforward, and a number of informants wrestled with the concepts such as the doctrine of *karma* and a notion of loving God in the light of their suffering, questioning the validity of their beliefs, at least initially. The readings, rituals and support of others were all important factors in their ultimate acceptance and adjustment to the situation. Living in a post-Christian culture with a medical view of death as something to be postponed at almost any cost rather than accepted added to the dilemmas created by the changes they had to face.

10.2. Practical implications for the future

In Chapter 7 we examined some of the problems confronting Hindus facing long-term and terminal illness and the difficulties over hospital care, using the two Case Studies of Ramesh and Maya and Nalini as examples. Certain issues emerged from this chapter: quality of nursing care, problems of diagnosis and disclosure, communication and interpretation, and perceived racism. There may also be a conflict of interest between relatives who wish to perform the last rites at the deathbed and the medical staff who wish to maintain the peace and comfort of the patient and the ward.

Within an extended family in India there are several people who can help to care for a dying person, although this can be idealised and I have observed cases of severe neglect. Hospital patients are cared for by their own relatives and are frequently sent home to die. In Britain there may be a reluctance to send or take terminally ill patients home if there is some hope that the person can be helped by medical treatment. Home care is often impractical for working families, but it is important that the ideal model is recognised, and if Hindus wish to care for the dying at home, adequate services should be provided and families informed of the provisions that are available to them. Hospices, in principle, provide for the emotional and spiritual needs of dying patients, as well as providing space and care for relatives. Elderly Hindus may wish to fast at the end of life, and in a hospital setting this may be disturbing to nurses who see their function as providing nourishment and care. The importance of being conscious at death also has implications for pain control, and hospices are often best placed to deal with this problem. yet there is a low take-up of hospice places by Asian patients. There may be several reasons for this. If the hospices are religious foundations, it may be feared that there will be pressure to convert, or lack of sympathy for Hindu beliefs and practices and dietary and purity requirements. It may also be felt that a referral to a hospice is tantamount to a death sentence. Yet high quality palliative care, as championed by the hospice movement, places a premium on the holistic approach, which includes a spiritual dimension, and is thus particularly suitable for Hindus.

The holistic, patient-centred approach is already part of the Asian traditions we have been discussing, and Hindus have as much to contribute to an understanding of death and bereavement, as they have to receive from high quality care. It is vitally important, as palliative care develops, that it should be accessible to all sections of the community, regardless of age, diagnosis or ethnic group. The NCSPCS report, *Opening Doors*,[9] suggests that many general practitioners, the main gate-keepers, often do not refer Asian patients to hospice and palliative care services because they do not have the necessary information or think it appropriate. "They also do not at times listen sufficiently to their patients, either because they cannot understand what they are saying or because of other language difficulties, resulting in missed diagnosis and subsequent late referral to hospital."[10]

Many of the problems which arise in medical and nursing care are due to ignorance on both sides, stereotypical thinking and poor communication, issues which are raised repeatedly in the NCSPCS report. Blakemore and Boneham point out that ethnic minority patients themselves have to learn appropriate roles in a social process "involving social rules, values and a culture".[11] However, they emphasise that the medical staff, who may themselves come from ethnic minority groups, are equally products of their culture and not just rational, impartial or,

> 'affectively neutral' actors in relationships with patients, while the patients themselves are pictured as the ones bringing to the encounter emotion, pain, values and particular cultural attitudes - whether they are English, Welsh, Cypriot or Sikh. Yet we know, from sociological research ... that doctors have been observed to behave quite differently towards patients with the same kinds of medical condition as a result of the doctors' assessments of the social worth, personal behaviour or ethnic group of each patient.[12]

The problem of stereotyping Asian patients is also commented on by Patel as

---

[9] The report, *Opening Doors*, 1995, by the National Council for Hospice and Specialist Palliative Care Services (NCSPCS) notes that Asian women were particularly disadvantaged, both as patients and carers: "a heavy burden is also placed on the daughter-in-law, who, if the mother -in-law is the patient, has to do everything in the house and really cannot cope with the patient at home" p.37.

[10] NCSPCS report, *Opening* Doors, 1995:17.

[11] Blakemore and Boneham 1994:103-4.

[12] Blakemore and Boneham 1994:105.

having a racist dimension.[13] She cites comments by nurses very similar to those reported by Maya (7.1.2). Racist attitudes exist in individuals who may not be aware of them, but are also institutionalised.[14] At the individual level much of this is due to ignorance. I spent two days on informal research in a large general hospital in Westmouth talking to doctors and nurses who came into contact with Asian patients. Few of the doctors knew the difference between their Hindu, Muslim and Sikh patients (unless the latter wore a turban), and felt that they had no time to make a study of them in any case. This is not just a question of institutionalised racism, however, - it is a reflection of the pressure on doctors within the present structures, which allows for little time with any patients. The nurses made efforts to understand the needs of Asian patients, but had not, at that time, had any multicultural training. Booklets and check-lists on the needs of Asian patients may give some guidance in patient care, but may also reinforce stereotypes. Mcnamara and Waddell warn against the "stereotypical fallacy", of assuming that members of one cultural group share all the same beliefs, practices and needs.[15] Chapter 2 pointed out the enormous variations in language, culture, history and educational backgrounds among British Hindus. Not all Hindus want to die on the floor, for example - some who have grown up in the West do not even realise this is an Indian tradition. Patients may feel powerless and vulnerable, partly because their condition creates pain and fear, but also because of the authoritarian role of the medical staff, especially in a hospital setting. Communication and language difficulties exacerbate this. Blakemore and Boneham comment: "When the patient may feel stigmatised or unwanted, or is actually treated as such by hospital staff, the distress and bewilderment which often accompany hospitalization can be doubled."[16]

One of the most fundamental issues is communication, involving, at best, medical staff listening patiently to ensure that the problems are understood, and explaining the diagnosis and prognosis carefully to the patient and his or her family, to ensure everything is understood. This is not just an issue for Asian patients; it is a fundamental problem in all health-care relationships. Disclosure is often extremely difficult for doctors, especially those who have not come to terms with their own

13 Patel 1993:124-6.

14 Cf. Ahmed 1994:11ff.; Blakemore and Boneham 1994:103ff..

15 Mcnamara and Waddell 1997:155.

16 Blakemore and Boneham 1994:105.

anxieties about death, or who fear emotional upsets in their patients or their relatives. There is still little training in how to deal with this.[17].

In a cross-cultural context, as noted in Chapter 7, communication difficulties are exacerbated by different expectations, non-verbal signals, gender attitudes and different use of language and metaphors, requiring some knowledge of the patient's cultural background. It is essential to ensure that adequate and trained interpreters are available when necessary, who can not only deal with translating the language and medical terminology, but who also understand the cultural tradition on both sides. Often Hindu doctors are called upon to act as interpreters, which is not their function, but the use of family members can be problematical, as can volunteers from the community who, it is feared, might gossip. A system of trained patient advocates is particularly useful, but demands considerable resources in a multilingual society.

Western doctors also have to be aware, not only of the different metaphors which may be used to describe both psychological and physical conditions, as was seen in 9.1, but of the possibility that psychological distress may be somatised so that depression may not be recognised.[18] However, this has been challenged as too simplistic by some writers, who point out that patients may try to communicate in ways they believe to be acceptable to the doctor, and that both the patients and the professionals may be influenced by racism.[19] According to the NCSPCS report Asian doctors themselves may not show adequate respect to Asian patients, especially if they are of a different caste.[20]

Traditional Hindus are less likely to see themselves as autonomous individuals than members of a structured family unit, which may affect the way they respond to care, especially if the family is excluded from discussion about and involvement in their care. This is also true of other Asian traditions, as Mcnamara and Waddell show in an Australian study of white and Chinese Australians in which marked differences emerged in attitudes to autonomy. In contrast to white Australians, the

---

[17] On problems of disclosure, see Buckman 1993:172; Maguire and Faulkner 1993; 180-185; 186-191; Dickenson 1993:25ff.; Katz 1993:15-44.

[18] Kleinman 1986:51ff.; Ineichen 1993:184-6; cf. 16.1.

[19] Littlewood and Lipsedge 1993:258-260; Ahmed 1993:5.

[20] NCSPCS report, *Opening* Doors, 1995:17.

latter were found to have "tendencies to strict social hierarchy and family solidarity which includes the notion of filial piety or respect for elders; a more submissive and collectivist approach which discourages individualism and autonomy."[21] While such parallels should not be stretched tooo far, they illustrate differences in attitudea to autonomy and family structures which are also true of British South Asians which have an important bearing on the care of patients and their relatives. Discussion of treatment and issues of disclosure and attitudes to care have to take these differences into account, as well as the different ways of expressing feelings. Hospital staff may have problems dealing with emotional and noisy relatives, and one solution would be to set aside a room for the dying patient, and if requested, allow him or her to have a mattress on the floor. This can minimise the disruption caused by numbers of visitors and religious rituals. If communication is good, the need for restricting numbers can be explained, although this may take time. Blakemore and Boneham point out that the Asian model of hospital care in which the relatives do everything for the patient may be therapeutically sound, but they ask whether "patients' or health service consumers' representatives, including people from the minority ethnic communities, had ever been consulted about how visiting by large family groups could be best handled".[22] This needs a high degree of understanding and sensitivity, both at the administrative level and on the part of doctors and nurses caring for the patients.

A multicultural component in training and on in-service or post-graduate courses, particularly those on death and bereavement, can help to develop awareness not only for nurses and social workers, but for doctors as well. It has to include recognition of the spiritual and religious dimensions of patient needs which may be challenging to carers whose own world view does not include the possibility that there is continuity and life after death. However tolerant they try to be, they may find it difficult to enter imaginatively into a world that depends on such complex beliefs and practices as have been discussed in this work.

After death there can be a number of problems associated with the disposal of the body. In most areas deaths cannot be regestered at weekends or on bank holidays, causing further delays. This is a greater problem for Muslims, who, like Jews, wish

[21] Mcnamara and Waddell 1977:154.
[22] Blakemore and Boneham 1994:106.

to bury their dead immediately, and are deeply upset by the delays in Britain.[23] Although Hindus do not have the same intensity of feeling about post-mortems that Muslims do, there may be anxiety about them (7.2). Pathologists need to realise that the body will be bathed and dressed by relatives, and leave it as tidy as possible, as tubes left in place and crude stitching can be very upsetting.

Funeral directors usually do their best to accommodate their Hindu clients within the constraints of time and the practical arrangements of busy crematoria. However, neither they nor crematorium staff are always aware of the problems caused by the delays in arranging a cremation, perhaps because the Hindu community are not vociferous about their needs, and do not wish to draw undue attention to themselves. The new crematoria in Basingstoke and Bedford are designed with these requirements in mind, and Hindu run crematoria have opened in London and Leicester which may allow for quicker cremations. It is, after all, sound business sense to take into account ethnic minority needs in the services offered.

Employers also need to understand the requirements of Hindus to have enough time to mourn, even for relatives who, in white British society, might not be regarded as sufficiently close to permit time off. It is useful to note Eisenbruch's observation that the Puerto Rican immigrants in the United States believe the three days normally allowed by businesses for mourning are totally inadequate, interfering with their ability to grieve properly.[24] Allowing more time, however, can create problems for employers, especially those whose employees experience several bereavements within a short time. Dialogue and mutual understanding are necessary.

10.3. Concluding remarks

For Hindus death is not the end of life but a transition to another life, for which it is possible to prepare in advance through discipline, detachment and religious practice. A good death can be profoundly satisfying, both for the dying person and his or her family, assured of the safety and continuity of the soul of the deceased and the future well-being of the living who have done their duty. This seems to assist recovery,

---

[23] Interrestingly, this desire for immediate burial does not extend to those who want to take the body back to, e.g. Pakistan or Bangladesh, since there are inevitable delays in making the appropriate arrangements.

[24] Eisenbruch 1981 II:335.

whereas an unsatisfactory death can be devastating for the survivors. Eisenbruch shows that this is common to other expatriate communities, and advises professionals to take into account aspects such as "the fear of incomplete mourning [which] suggests a vulnerable point in the bereavement practices".[25] Professionals have a responsibility to their patients or clients, as they can make or break an otherwise good death and exacerbate a bad one, making the process of bereavement more straightforward or complicated.

Continuity with Indian traditions is maintained through the priests as well as through the older generation of relatives living here, and relatives in India with whom the British Hindus remain in contact; all of these are vital resources for information and guidance at the time of death. The *śrāddha*, more than the funeral and cremation, provides a strong thread of continuity with India and seems likely to continue to do so, especially when it is performed in conjunction with taking the ashes to the Ganga. Many Hindus, however, dispose of the ashes in British rivers for reasons of expense and convenience, and it remains to be seen whether this increases as more Hindus die in Britain.

Such links with India are an important way of maintaining Hindu identity, although Blakemore and Boneham point out that by doing so, Hindus risk retaining the status of an immigrant community rather than an autonomous minority like the Jewish community, defining "their aspirations and standard of living more in relation to their ancestral or old country than to the majority in the host country".[26] These links are also strengthened if money is sent to India and marriage partners are sought there for sons and daughters. Expectations are changing, particularly for women. It will be interesting to see in the next generation whether younger educated women, and widows in particular, have more freedom and opportunities than their Indian sisters.

Second or third generation Hindus who have not maintained their religious beliefs and practices may feel alienated and disorientated at the time of a death and uncomfortable with traditional expressions of grief, although it is at the time of death that the strength and social cohesion of the community is most evident. At the same time, many of them discover aspects of their faith of which they were unaware, and attempt to find a new 'language' which integrates traditional beliefs and practices

---

[25] Eisenbruch 1984 II:333.

[26] Blakemore and Boneham 1994:36.

and their own particular religious and spiritual insights with their experiences and life-style in Britain.

The Hindu model of a good death provides a useful philosophical approach to death at a time when there is a growing awareness, particularly in the hospice and palliative care movements, of the need to help people to find spiritual meaning in the experience of dying and to die with dignity. An experienced English counsellor said, "When I read accounts of Hindu approaches to death I felt sad to think how badly we had failed members of my own family who died recently."[27] For this reason, if for no other, the Hindu approach to death in all its dimensions: conceptual, spiritual, cognitive, ritual and social, can provide new insights and understanding. In a secular culture in which death is highly medicalised, there is a risk of seeking rational explanations for illness and death in terms of physical causes which can lead to a separation of religion from the rest of life and a devaluation of religious experience and spirituality, although in the hospice and palliative care movements there is a growth of interest in the latter. If death is not seen as inevitable, at least at the end of life, then there will not be opportunities for preparation. At the same time the lack of British expertise for helping enabling Hindus (and other ethnic minorities) to face death and bereavement in ways which are appropriate to their needs cannot be explained away by lack of funds or the argument of numbers. Hindu strategies for coping with death and bereavement can make a valuable contribution to cross-cultural studies of death and bereavement, and even if they do not claim it expressly, they have a right to be helped in situations of distress caused by death. They should be able to expect a level of care and recognition of their needs in line with our understanding of holistic principles which recognise the spiritual, social and emotional needs of both patient and families, which have always been part of the Hindu approach to death. Adaptation need not and should not be a one-way process: the host community also needs to adapt and learn.

---

[27] Cf. Firth 1989; 1993a.

Appendix
National Council of Hindu Temples (UK) Funeral Rite[1]

Introduction

Death is an unavoidable fact. This results in a lot of grief, emotional stress, shock and feelings of hopelessness and helplessness. In Sanatan Dharma, the last rites are very important facets of human life. They are to be performed in a particular way in order to provide peace to the departed soul and to provide chances for the near relatives to get actively and intimately involved by bringing them closely in contact with the remains of the departed soul. By doing so, they are being prepared to bear the shock by lessening the intensity of their grief to some extent. It is written in all ancient religious Scriptures that properly performed last rites provide peace to the departed soul and solace to the relatives. The following steps are taken to prepare the material remains for cremation:

1. The rites depend on time, place and circumstances. The body should be brought home from the funeral directors.

2. The dead body should be placed in such a way so that the head is towards the North and the feet towards the South;

3. The next of kin should be asked to come to perform the rites.

4. Light a *dīpak* (light) and place on the right side of the body in close proximity to its head.

5. Put some grain near the body by the *dīpak* (light).

6. The next of kin should be made to sit on the right side to offer *piṇḍas* to the departed soul. The *piṇḍas* consist of the mixture of what flour, linseed (*til*) and sugar. Six *piṇḍas* are offered to the body by placing them on the ground or on the chest. Nobody should cry at the time of *piṇḍa* ceremony. Six *piṇḍas* are meant for (the body, the exit door, the crossroads, the resting place, the cremation place, and the pyre) which are to be placed in the coffin box.

7. Then this *saṃkalpa* is recited:-
(Name)...(*gotra*)... *pretasya pretatva-nivṛtty-artham uttama-loka-prāpty-artham aurdhvadaihikaṃ kariṣye*
"I shall perform the funeral of the deceased X of lineage Y so that s/he may cease to be a *preta* and attain the highest world"

8. Then the next of kin takes flowers or dry grass straws (*kuśa*) to sprinkle water over the body. This *mantra* should be recited:-

> *Om. āpo hi ṣṭhā mayobhuvas tā na ūrje dadhātana / mahe raṇāya cakṣaṣe // yo vaḥ śivatamo rasas tasya bhājayateha naḥ / uśatīr iva mātaraḥ // tasmā araṃ gamāma vo yasya kṣayāya jinvatha / āpo janayathā ca naḥ //*

[1] Dermot Killingley has standardised the transliterations of the original service. Some of the original translations have also been modified.

(ṚV 10.9.1-2)
" Waters, you are refreshing; then fit us for nourishment, to see great joy. Let us partake of your most auspicious fluid, like willing mothers. Let us go to the aid of him for whose dwelling you enliven us, O waters, and give us birth."

9. Then put *tulasī* leaves in the Ganges water and pour some in the mouth of the body. Recite these mantras three times:-

Oṃ keśavāya namaḥ.
Oṃ nārāṇāya namaḥ.
Oṃ mādhvāya namaḥ

"*Oṃ*. Homage to Keśava (=Kṛṣṇa). *Oṃ*. Homage to Nārāyaṇa (=Viṣṇu).*Oṃ* Homage to Mādhava (=Kṛṣṇa)."

Put a *Tulasī mālā* around the neck of the body, put sandal paste on the forehead, and place sandalwood and sandal powder [on the body]. Then *ghī* offerings are made like the Agnihotra to the body reciting these mantras:-

Oṃ. prajāpataye svāhā. idaṃ prajāpataye na mama.
Oṃ. indrāya svāhā. idaṃ indrāya na mama.
Oṃ. agnaye svāhā. idaṃ agnaye na mama.
Oṃ. somāya svāhā. idaṃ somāya na mama.
Oṃ. yamāya svāhā. idaṃ yamāya na mama.
Oṃ. mṛtyave svāhā. idaṃ mṛtyave na mama.
Oṃ. brahmaṇe svāhā. idaṃ brahmaṇe na mama.

"*Oṃ*. To Prajāpati, *svāhā.*[2] This is for Prajāpati, it is not mine" (Similarly for Indra, Agni, Soma, Yama, Death, Brahman).
After this, three more offerings of *ghī* are made with these mantras:-

Oṃ bhūḥ svāhā. idaṃ agnaye na mama.
Oṃ. bhuvaḥ svāhā. idaṃ vāyave na mama.
Om. svaḥ svāhā. idaṃ sūryāya na mama.

"*Oṃ. bhūḥ svāhā.* This is for Agni, it is not mine. *Oṃ. bhuvaḥ svāhā.* This is for Vāyu [wind], it is not mine. *Oṃ. svaḥ svāhā.* This is for Sūrya [sun], it is not mine."

10. After this give the offering with the *havan samagrī* reciting this mantra:-

Om. āyur yajñena kalpatām. prāṇo yajñena kalpatām. cakṣur yajñena kalpatām. śrotraṃ yajñena kapatām. vāg yajñena kalpatām. mano yajñena kalpatām. ātmā yajñena kalpatām. brahmā yajñena kalpatām. pṛṣṭho yajñena kalpatām. yajño yajñena kalpatām.(VS 18.29).

" *Oṃ*. May life accord with the sacrifice. May breath accord with the sacrifice. May the eye accord with the sacrifice. May the ear accord with the sacrifice. May the voice accord with the sacrifice. May the mind accord with the

[2] *Svāhā,* often translated 'Hail!' is a ritual utterance spoken when placing an offering in the fire.

sacrifice. May the self accord with the sacrifice. May Brahman accord with the sacrifice. May the back accord with the sacrifice. May sacrifice accord with the sacrifice."

11. After this take a dry coconut, fill it with *til* [sesame] seeds and *ghī*, place it on the forehead and recite these mantras:-

asau svargāya lokaya svāhā (VS 35.22)[3]

"May he [be born again] into a heavenly world."

12. Pour *ghī dhara* and recite these mantras:-

oṃ. vasoḥ pavitram asi śata-dhāram. vasoḥ pavitram asi sahasra-dhāram. devas tvā savitā punātu vasoḥ pavitreṇa śatadhāreṇa supvā. kām adhukṣaḥ. svāhā. (VS 1.3)

Oṃ. You are Vasu's purifier with a hundred streams. You are Vasu's purifier with a thousand streams [addressing the strainer used for milk at the new-moon or full moon sacrifice]. May the god Savitṛ purify you with a cleansing purifier with a thousand streams [addressing the milk]. Which one did you milk [addressing the person who milks three cows for this sacrifice]? *Svāhā.*"

13. After this the body should be taken to the Cremation ground. On the way the following mantras should be recited:-

rām nām satya hai. hari oṃ tat sat. oṃ namaḥ śivāya.
ṣrī rāma jaya rāma jaya jaya rāma.

" Rāma's name is truth. Hari (=Viṣṇu) *Oṃ*, that is the true. *Oṃ*, homage to Śiva. Victory to Rāma."

Procedures at the cremation hall

These mantras are to be recited at the Cremation Hall before the body when the whole assembly sits down:-

1. *tryambakam yajāmahe sugandhiṃ puṣṭi-vardhanam / urvārukam iva bandhanān mṛtyor mukṣīya māmṛtāt //* (ṚV 7.59.12)

" We worship Tryambaka (=Rudra) the fragrant, who increases prosperity. As a melon from its stalk, may I be freed from death, not from deathlessness.

2. *tvam ādi-devaḥ puruṣaḥ purāṇas tvam asya viśvasya paraṃ nidhānam/ vettā 'si vedyaṃ ca paraṃ ca dhāma tvayā viśvam ananta-rūpa //* (BG 11.38)

"You are the eternal God, ancient being. You are the resting place of this universe. You are the knowledge, the knower and the supreme abode. You have infinite forms and you pervade the whole universe.

---

[3] The service book adds '*javaltu pavke*', which is not clear.

3. *vāsāṃsi jīrṇāni yathā vihāya navāni gṛhṇāti naro 'parāṇi / tathā śārīrāṇi vihāya jīrṇāny anyāni saṃyāti navāni dehī //* (BG 2.22)

"As a man leaves old garments and takes new ones so the soul leaves old bodies and goes to new ones.

4. *na jāyate mriyate vā kadācin nāyam bhūtvā bhavitā vā na bhūyaḥ / ajo nityaḥ śāśvato 'yaṃ purāṇo na hanyate hanyamāne śarīre //* (BG 2.20)

"It is never born, and never dies; once having been, it will not cease to be. Unborn, constant, eternal, ancient, it is not killed when the body is killed"

5. *nainaṃ chindanti śastrāṇi nainaṃ dahati pāvakaḥ / na cainaṃ kledayanty āpo na śoṣayati mārutaḥ //* (BG 2.23)

"Weapons cannot cut the soul, fire cannot burn it. Water cannot wet it and wind cannot make it dry."

6. *avyaktādīni bhūtāni vyakta-madhyāni bhārata / avyakta-nidhanāny eva tatra kā paridevanā //* (BG 2.28)

"The end and the beginning of being is unknown. We witness only the intervening manifestations. Then why should there be grief?"

7. *oṃ. ya ātma-dā bala-dā yasya viśva upāsate praśiṣam yasya devāḥ / yasya chayāmṛtaṃ yasya mṛityuḥ kasmai devāya haviṣā vidhema //* (ṚV 10.121.2).

"*Oṃ.* He who gives life, who gives strength, whose command all the gods revere, whose shadow is the immortal and the mortal - to what god shall we offer the oblation?"

8. *oṃ. sūrye cakṣur gacchatu vātam ātmā dyāṃ ca gaccha pṛthivīṃ ca dharmaṇā / apo vā gaccha yadi tatra te hitam oṣadhīṣu prati tiṣṭha śarīraiḥ //* (ṚV 10.16.3)

"*Oṃ.* May your eye go to the sun, your self to the wind; go to the sky and to the earth, in due order. Or go to the waters, if that has been ordained for you; take your place in plants with your body."

9. *Oṃ. śam agne paścāt tapa śaṃ purastāt śam uttarāc cham adharāt tapainam / ekas tredhā vihito jātavedaḥ samyag enaṃ dhehi sukṛtam u loke //* (AV 18.4.11)

"*Oṃ.* Agni, blaze peacefully on him in front, peacefully behind, peacefully above, peacefully blaze below. Agni, who are one and placed as three, place him rightly in the world of good deeds."

10. *Oṃ. saṃgacchasva pitṛbhiḥ śaṃ yameneṣṭāpurtena parame vyoman / hitvāyāvadyaṃ punar astam ehi saṃ gacchasva tanvāṃ suvarcāḥ //* (ṚV 10.14.8)

"Oṃ. Join with your fathers, with Yama, with your sacrifices and good deeds in the highest heaven. Leave what is bad and go back home; join with a body, radiant."

11. *Oṃ. vāyur anilam amṛtam athedaṃ bhasmāntaṃ śarīram / oṃ krato smara kṛtaṃ smara krato smara kṛtaṃ smara //* (*Īśā* Up.)

"*Oṃ*. Wind; immortal breath; and this body which ends in ashes. Oṃ, Power, remember what has been done, remember, Power, remember what has been done, remember."

12. *eka eva suhṛd dharmo nidhane 'py anuyāti yaḥ / śarīreṇa samaṃ nāśaṃ sarvam anyad dhi gacchati //* (*Manu* 8.17)

"*Dharma* is the one friend who follows one even in death; for everything else dies with the body."

13. *nir-māṇa-mohā jita-saṅgha-doṣā adhyātma-nityā vinivṛtta-kāmāḥ / dvandvair vimuktāḥ sukha-duḥkha-saṃjñair gacchanty amūḍhāḥ padam avyayaṃ tat //* (BG 4.2.22-24)

"Free from pride and delusion, victorious over the evil of attachment, dwelling constantly in the self, their desires having completely turned away freed from the pairs of opposites known as pleasure and pain, the undeluded reach the eternal goal."

14. *Oṃ. asato mā sad gamaya tamaso mā jyotir gamaya mṛityor mā 'mṛitaṃ gamaya //* (Bṛ Up. 1.3.28)

"*Oṃ*. From the unreal lead me to the real. From darkness lead me to light. From death lead me to immortality."

15. *Oṃ. dyauḥ śāntir antarikṣaḥ śāntiah pṛithvī śāntir āpaḥ śāntiḥ vanaspatayaḥ śāntir viśvedevāḥ ṣāntir brahma śāntiḥ sarvaṃ śāntiḥ śāntir eva śantiḥ sā mā śāntir edhi* (VS 36.17)

"*Oṃ*. The sky is peace, the atmosphere is peace, the earth is peace, the waters are peace, the trees are peace, the All-gods are peace, Brahman is peace, peace itself is peace. May I have peace."

Oṃ śāntiḥ śāntiḥ śāntiḥ. Oṃ namaḥ śivāya. Oṃ namaḥ śivāya. Oṃ namaḥ śivāya.

"*Oṃ*. Peace, peace, peace. *Oṃ*. Homage to Śiva. *Oṃ*. Homage to Śiva. *Oṃ*. Homage to Śiva."

Glossary of key terms

Sects have not been included as the principle ones are described in Ch. 2.1.

Agarbattī: incense.
Agni: fire, the god of fire.
Agni saṃskāra: sacrifice of the deceased to Agni.
akāla mṛityu: untimely death.
akhaṇḍ pāṭh: the continuous reading of the Sikh scripture, the Gurū Granth Sahib, over a period of forty-eight hours.
Akṣardhām: the heaven of Swāmīnārāyaṇa, a form of Viṣṇu.
Amṛta Varṣa: an Arya Samaj text written and compiled by *Puri et al.*, including poems from the Sikh Scripture, *Guru Granth Sahib,* and poems by Tusi Das and Kabir.
antyeṣṭi saṃskāra: the last *saṃskāra* or life cycle rite.
arghya: water used in the *śrāddha* ritual for purification.
ārtī: a ritual conducted at the end of worship in which a tray with a lighted lamp(s) rotated in front of the image(s).
ātman (Hindi *ātma*): the eternal spirit or soul, identified in the Upaniṣads with Ultimate Reality, Ātman or Brahman.
āśrama: one of the four stages of life for a Hindu man: student, householder, forest dweller and renouncer. Also a religious community or retreat.
asthisañcayana: rituals associated with the collection and disposal of the ashes.
avatāra: an incarnation of the divine, particularly associated with Viṣṇu, who appears on earth whenever there is unrighteousness. The most popular *avatāras* are Kṛṣṇa and Rāmā.
bhajans: religious songs or hymns.
bhakti: devotion, associated with devotional cults, with one of the three paths (*marga* or *yoga*) to salvation.
bhūmi-dāna: gift of land.
bhūta preta (*H. bhūt pret*): the unincorporated ghost of the dead.
Bhagvan: the supreme Lord.
brahmarandhra: the point at the top of the skull where the bones join, said to be the point from which the *ātman* leaves in an ideal death.
Brahmin: the purest and highest ranking of the four classes, *varṇas*. Not all Brahmins are pandits (priests), but priests have to be Brahmins.
Brahman: an impersonal neuter term for the Ultimate Reality underlying all phenomena.
Caitanya-mṛtyu: conscious death.
Chitragupta: Yama's scribe who records all an individual's good and bad deeds.
dakṣiṇā: the honorarium given to the pandit who officiates at a ritual.
dakṣiṇāyana: the six months of the year when the sun moves in its southern path
dāna (H.*dān*): an unreciprocated gift or offering which aquires merit for the giver.
darśana (H.*darśan*): looking at or being in the sight of a deity, an important part of religious ritual.

dharma: moral and religious law and duty. There are different types of *dharma* for different stages and roles.

dīvā, dīpā: Gj. *dīyā*: a *ghī* lamp.

duḥkha: sorrow.

ekoddiṣṭa śrāddha: *śrāddha* for one ancestor.

gangā-jal: Ganga water.

gārhasthya: housholdership, the second of the four *āśramas*.

Gāyatrī Mantra: an invocation to the sun considered to be particularly sacred. It is a very popular prayer from ṚV III.62.10, and is chanted when the coffin is brought to the home.

ghī: melted butter, regarded as exceptionally pure.

gō-dāna: the gift of a cow.

gotra: lineage.

guṇas: three elements or qualities forming the basis of matter or nature (*prakṛti*).

guru: a religious guide or teacher.

havan: the Vedic fire ceremony accompanying important rituals. It was popularised by Dayanand Saraswati and is used in Arya Samaj rituals.

Icchā: wish, will; *Icchā-mṛtyu*: willed death.

*jap:*the repetition of the name of a deity, *mantra* or sacred text.

jāti, Gj. *gnāti*, a caste group.

jivātman: the individual soul as distinct from Ātman/Brahman, the Ultimate Reality.

jñāna, H. *gyān:* knowledge, particularly the intuitive knowledge achieved through spiritual discipline.

kali yuga: the last of the four ages of the universe, said to be one of moral degeneration.

kapāla kriyā: the rite of breaking the skull by the chief mourner during the cremation.

karma: the causal moral law by which good deeds store up good effects and merit and bad deeds bad effects, particularly in the next life.

karma kāṇḍa: the pandit's ritual text according to a particular school.

khattri: a Panjabi merchant caste associating itself with *kṣatriya* status.

kismat: fate or luck (also *nasib*).

kṣatriya: the warrior and kingly class, the second *varṇa*.

kumbha: water pots used in rituals.

Kuśa/dharba: a sacred grass used in many rituals.

laukika: popular practice, not from the scriptures.

liṅgam (H. *liṅga, liṅg*): a stone phallus representing the creative power of Śiva.

loka (H. *lok*): one of the three worlds (heaven, earth and the underworld), but also one of many heavens. *Yama loka* is Yama's world, *pitṛ loka* is the abode of ancestors.

mahābrāhmaṇa: specialist funeral priest.

mandir: a Hindu temple, or the shrine in the house.

mantra: a short phrase or syllable, usually Sanskrit, used in worship or meditation.
mātā: mother, a term also used for the mother goddess.
mokṣa, mukti: liberation, salvation.
mṛtyu: death.
mukti: *mokṣa*, liberation from the *saṃsāra*, the cycle of birth and death.
mūrti: the divine image used as a focus for worship after being properly installed.
naraka loka: hell, or one of many hells.
nārāyaṇa bali: a powerful ritual performed after a 'bad' or unnatural death.
navarātri: the festival of nine nights in September/October in honour of the mother goddess, particularly popular among Gujaratis. In some regions it celebrates the story of Rāmā.
niyoga: a relationship between a young widow and the deceased husband's younger brother in order to produce heirs.
pagrī: turban.
pañcamṛta: a mixture of five items: milk, honey, *ghī*, sugar, yoghurt.
pañca-gavya: five sacred products of a cow: urine, cowdung, milk, yoghurt and *ghī*.
pañca-dāna: five gifts before or after death, including land, money, a cow, etc.
pañcaka: a set of five lunar asterisms in which it is very inauspicious to die, or to cremate a body.
pañcaka śānti: a rite to set at rest the ghost of on who died during *pañcaka*.
Paramātman: the Supreme Being, Ultimate Reality.
pati-vratā: a woman who has vowed to dedicate herself to her husband.
piṇḍa: a ball of rice, wheat or barley, mixed with substances like honey and *ghī* offered to the deceased. It also means 'embryo'.
piṇḍa dāna: the rite of giving the *piṇḍa*.
pitṛ: ancestor.
pitṛ pakṣa, the fortnight of the ancestors.
prāṇa: the breath of life. There are a number of these.
prāyaścitta: act of penance.
pradakṣiṇā: clockwise circumambulation of a deity or a corpse.
prasāda: food that is blessed by the deity and shared with the worshippers.
preta: the newly dead ghost before it becomes incorporated as an ancestor.
pūjak: the performer of rituals, the chief mourner in this book.
puṇya: merit.
pūjā: act of worship or homage before an image.
purohita: family pandit.
ṛṇa: sacred obligation or debt to the gods, the sages, the ancestors and mankind.
sadgati: a good end.
sādhāraṇ pāṭh: reading of the Sikh scripture, the Gurū Granth Sahib over a period of time - usually eight to ten days following a death.
Śakti: female personification of divine energy and power, usually seen in relation to Śiva.
saṃsāra: the cycle of birth, deth and rebirth.

saṃskāra: One of sixteen life cycle rites. *Anyeṣṭi saṃskāra* (H. *antim saṃskāra*) is the last rite at death.
saṃkalpa: a ritual declaration of intention.
Sann maran: good death.
sannyāsa (H. *sannyās*): the fourth stage of life; the abandonment of normal earthly ties in pursuit of liberation.
sannyāsī: an ascetic who has renounced all attachments, either early in life or as the fourth stage.
śantī: peace.
Śāstras: Authoritative texts including the Vedas but especially the law books *(dharmaśāstra)*.
Satī: a goddess symbolising the perfect woman. The term is also used for the voluntary act of immolation as such a woman becomes Satī on the pyre.
satī-strī: a good woman and perfect wife who is dedicated to her husband as a god.
satsaṅg: a gathering to sing hymns together and discuss religious texts.
śmaśāna: cremation ground.
śoka: grief, sorrow.
śrāddha: the rites for the dead which enable them to become ancestors.
śraddhā: faith.
śūdra: peasants/ labourers, the fourth of the four classes (*varṇas*). 'Untouchables' were a sub-group who performed unclean tasks.
sūtaka: a period of ritual impurity following death.
sūtra: a set of rules for rituals.
sūkta: a Vedic hymn.
svāhā: an exclamation made during ritual offerings which is thought to have divine power.
svarga: heaven.
tarpaṇa: a water libation to gods and ancestors.
thālī: a stainless steel or copper dish or small round tray used to contain several substances in rituals.
tithi: the anniversary of a death according to the lunar calender.
tulasī(H.*tulsī*): a type of basil which is sacred to the worship of Kṛṣṇa and Viṣṇu.
upanayana: the sacred thread ceremony initiating a Hindu male of the top three classes into twice-born status.
uttarāyaṇa: the northern path of the sun during the six months of the year following the winter solstice.
Vaikuṇṭha: Viṣṇu's heaven.
Vaiṣṇava: a devotee of Viṣṇu.
Vaitaraṇī nadi: the horrible river of death filled with blood and pus. The Vaitaraṇī cow tows the *preta* across it.
varṇa: the four great classes, *brāhmanas* (priestly class), *ḳsatriya* (kingly and warrior classes), *vaiśyas* (mercantile classes) and *śūdras* (labourers).

varṇāśramadharma: a term combining the concepts of class (*varṇa*) stage of life (*āśrama*), and duty/obligation (*dharma*), representing the system of life for each upper-class Hindu.

vaiśya: mercantile classes, the third of the four *varnas*.

Yama: the first mortal to die and originally ruler of svarga, heaven; later the terrifying king of the underworld, Yama Rājā.

Yamdūt: the mesenger of Yama.

yoga: a spiritual path or discipline. The three principle spiritual paths or margas are devotion (*bhakti*), knowledge (*jñāna*) and action (*karma*).

yuga: the ages of the universe.

Bibliography

Abbot, J., 1984, *Indian Ritual and Belief*, New Delhi, Usha Press.

Ahmed, Waqar, I.U. (ed.), 1993, *'Race' and Health in Contemporary Britain*, Buckingham, Open University Press.

Ainsworth-Smith, Ian and Peter Speck, 1982, *Letting Go: Caring for the Dying and Bereaved*, London, SPCK.

Albery, N. *et al.* (eds.), 1993, *The Natural Death Handbook*, London, Virgin.

Altekar, A.S. 1956, *The Position of Women in Hindu Civilization: From Prehistoric Times to the Present Day*, Delhi, Motilal Banarsidass.

Ariès, Philippe, 1974, *Western Attitudes to Death from the Middle Ages to the Present*, Baltimore, Johns Hopkins.

---1981, *The Hour of Our Death*, London, Peregrine Books.

Ariès, Philippe, 1974, *Western Attitudes to Death from the Middle Ages to the Present*, Baltimore, Johns Hopkins University Press.

---1981, *The Hour of Our Death*, London, Peregrine Books.

Ashby, P., 1974, *Modern Trends in Hinduism*, New York, Columbia University Press.

Āśvalāyana-Gṛhya-Sūtram, in *Gṛhya-Sūtras: Rules of Vedic Domestic Ceremonies*, SBE, 1892, Vol. XXIX; 1886, Vol XXX, tr. by Oldenburg, Herman, Delhi, Motilal Banarsidass,

Atharva-Veda-samhita, The, 1905, tr. by Whitney, William Dwight and C.R. Lanham, Harvard Oriental Series, Vol. VIII, ed. C.R. Lanman, Cambridge, Mass., Cambridge University Press.

Athavale, Parvati, 1986, *Hindu Widow: An Autobiography*, tr. by J.E. Abbott, New Delhi, Reliance Publishing House.

Badham, Paul (ed.), 1989, *Religion, State, and Society in Modern Britain*, Lampeter, Edwin Mellen Press.

Badham, Paul and Linda Badham (eds.), 1987, *Death and Immortality in the Religions of the World*, New York, Paragon House Publishers.

Balarajan, R. *et al.*,1984, 'Patterns of Mortality Among Migrants to England and Wales from the Indian Subcontinent', *British Medical Journal*, Vol. 289, 3 November 1984, pp. 1185-1187.

Balasubramanian, R., 1987, The Advaita View of Death and Immortality', in Badham, Paul and Linda Badham (eds.), pp. 109-127.

Ballard, Roger, 1986, 'Changing Life-styles among British Asians', *New Community*, Vol. 13, No.2, pp. 301-303.

---(ed.),1994, Desh Pardesh: *The South Asian Presence in Britain*, London, Hurst and Company.

Banerji, Brojendra Nath, 1979, *Hindu Culture, Custom and Ceremony*, Delhi, Agam Kala Prakasham.

Barker, Jonathan, 1984, *Black and Asian Old People in Britain*, Research Perspectives on Ageing, London, Age Concern Research Unit.

Barot, Rohit, 1980, 'The Social Organization of a Swaminarayan Sect in Britain', Unpublished PhD thesis, London, University of London (SOAS).

---1987, 'Caste and sect in the Swaminarayan movement' in Burghart, Richard (ed.), pp. 67-80.

---(ed.), 1993, *Religion and Ethnicity: Minorities and Social Change in the Metropolis*, Kampon, Kok Pharos.

Barot, Rohit, Harriet Bradley and Steve Fenton 1997-8, *Ethnicity, Gender and Social Change*, Macmillan.

Barz, R, 1976, *The Bhakti Sect of Vallabhacharya*, Faridabad, Thompson Press.

Basham, A.L., 1967, *The Wonder That Was India*, London, Sidgewick and Jackson.

Bayly, C.A., 1981, 'From ritual to ceremony: death ritual and society in Hindu North India Since 1600' in Whalley, Joachim (ed.), pp. 154-186.

Bennett, P.J., 1983, 'Temple Organization and Worship among the Pustimargiya-Vaisnavas of Ujjain', unpublished PhD thesis, London, University of London (SOAS).

Berger, Arthur, Paul Badham, Austin H. Kutscher, Joyce Berger, Michael Perry and John Beloff, (eds.), 1989, *Perspectives on Death and Dying: Cross-cultural and Multi-disciplinary Views*, Philadelphia, Charles Press.

Berger, Peter, 1969, *The Social Reality of Religion*, London, Faber and Faber.

Berger, Peter and Arthur Luckman, 1967, *The Social Construction of Reality: A Treatise on the Sociology of Knowledge*, Harmondsworth, Penguin Books.

Bhachu, Parminder, 1985, *Twice Migrants: East African Sikh Settlers in Britain*, London, Tavistock Press.

Bhadwar, Inderjit, 1986, 'Varanasi: The dues of death' in *India Today*, April 15, 1986, pp. 72-80.

Bhagavad Gita, The, 1962, tr. by Mascaró, Juan, Harmondsworth, Penguin

Bhagavad Gita, The, 1948, tr. By Radhakrishnan, Sarvapalli, 1948, New York, Harper & Bros.

Bharati, Agehananda, 1972, *The Asians in East Africa*, Chicago, Nelson Hall.

---1976, 'Ritualistic tolerance and ideological rigour: The paradigm of the expatriate Hindus in East Africa', *Contributions to Indian Sociology*, (NS) Vol. 10 No, 2 (1976), pp. 317-339.

Bijlert, Victor A. van, 1989, 'Hindus in the Netherlands', in *South Asia Newsletter*, No 3, August 1989, pp. 16-21.

Black, John, 1987, 'Broaden Your Mind About Death and Bereavement in Certain Ethnic Groups in Britain', *British Medical Journal*, Vol. 295, Aug. 29, 1987, pp. 536-539.

Blakemore, Ken and Margaret Boneham (eds.), 1993, *Age, Race and Ethnicity: A Comparative Approach*, Rethinking Ageing Series, Buckingham, Open University Press.

Bloch, Maurice and Jonathan Parry (eds.), 1982, *Death and the Regeneration of Life*, Cambridge, Cambridge University Press.

Borman, William A., 1989, Upanishadic eschatology: the other side of death', in Berger, Arthur, *et al.* (eds.), pp. 89-100.

Bowen, David (ed.), 1981, *Hinduism in England*, Bradford College.

---1987, 'The evolution of Gujarati Hindu organizations in Bradford', in Burghart, Richard (ed), pp. 15-31.

Bowes, Pratima, 1982, *Between Cultures*, New Delhi, Allied Publishers Private Ltd.

Bowker, John, 1970, *Problems of Suffering in the Religions of the World*, Cambridge, Cambridge University Press.

---1983, *Worlds of Faith: Religious Belief and Practice in Britain Today*, London, BBC, Ariel Books.

---1991, *The Meanings of Death*, Cambridge, Cambridge University Press.

Bowlby, John, 1961, 'Processes of Mourning', *International Journal of Psycho-Analysis*, Vol. 42, pp. 44:317.

---1969, *Attachment and Loss*, 1972, Vol.1, *Attachment*; 1980, Vol. 2, *Separation: Anxiety and Anger*; Vol. 3, *Loss, Sadness and Depression*, London, Hogarth.

Bradbury, Mary, 1993, 'Contemporary representations of "good" and "bad" death', in Dickenson, Donna and Malcolm Johnson (eds.), pp. 68-71.

Brockington, John, 1981, *The Sacred Thread: Hinduism in its Continuity and Diversity*, Edinburgh, Edinburgh University Press.

Buckman, Robert, 1993, 'Why is breaking bad news so difficult?' in Dickenson, Donna and Malcolm Johnson (eds.), pp. 172-179.

Burghart, Richard, (ed.) 1987, *Hinduism in Great Britain: The Perpetuation of Religion in an Alien*

Cultural Milieu, London, Tavistock.
--- 1987a 'Introduction: the diffusion of Hinduism to Great Britain' in Burghart, Richard (ed.), pp. 1-14.
—1987b: 'The Perpetuation of Hinduism in an alien cultural milieu', in Burghart, Richard (ed.), pp. 224-251.
Burke, Aggrey, (ed.), 1983, *Transcultural Psychiatry: Racism and Mental Illness,* 30th Anniversary Double Issue of the International Journal of Social Psychiatry, Vol 30, 1-2.
Carey, Séan, 1987, 'The Indianization of the Hare Krishna movement in Britain', in Burghart, Richard (ed.), pp. 81-99.
Carstairs, G.M., 1955, 'Attitudes to death and suicide in an Indian cultural setting', International Journal of Social Psychiatry, pp. 33-41.
---1958, *The Twice Born: a Study of a Community of High Caste Hindus*, Bloomington, Indiana University Press.
Chadha, Prem Nath, 1978, *Hindu Law*, Lucknow, Eastern Book Co., 4th ed. 1974 with 1978 supplement.
Chen, Marty and Jean Drèze, 1992, *Widows and Well-Being in Rural North India*, London, The Development Economics Research Programme, London School of Economics, No 40.
Clark, David, (ed.) 1993, *The Future for Palliative Care: Issues of Policy and Practice*, Milton Keynes, Open University Press.
Clarke, Colin, Ceri Peach and Steven Vertovec (eds.), 1990, *South Asians Overseas: Migration and Ethnicity*, Cambridge, Cambridge University Press.
Cole, W. Owen and Piara Singh Sambhi, 1978, *The Sikhs, Their Religious Beliefs and Practices*, London, Routledge and Kegan Paul.
Connolly, Peter and Sue Hamilton (eds.), 1997, *Indian Insights: Buddhism, Brahminism and Bhakti*, (Papers from the Annual Spalding Symposium in Indian Religions), London, Luzac Oriental).
Currer, Caroline, 1983, 'Pathan women in Bradford: factors affecting mental health with particular reference to the effects of racism', in Burke, Aggrey (ed.), pp. 72-76.
Dandavate, Pramila, Ranjana Kumari and Jamila Verghese (eds.), 1989, *Widows, Abandoned and Destitute Women in India*, New Delhi, Radiant Publishers.
Datta, V.N., 1988, *Sati: A Historical, Social and Philosophical Enquiry into the Hindu Rite of Widow Burning*, New Delhi, Manohar Publications.
Das, Veena, 1976, 'The uses of liminality: society and cosmos in Hinduism', *Contributions to Indian Sociology* (NS), Vol. 10. No. 2 (1976), pp. 245-263.
---1977, *Structure and Cognition: Aspects of Hindu Caste and Ritual*, Delhi. Oxford University Press.
Dasgupta, Surendra Nath, 1921-52, *A History of Indian Philosophy,* 5 Vols.,Cambridge, Cambridge University Press.
Denton, Lynn Teskey, 1991, 'Varieties of Hindu female asceticism', in Leslie, Julia (ed.), pp.211-231.
Derrett, C.M.H.L, 1970, *A Critique of Modern Hindu Law*, Bombay, N.H. Tripathi,
Derrett, J.D.M., 1979, 'Unity in Diversity: The Hindu Experience', *Bharata Manusha*, Vol. V.1, April 1979, pp. 21-36.
Desai, R.1963, *Indian Immigrants in Britain*, London, Oxford University Press.
Deussen, Paul, 1972 (1905), *The Philosophy of the Upanisads, Sacred Books of the Aryans, II.*, 1972, Delhi, Oriental Publishers.
Dhavamony, Mariasusai, 1987, 'Death and immortality in Hinduism', in Badham, Paul and Linda Badham (eds.), pp. 93-108.

Dickenson, Donna, 1993, *Preparing for Death,* Death and Dying, Workbook 2, Milton Keynes, Open University, Department of Health and Social Welfare.

Dickenson, Donna, and Malcolm Johnson (eds.), 1993, *Death and Dying*, London, Sage.

Donaldson, Liam and Marie Johnson, 1990, 'Elderly Asians', in McAvoy, Brian and Liam J. Donaldson (eds.), pp. 237-249.

Donovan, Jenny, 1986, 'Black people's health: a different approach', in Rathwell, Thomas and David Phillips (eds.), pp. 117-136.

Douglas, M., 1966, *Purity and Danger: an Analysis of Concepts of Pollution and Taboo*, New York, Praeger.

Drèze, Jean, 1990, *Widows in Rural India*, London, The Development Economics Research Programme, London School of Economics, No 26.

Drury, Naama, 1981, *Sacrificial Ritual in the Satapatha Brahmana*, Delhi, Motilal Banarsidas.

Dube, S.C., 1965, *Indian Village,* London, Routledge and Kegan Paul.

Dubois, Abbe J.A., 1906 (1816), *Hindu Manners, Customs and Ceremonies*, tr. by Henry K. Beachamp, Oxford, Clarendon Press, 3d Edition..

Dumont, Louis, 1972, *Homo Hierarchicus: The Caste System and its Implications*, London, Weidenfeld and Nicholson.

---1983, 'The debt to ancestors and the category of sapinda', in Malamoud, Charles (ed.) pp. 1-20.

Dumont, Louis and David Pocock, 1959, 'Pure and impure', *Contributions to Indian Sociology* (NS), 5, pp. 58-78.

Durkheim, Emile, 1961, *The Elementary Forms of Religious Life*, tr. by J. Swain, New York, Free Press, first published 1912.

Dvivedi, J.P. (ed.), 1973, *Sri Sraddhakaumudi Sutaka Nirnaya Samhita*, Surat, B.J. Dvivedi.

Dwyer, Rachel, 1994, 'Caste, religion and sect in Gujarat: followers of Ballabhacharya and Swaminarayan,' in Ballard, R. (Ed.), London, C. Hurst & Co.

Eck, Diana L, 1983, *Banaras: City of Light,* London, Routledge and Kegan Paul.

Eisenbruch, Maurice, 1984a, 'Cross-cultural aspects of bereavement I: a conceptual framework for comparative analysis', *Culture, Medicine andPsychiatry* Vol. 8 No.3, September, pp. 283-309.

---1984b, 'Cross-cultural aspects of bereavement II: ethnic and cultural variations in the development of bereavement practices', *Culture, Medicine and Psychiatry* Vol. 8 No.4, December, pp. 315-347.

Eliade, Mircea, 1977, 'Mythologies of death: an introduction' in Reynolds, Frank E. and Earle H. Waugh (eds.), pp. 13-23.

---'Rites of Passage', 1987 in *Encyclopedia of Religion*, Eliade, M. (ed.), New York: Macmillan.

Embree, Ainslie, 1994, 'Widows as cultural symbols', in Hawley, John Stratton (ed.), pp.149-158.

Evison, Gillian, 1989, 'Indian Death Rituals: The Enactment of Ambivalence', unpublished DPhil thesis, Oxford, Oxford University.

Feifel, Herman, (ed.), 1965, *The Meaning of Death*, New York, McGraw Hill Paperback Edition.

Ferro-Luzzi, (ed.), 1990, *Rites and Beliefs in Modern India*, Delhi, Manohar.

Field, David and N. James, 1993, 'Where and How People Die', in Clark, David (ed.), pp. 6-29.

Firth, Shirley, 1988, 'Asian women and changing marriage patterns', for *World Religions in Education: Women in Religion*, Shap.

---1989, 'The good death: approaches to death, dying and bereavement among British Hindus', In Berger, Arthur *et al.* (eds.), 1989 pp. 66-83.

---1991, 'Changing patterns of Hindu death rituals in Britain,' in Killingley, Dermot, Werner Menski and Shirley Firth, pp. 51-84.

---1993a, 'Approaches to death in Hindu and Sikh communities in Britain', in Dickenson, Donna, and Malcolm Johnson (eds.), pp.26-32.

---1993b, 'Multicultural appraches to bereavement,' in Dickenson, Donna and Malcolm Johnson

(eds.), pp.254-261.
---1993c, 'Cultural issues in terminal care', in Clark, David, (ed.), pp. 98-110.
---1994, 'Death, Dying and Bereavement in a British Hindu Community', unpublished PhD thesis, London, School of Oriental and African Studies.
---1995, 'The good death: attitudes of British Hindus.', 1995 in Jupp, Peter, and Glennys Howarth (eds.), pp. 96-107.
---1997/8, 'Hindu widows,' in Barot, Rohit, Steve Fenton and Harriet Bradley (eds.)
Flood, Gavin, 1996, *An Introduction to Hinduism*, Cambridge, Cambridge University Press.
Freemantle, Francesca and Chogyal Trungpa (tr.), 1975, *The Tibetan Book of the Dead: The Great Liberation Through Hearing in the Bardo*, by Guru Rinpoche according to Karma Lingpa, Boulder and London, Shambala.
Freud, S, 1917, *On Mourning and Melancholia*, reprinted in *On Metapsychiatry, The Theory of Psychoanalysis*, Pelican Books, 1984, reprinted in 1987.
Fuller, C.J., 1992, *The Camphor Flame: Popular Hinduism and Society in India*, Princeton, N.J., Princeton University Press.
---1984, *Servants of the Goddess: the Priests of a South Indian Temple*, Cambridge, Cambridge University Press.
Ganapati, R.,1981, *Baba Sathya Sai: His Early Life and Subsequent Life Through his Devotees' Lives,* from the Tamil book *Svami,* by H. Ramamorthy and R. Ganapathy, Madras, Satya Jyoti.
Gandhi, M.K., 1958, *Women*, Ahmedebad, Navajivan Publishing House.
Garuḍa Purāṇa, Part II, 1979, Part III, 1980: tr. by a board of scholars, Varanasi, Motilal Banarsidass.
Garuḍa Purāṇa (Sāroddhāra) with English translation, 1911, tr. by Good, E. and S. Subrahmanyam, Sacred Books of the Hindus v. IX, Allahabad, Sudhindra Natha Vasu.
Geertz, Clifford, 1966, 'Religion as a cultural system' in *Anthropological Approaches to the Study of Religion*,. M. Banton (ed) London, Tavistock.
---1973, *Interpretation of Culture*, New York, Basic Books.
Glasenapp, Helmuth von, 1984, *Doctrines of Vallabhacharya*, tr. by Amin, Ishverbhai, Baroda, Shri Vallabha Publications.
Glaser, B.G. and A. Strauss, 1965, *Awareness of Dying*, Chicago, Aldine Publishing Co..
---1968, *Time for Dying*, Chicago, Aldine Publishing Co..
Glucklich, Ariel, 1984, 'Karma and pollution in Hindu dharma: distinguishing law from nature', in *Contributions to Indian Sociology* (NS) 18.1, 1984, pp. 25-43.
Gold, Ann Grodzins, 1988, *Fruitful Journeys: the Ways of Rajasthani Pilgrims*, Berkeley: University of California Press.
Gonda, Jan, 1975, *Vedic Literature (Saṃhitas and Brāhmaṇas)*, Weisbaden, Otto Harrassowitz.
---1977, *The Ritual Sūtras*, (A History of Indian Literature, Vol. I facs. 2), Weisbaden, Otto Harrassowitz.
---1980, *Vedic Ritual: the Non-solemn Rites*, Leiden-Köln, E Brill.
Goody, Jack, 1962. *Death, Property and the Ancestors*, Stanford, CA, Stanford University Press.
Gorer, Geoffrey, 1965, *Death, Grief and Mourning,* London, Cresset.
Gough, Kathleen E., 1958, 'Cults of the Dead Among the Nayars', *Journal of American Folklore*, Vol.71, pp. 446-78.
Green, Jennifer, 1991, *Death with Dignity: Meeting the Spiritual Needs of Patients in a Multi-cultural Society,* 2 Vols., Nursing Times, London, Macmillan Magazines Ltd.
Green, J. and Green, M., 1992, *Dealing with Death: Practice and Procedures*, London, Chapman

and Hall.
Grof, Stanislav and Joan Halifax, 1977, *The Human Encounter With Death*, London, Souvenir Press (E & A) Ltd.
Grove, Kanta 1990, *Burning Flesh*, New Delhi, Vikas Publications.
Gupta, A.R. 1982, *Women in Hindu Society: A Study of Tradition and Transition*, New Delhi, Jyotsna Prakashan.
Hawley, John Stratton (ed.), 1994, *Sati, the Blessing and the Curse: The Burning of Wives in India*, Oxford, Oxford University Press.
Henley, Alix, 1979, *Asian Patients in Hospital and at Home*, London, King Edward's Hospital Fund for London.
Hertz, Robert, 1960 (1909), *Death and the Right Hand*, tr. by R. and C. Needham, with an introduction by Evans-Pritchard, New York, New York Free Press.
Hiriyanna, M., 1932, *Outlines of Indian Philosophy*, London, George Allen and Unwin.
---1985 (1949), *Essentials of Indian Philosophy*, London, George Allen and Unwin..
Hockey, H., 1996a, 'The view from the West: Reading the anthropology of non-western death ritual', in Howarth, Glennys and Peter Jupp, (eds.).
----1996b, 'Accounting for the time of bereavement', unpublished paper.
Howarth, Glennys and Peter Jupp, (eds.). 1996, *Contemporary Issues in the Sociology of* Death, *Dying and Disposal*, London, Macmillan.
Humphrey, Christmas, 1970, *The Wisdom of Buddhism*, London, Rider and Co.
Huntington, Richard and Peter Metcalf, 1979, *Celebrations of Death: The Anthropology of Mortuary Ritual*, Cambridge, Cambridge University Press.
Ineichen, Bernard, 1993, 'Responding to adversity: Mental illness, religion and social change among British Asians', in Barot, Rohit (ed.), pp. 183-195.
Irish, Donald P., Kathleen F. Lundquist and Vivian Jenkins Nelson (eds.), 1993, *Ethnic Variations in Dying, Death and Grief*, Bristol, PA, Taylor and Francis Inc.
Jackson, Edgar N., 1965, 'Grief and religion' in Feifel, Herman (ed.), *The Meaning of Death*, New York, McGraw Hill Paperback, pp. 218-233.
Jackson, Robert and Dermot Killingley, 1988, *Approaches to Hinduism*, London, John Murray.
Jackson, Robert and Eleanor Nesbitt, 1993, *Hindu Children in Britain*, Stoke-on-Trent, Trentham Books.
Jones, Kenneth W., 1976, *Arya Dharm: Hindu Consciousness in 19th Century Punjab*, Berkeley, University of California Press.
Joshi, Ramashankar, 1970, *Sraddha Kalpadrum*, Surat, Harihar Pustakalaya.
Jung, Carl G., 1961, *Modern Man in Search of a Soul*, London, Routledge and Kegan Paul Ltd., first published in 1933.
---1965, 'The soul and death', in Herman Feifel (ed.), pp. 3-15.
Kakar, Sudhir, 1978, *The Inner World: A Psychoanalytic Study of Childhood and Society in India*, Delhi, Oxford University Press.
---1990. 'Stories from Indian psychoanalysis: context and text', in Stigler, James W. *et al.*, (eds.), pp. 427-443.
Kalsi, Seva Singh, 1992, *The Evolution of a Sikh Community in Britain: Religious and Social Change Among the Sikhs of Leeds and Bradford*, Monograph Series, Community Religions Project Collection, Leeds, Department of Theology and Religious Studies, University of Leeds.
---1996, 'Funeral rites of the Sikhs in Britain', unpublished paper given at a conference on The Social Context of Death, Dying and Disposal, Mansfield College, Oxford, April 1993.
Kaminer, H. and Lavie, P, 1993, 'Sleep and dreams in well-adjusted holocaust survivors', in Stroebe, M. (eds.) *et al.*

Kane, P.V., *History of the Dharmashastra*, 1941-1953, in five Vols., Poona, Bhandarkar Oriental Research Institute.

---1973, Kane, P.V., *History of the Dharmashastra*, Vol. IV, 2nd ed., Poona, Bhandarkar Oriental Research Institute.

Kanitkar, V.P. (Hemant), 1984, *Hindu Festivals and Sacraments*, Barnet, Kanitkar.

Kapur, B.L., 1984, *Hanuman Chalisa: The Desert of Grace,* New Delhi, Trimurti Publications.

Katz, Jeanne, 1993, *Caring for Dying People*, Death and Dying, Workbook 3, Milton Keynes, Open University, Department of Health and Social Welfare.

Katz, Jeanne, Alison Peberdy and Moyra Siddell, *Life and Death,* Death and Dying, Workbook 1, Milton Keynes, Open University, Department of Health and Social Welfare.

Kaushik, Meena, 1976. 'The Symbolic representation of death', *Contributions to Indian Sociology* (NS) Vol. 10 No. 2 (1976), pp. 265-292.

Keith, Arthur Berriedale, 1925, *The Religion and Philosophy of the Vedas and Upanishads*, Harvard Oriental Series, Vol 32, Cambridge Mass., Harvard University Press.

Khare, R.S. 1976, *The Hindu Hearth and Home*, New Delhi, Vikas.

Killingley, Dermot H., 1985, 'Unity and diversity, change and continuity', *Understanding the Hindu Tradition: Papers of the third 'York Shap' Conference*, York, Shap, York Religious Education Centre, The College, York. pp. 3-11.

---1991a, 'Introduction', in Killingley, Dermot, Werner Menski and Shirley Firth, pp. 1-6.

---1991b 'Varna and caste in Hindu apologetic' in Killingley, Dermot, Werner Menski and Shirley Firth, pp. 1-31

---1992, 'The paths of the dead and the dive fires', paper presented at the Indian Symposium, Oxford.

Killingley, Dermot, Werner Menski and Shirley Firth, 1991, *Hindu Ritual and Society*, Newcastle upon Tyne, S.Y. Killingley.

Kingsley, David R., 1973, '"The death that conquers Death": dying to the world in medieval Hinduism', in Reynolds, Frank. E and Earle H. Waugh (eds.), pp. 7-110.

Klass, D., 1988, *Parental Grief: Solace and Resolution*, New York, Springer Publication Co.

Klein, Melanie, 1940, 'Mourning and its relationship to manic depressive states', *International Journal of Psycho-analysis,* Vol. 21, pp. 125-153.

Kleinman, Arthur, 1977, 'Depression, somatization and the "new cross-cultural psychiatry"', *Social Science and Medicine*, Vol. 11 pp. 3-10.

---1980, *Patients and Healers in the Context of Culture*, Berkeley, University of California Press.

Knipe. D.M., 1977, '*Sapiṇḍīkaraṇa*: The Hindu rite of entry into heaven.' in Reynolds, Frank E. and Earle H. Waugh (eds.), pp. 112-124.

Knott, Kim, 1986a, *Hinduism in England: The Hindu Population in Leeds*, Department of Sociology, Religious Research Papers, Leeds, University of Leeds.

---1986b, *Hinduism in Leeds: A Study of Religious Practice in the Indian Hindu Community and in Hindu Related Groups*, Monograph Series, Community Religions Project, Leeds, Department of Sociology and Religious Studies, University of Leeds.

---1986c, *My Sweet Lord: The Hare Krishna Movement*, Wellingborough, Aquarian Press.

---1987, 'Hindu temple rituals in Britain: the reinterpretation of tradition' in Burghart, Richard (ed.), pp. 157-179.

---1989, 'The Hindu community in Britain' in Badham, Paul (ed.), pp. 243-258.

Krause, Inga-Britt, 1989, 'Sinking heart, a Panjabi communication of distress', in *Social Science and Medicine,* Volume 29, No.4, pp. 563-575.

Krishnakumari, N.S., 1988, *Status of Single Women in India* (*A Study of Spinsters, Widows and*

Divorcees), New Delhi, Uppal Publishing House.
Kübler-Ross, Elisabeth, 1970, *On Death and Dying,* London, Tavistock.
---1975, *Death: The Final Stage of Growth*, London, Prentice Hall.
Laungani, Pittu, 1996, 'Death and berevement in India and England: a comparative analysis' in *Mortality,* Vol.1. No.2, July.
---1997, 'Death in a Hindu family', in Parkes, Laungani and Young, pp. 52-72
Leicester Mercury, July 31, 1997
---1997, 'Death in a Hindu family', in Parkes, Murray, Pittu Laungani and Bill Young, pp.52-72.
Leslie, Julia, 1987/88, 'Suttee or Sati: victim or victor?', *Bulletin of Center for the Study of World Religions,* Harvard University, Vol.14, No.2, pp. 5-24.
---1989, *The Perfect Wife: The Orthodox Hindu Woman According to the Stridharmapaddhati of Tryambkayajvan,* Delhi, Oxford University Press.
---(ed.), 1991a, *Roles and Rituals for Hindu Women*, London, Pinter.
---1991b, 'Religion, gender and *dharma*: the case of the widow-ascetic', British Association for the Study of Religion, Occasional Papers 4.
Lingat, Robert, 1973, *The Classical Law of India*, Berkeley, University of California Press.
Long, J. Bruce, 1977, 'Death as a necessity and a gift in Hindu mythology', in Reynolds, Frank E. and Earle H. Waugh (eds.), pp. 71-96.
---1981, 'The concepts of action and rebirth in the Mahabharata', in O'Flaherty, Wendy (ed.), pp.38-62.
Madan, T.N., (ed.), 1982, *Way of Life: King, Householder, Renouncer*, Delhi, Vikas Publishing House.
---1987, *Non-renunciation: Themes and Interpretations of Hindu Culture,* Oxford, Oxford University Press.
Maguire, Peter and Ann Faulkner, 1993, 'Communicating with cancer patients: 1. Handling bad news', pp. 180-185; 'Communicating with cancer patients'; 2. 'Handling uncertainty, collusion and denial, pp. 186-191, in Dickenson, Donna and Malcolm Johnson (eds.).
Malamoud, Charles (ed.), 1983, 'The theology of debt in Brahmanism' in Malamoud, Charles (ed.), pp. 21-40.
Mandelbaum, David, 1965, 'Social uses of funeral rites', in Feifel, Herman, (ed.), pp. 189-217.
---1970, *Society in India*, 2 Vols., Berkeley, University of California Press.
Marriott, McKim (ed.), 1955, *Village India: Studies in the Little Community*, London, Chicago University Press.
McAvoy, Brian R. and Liam J. Donaldson, 1990, *Health Care for Asians*, Oxford, Oxford University Press.
McAvoy, Brian R. and Akram Sayeed, 1990, 'Communication', in McAvoy, Brian and Liam J. Donaldson (eds.), pp. 57-71.
McGirk, Tim, 1991. 'Politicians falter before the keeper of death', *The Independent*, May 17, p.15.
---1992, City of widows', *The Independent Magazine,* 29 August, 1992, pp. 29-33.
Mcnamara, Beverley, 1997a, 'The "good enough" death in hospice and palliative care': paper given at the 3rd International Conference on the Social Context of Death, Dying and Disposal, Cardiff.
McNaught, Allan 1990, 'Organization and Delivery of Care', in McAvoy, Brian, and Liam J. Donaldson (eds.), pp. 31-39.
Menski, Werner 1984, 'Role and Ritual in the Hindu Marriage', unpublished PhD thesis, London, London University (SOAS).
---1987, 'Legal pluralism in the Hindu marriage' in Burghart, Richard (ed.), pp. 180-200.
---1987, 'Is there a customary form of widow-remarriage for Hindus?' Kerala Law Times, pp.69-71
---1991, 'Change and continuity in Hindu marriage rituals' in Killingley, Dermot, Werner Menski and

Shirley Firth, pp. 32-51.
---1995, 'Widow's right to property: prejudices against remarried Women', in Manushi,V.I. 89, July, August, 1995.
---1996, Review of Hawley, John Stratton (ed.), 1994, in *The Bulletin of South Asian Studies.*
Michaelson, Maureen, 1983, 'Caste, Kinship and Marriage: A Study of Two Gujarati Trading Castes in England', unpublished PhD thesis, London, University of London, SOAS.
---1987, 'Domestic Hinduism in a Gujarati trading caste' in Burghart, R., (ed.), pp. 32-49.
Mines, Diana Paul, 1989, 'Hindu periods of death "impurity"', *Contributions to Indian Sociology*, (NS) 23, No. 1, pp. 103-130.
Mishra, Neerja (1989), 'The murder of Roop Kanwar' in Dandavate, Pramila *et al.*,
Monier-Williams, 1884, *Brahminism and Hinduism*, London, John Murray.
---1876, 'Sraddha ceremonies at Benares and Gaya', in *Indian Antiquary* V, pp. 200ff.
---1899, *A Sanskrit-English Dictionary*, Oxford, Clarendon Press, 2nd ed.
Moffatt, B., 1968, 'Funeral Ritual in South India', Unpublished B. Litt thesis, Oxford, Oxford University.
Murphet, Howard, 1971, *Sai Baba: Man of Miracles*, London, Muller.
Nandy, Ashis 1994, 'Sati as profit versus sati as a spectacle: the public debate on Roop Kanwar's death', in Hawley (ed.), pp. 131-149.
National Council for Hindu Temples (UK), 1987, *Hindu Funeral Rites*, Leicester, Shree Sanatan Mandir.
National Council for Hospice and Specialist Palliative Care Services, 1995, by Hill, Dawn and Dawn Penso, *Opening Doors: Improving Access to Hospice and Specialist Palliative Care Services by Members of the Black and Ethnic Minority Communities*, Occasional Paper 7.
Nesbitt, Eleanor, 1991, *'My Dad's Hindu, my Mum's Side are Sikhs'*, *Issues in Religious Identity, Arts, Culture,* Education Research and Curriculum Papers, Coventry, National Foundation for Arts Education.
---1993, 'Children and the world to come: the views of children aged 8 to 14 years on life after death', *Religion Today*, Issue 3, Summer 1993, pp. 10-14.
Neuberger, Julia, 1987, *Caring for Dying People of Different Faiths*, London, Lisa Sainsbury Foundation, Austin Cornish Publishers Ltd.
Nicholas, Ralph W., 1982, 'Sraddha, impurity, and relations between the living and the dead', in T.N. Madan, (ed.), pp. 66-79.
Nye, Mallory, 1992a, '"A Place for Our Gods": The Construction of a Hindu Temple Community in Edinburgh', unpublished PhD thesis, Edinburgh, University of Edinburgh.
---1992b, 'Hindu religious traditions in a diaspora context', unpublished paper given to the British Association for the Study of Religions, Winchester, September.
---1993, 'A place for our Gods: tradition and change among Hindus in
Edinburgh', in Barot, Rohit (ed.), pp. 123-137.
---1995, *A Place for Our Gods: The Construction of an Edinburgh Hindu Temple Community*, London, Curzon Press.
Obeyesekere, Gananath, 1980, 'The rebirth eschatology and its transformations: a contribution to the sociology of early Buddhism', in O'Flaherty, Wendy (ed.), pp. 137-164.
O'Dea, Thomas and Janet O'Dea Aviad, 1983, *The Sociology of Religion*, New Jersey, Prentice Hall.
Office of Population Census and Surveys, 1991, *Mortality Statistics: General Review of the Registrar General on Deaths in England and Wales,* London, HMSO.
O'Flaherty, Wendy, (ed.), 1980, *Karma and Rebirth in the Indian Classical Tradition*, Berkeley, Los

Angeles and London, University of California Press.
---1980, 'Karma and rebirth in the Vedas and Puranas' in O'Flaherty, Wendy (ed.), pp. 3-37.
O'Hanlon, Rosalind, 1988, 'Issues of widowhood: gender, discourse and resistance in colonial western India', unpublished paper given at post-graduate seminar on Women, Colonialism and Commonwealth, University of London, Institute of Commonwealth Studies.
Ojha, Catherine 1981, 'Feminine asceticism in Hinduism: its tradition and present condition' in *Man In India*, Sept. 1981, pp.254-285.
Oldenburg, Veena Talwar, 1994, 'The continuing invention of the sati tradition', in Hawley, pp.159-173.
Padfield, J. 1908, *The Hindu at Home,* London, Simkin, Marshall, Hamilton, Kent and Co.
Pandey, Raj Bali, 1969, *The Hindu Samskaras: Socio-religious Study of the Hindu Sacraments*, Delhi and Varanasi, Motilal Banarsidass.
Parkes, Colin Murray, 1986, *Bereavement: Studies of Grief in Adult Life*, Harmondsworth, Penguin Books, 2nd. ed.
---1993, 'Bereavement as a psychosocial transition: processes of adaptation to change', in Dickenson, Donna and Malcolm Johnson (eds.), pp. 241-247.
Parkes, Colin Murray, Pittu Laungani and Bill Young, 1997, *Death and Bereavement Across Cultures*, London, Routledge.
Parkes, Colin Murray and R.S. Weiss, 1983, *Recovery From Bereavement*, New York, Basic Books.
Parrinder, Geoffrey, 1973, *The Indestructible Soul*, London, Allen and Unwin.
Parry, Jonathan, 1980 'Ghosts, greed and sin: the occupational identity of the Banaras funeral priests', *Man* (NS), Vol. 15 No.1, pp.88-111.
---1981, 'Death and cosmogony in Kashi', *Contributions to Indian Sociology*, Vol. 15, pp. 337-65.
---1982, 'Sacrificial death and the necrophagous ascetic', in Bloch, Maurice and John Parry (eds.), pp. 74-110.
---1985, 'Death and the digestion: the symbolism of food and eating in north Indian mortuary rites'. *Man* (NS) Vol. 20, pp. 612-630.
---1986, 'The *gift*, the Indian gift and "the Indian gift"', *Man* (NS), Vol. 20, No. 3, pp. 453-473.
---1989, 'The end of the body', in Feher, Michael, Ramona Naddaff and Nadia Tazi (eds.), *Fragments for a History of the Human Body*, Part 2, New York, Urzone Inc., pp. 491-517.
---1991, 'On the inauspiciousness and Impurity of death', unpublished paper.
Parsons, Talcott, 1965, 'Introduction' in Weber, Max, pp. xix-lxvii.
Peach, Ceri, Vaughan Robinson, Julia Maxtead and Judith Chance, 1988, 'Immigration and ethnicity', in Halsey, A.H. (ed.), *British Social Trends Since 1900*, Houndmills, Macmillan, pp. 561-615.
Peberdy, Alison, 1993, 'Spiritual care of dying people', in Dickenson, Donna and Malcolm Johnson, (eds.), pp. 219-223.
Pegg, Patricia F. and Erno Metze, 1981, *Death and Dying: a Quality of Life*, London, Pitman Books Ltd.
Planalp, J., 1956, 'Religious Life and Values in a North Indian Village'. Part 2, unpublished PhD thesis, Ithaca, Cornell University.
Pocock, D.F., 1976, 'Preservation of the religious life: Hindu immigrants in England', Contributions to Indian Sociology (NS) Vol.10 No.2, pp. 341-365.
Poulter, Sebastian, 1986, *English Law and Ethnic Minority Customs*, London, Butterworth.
---1989-1990, 'The Scattering of cremation ashes, river pollution and the law', Land Management and Environmental Law Report, pp. 82-85.
---1990, *Asian Traditions and English Law*, Runneymede Trust and Trentham Books.
Prabhavananda, Swami and Christopher Isherwood, 1954, *The Song of God: Bhagavad Gita*, New York, Mentor.

Prabhavananda, Swami and Frederick Manchester, 1948, *The Upanishads: Breath of the Eternal*, New York, Mentor Books.

Prashad, Jamuna, 1989, 'The Hindu concept of Death', in Berger, Arthur *et al.* (eds.), pp. 84-88.

Prickett, John (ed.), 1980, *Death*, Living Faiths Series, Guildford and London, Lutterworth Educational.

Prior, Lindsey, 1989, *The Social Organization of Death: Medical Discourse and Social Practice in Belfast*, London, Macmillan.

---1993, 'The social distribution of sentiments', in Dickenson, Donna and Malcolm Johnson, Milton Keynes, Open University Press, pp. 248-253.

Puligandla, R.,1975, *Fundamentals of Indian Philosophy*, Nashville, Abingdon Press.

Puri, Shanti Devi, Pashpavati Handa and Sahagvanti Ghai, 1960, *Amṛta Varṣa*, 1960, Nairobi, Times Press Ltd.

Quayle, Brendan, Peter Phillimore and Anthony Good, 1980, *Hindu Death and the Ritual Journey,* Durham Working Papers in Social Anthropology 4. Durham, Department of Anthropology, University of Durham.

Rack, Philip, 1990, 'Psychological/ psychiatric disorders', In Brian McAvoy and Liam J. Donaldson (eds.), pp. 290-303.

Radhakrishnan, Sarvapalli and Charles Moore (eds.), 1973 (1953)., *A Source Book in Indian Philosophy*, Princeton, N.J., Princeton University Press.

Raheja, Gloria Goodwin, 1988, *The Poison in the Gift: Ritual Prestation and the Dominant Caste in a North Indian Village*, Chicago, University of Chicago Press.

Rahman, Fazlur, 1989, 'Islam and health/medicine: a historical perspective', in Sulivan, L.E, pp. 149-172.

Raphael, Beverley, 1984, *The Anatomy of Bereavement: A Handbook for the Caring Professions*, London, Hutchinson.

Rathwell, Thomas and David Philips (eds.), 1986, *Health, Race and Ethnicity*, London, Croom Helm.

Rees, W. Dewi, 1971, 'The hallucinations of widowhood,' *British Medical Journal*, October 1971, Vol.4, No. 13.

---1990, 'Terminal care and bereavement', in McAvoy, Brian R. and Liam J. Donaldson (eds.), pp. 304-321.

Reynolds, Frank E. and Earle H. Waugh, 1977, *Religious Encounters with Death: Insights from the History and Anthropology of Religion*, Pennsylvania State University Press.

Rig Veda, The, 1982, tr. by O'Flaherty, Wendy, Harmondsworth, Penguin Books.

Rig Veda, The Hymns of the, 1897, tr. by Griffiths, Ralph, Vol I, 1896, Vol II., Banaras, Lazarus & Co.

Robinson, Vaughan, 1986, *Transients, Migrants and Settlers: Asians in Britain,* London, Oxford University Press.

---1990, 'Boom and gloom: the success and failure of South Asians in Britain' in Clarke, Colin, Ceri Peach and Steven Vertovec, pp. 269-296.

Rosenblatt, P.C., 1988, 'Grief: The social context of private feelings', Journal of Social Issues, Vol. 44, No.3, 67-78.

---1993a, 'Cross-cultural variation in the experience, expression, and understanding of grief', in Irish, Donald P., Kathleen F. Lundquist and Vivian Jenkins Nelson (eds.), 1993, pp. 13-19.

---1993b, 'Grief: The social context of private feelings', in Stroebe, Margaret S. *et al.* (eds.), pp. 102-111.

Rosenblatt, P.C., R.P. Walsh and D.A. Jackson, 1976, *Grief and Mourning in Cross-cultural*

Perspectives, New York, HRAF Press.
Sambhi, Piara Singh and W. Owen Cole, 1990, 'Caring for Sikh patients', Serving People of Different Faiths Series, *Palliative Medicine*, 4, pp. 229-233.
Sandweiss, S.H., 1975, *Sai Baba - The Holy Man and the Psychiatrist*, San Diego, Birth Day Publishing Co.
Saraswati, Swami Dayanand, 1975, *Light of Truth*, New Delhi, Sarvadeshik Arya Pratimidhi Sabha.
---1976, *The Sanskar Vidhi*, (Sanskrit text with English translation) New Delhi, Sarvadeshik Arya Pratinidhi Sabha.
---n.d. *Arya Prayer,* New Delhi, Vedashankar, Nardev and Sookraj Chatai.
Saraswati, Pandita Ramabai, 1988, *The High-Caste Hindu Woman*, New Delhi, Inter India Publication.
Satapatha-Brahmana, 1900, tr. by Julius Eggeling, SBE, XLIV, Part V. Oxford, Clarendon Press.
Schulman, A., 1971, *Baba*, New York, Viking Press.
Shanker, Daya, 1989, 'Conquering death,' in Berger, Arthur *et al.* (eds.), pp. 101-107.
Shastri, Dakshina Ranjan, 1963, *Origin and Development of the Rituals of Ancestor Worship in India,* Calcutta, Bookland Private Ltd.
Sharma, Arvinda *et al* (eds.), 1988, *Sati: Historical and Phenomenological Essays*, New Delhi, Motilal Banarsidas.
Sharma, Najendranath, 1980, *Ancient India According to Manu*, New Delhi, Jawahar Naggar Publications.
Sharma, Naturam (ed.), 1964, *Sri Naimittikkarmaprakasa,* Vilkha Anand Ashram, Rajkot, Saurastra.
Sharma, Rajendranath, 1980, *Ancient Indian Rites According to Manu*, New Delhi, Nag Publishers.
Sharma, Ursula, 1978a, 'Theodicy and the doctrine of karma,' in Foy, Whitfield (ed.), pp. 24-45.
---1978b, 'The problem of village Hinduism: fragmentation and integration', in Foy, Whitfield (ed.), pp. 51-74.
Shastri, Dakshina Ranjan, 1963, *Origin and Development of Ancestor Worship in India*, Calcutta, Bookland Private Ltd.
Shekhewat, Prahlad Singh (1989), 'Sati in Rajasthan', in Dandavate, Pramila *et al* (eds.), pp 39-48.
Schneider, J., 1981, 'Growth from bereavement', in Pegg, Patricia and Erno Metze (eds.), pp.35-5.
Shuchter, Stephen R. and Sidney Zisook, 1993, 'The course of normal grief', in Stroebe, Margaret S. *et al* (eds.), pp. 23-43.
Siddell, Moyra, 1993, *Bereavement: Private Grief and Collective Responsibility,* Death and Dying, Workbook 4, Milton Keynes, Open University, Department of Health and Social Welfare.
Singh, Indu Prakash and Renuka Singh, 1989, 'Sati: its patri-politics', in Dandavate, Pramila *et al.*, pp.54-62.
Singh, Khushwant, 1989, *Train to Pakistan*, New Delhi, Time Books.
Singh, Kirpal, 1975, *Aging in India,* Calcutta, Minerva Association.
Sivananda, Swami, 1989, *What Becomes of the Soul After Death*, Divine Life Society.
Smith, Wilfred Cantwell, 1978, *The Meaning and End of Religion*, London, SPCK.
Sogyal Rimpoche, 1992, *The Tibetan Book of Living and Dying*, London, Rider.
Speck, Peter, 1978, *Loss and Grief in Medicine, London,* Ballière Tindall.
Srinivas, M.N., 1952, *Religion and Society among the Coorgs of South India*, Bombay, Asia Publishing House.
---1967, *Social Change in Modern India*, Berkeley, University of California Press.
Srinivas, M.N., S. Sesharah and V.S. Parthasarthy (eds.), 1977, *Dimensions of Social Change in India,* New Delhi, Allied Publishers Private Ltd.
Stannard, D., (ed.), 1974, *Death in America*, Philadelphia, University of Pennsylvania Press.
Stevenson, Sinclair, M., 1920, *Rites of the Twice-born*, London, Oxford University Press.

---(1930), *Without the Pale: the Life Story of an Outcaste*, London, Oxford University Press.
Stigler, James W., Richard A. Shweder, and Gilbert Herdt (eds.), 1990, *Cultural Psychology: Essays on Comparative Human Development*, Cambridge, Cambridge University Press.
Stroebe, Margaret S, 1994, 'Helping the bereaved to come to terms with loss: what does bereavement research have to offer?' Keynote address presented at the conference on Bereavement and Counselling, St. George's Hospital Medical School, London, 25th March, 1994.
Stroebe, Margaret S., Wolfgang Stroebe and Robert O. Hansson, 1993, *Handbook of Bereavement: Theory, Research, and Intervention*, Cambridge, Cambridge University Press.
Stutley, Margaret and James Stutley, 1977, *A Dictionary of Hinduism*, London and Henley, Routledge and Kegan Paul.
Sudnow, D., 1967, *Passing On: the Social Organisation of Dying*, New Jersey, Englewood Cliffs, Prentice Hall.
Sulivan, L.E., 1989, *Healing and Restoring: Health and Medicine in the World's Religions*, New York, Macmillan, pp. 149-172.
Taittirīya Samhitā, 1967 (1914), tr. by Keith, Arthur Berriedale, Harvard Oriental Series v. 18-19, Delhi, Motilal Banarsidass.
Tandon, Prakash, 1968, *Punjabi Century: 1857-1947*, Berkeley, University of California Press.
Taylor, Colette, 1990 'Asians in Britain - origins and lifestyles', in McAvoy, Brian and Liam J. Donaldson (eds.), pp. 3-27.
Taylor, Donald, 1987, 'Charismatic authority in the Sathya Sai Baba Movement' in Burghart, Richard (ed.), pp. 119-133.
Tinker, H., 1977, *The Banyan Tree: Overseas Emigration from India, Pakistan and Bangladesh*, London, Oxford University Press.
Tully, Mark 1992, *No Full Stops in India*, New Delhi, Penguin Books.
Turner, Victor, 1967, *The Forest of Symbols*, Ithaca, NY, Cornell University Press.
---1969, *The Ritual Process: Structure and Anti-structure*, Chicago, Aldine.
---1977, 'Death and the dead in the pilgrimage process', in Reynolds, Frank E. and Earle H. Waugh (eds.), pp. 111-124.
Upanisads, The Thirteen Principal, 1983 (1877), tr. by Hume, Robert Ernest, London, Oxford University Press.
Van der Burg, Christiaan J.G., 1993, 'Surinam Hinduism and the Netherlands and social change', in Barot, Rohit (ed.), pp.138-155.
Van Gennep, A., 1960, *The Rites of Passage*, tr. by M.B. Vizedom and G.L. Caffee, Chicago, University of Chicago Press (*Les Rites de Passage*, 1908).
Vatuk, S., 1980, 'Withdrawal and disengagement as a cultural response to aging in India', in Fry, C. (ed.), *Aging in Culture and Society,* New York, Praeger.
Vertovec, Steven, 1991a, 'Community and congregation in London Hindu temples: Divergent Trends', unpublished paper given at the British Association of South Asian Studies, London, SOAS.
---(ed.), 1991b, *Bound to Change? Aspects of the South Asian Diaspora*, New Delhi, Oxford University Press.
1992a, 'On the Reproduction and representation of "Hinduism" in Britain', unpublished paper, conference on Culture, Identity and Politics: Ethnic Minorities in Britain, Oxford, St. Anthony's College.
---1992b. 'Community and congregation in London Hindu temples: divergent trends', *New Community,* Vol. 18 No. 2, pp. 251-264.
Vidyarthi, L.P., 1979, *The Sacred Complex of Kashi*, New Delhi, Concept Publishers.

---(ed.), n.d. *Aspects of Religion in Indian Society*, Meerut, Kedar Nath.

Vidyasagara, Isvarachandra, 1976, *Marriage of Hindu Widows*, Calcutta, K.P. Bagchi & Co.

Waddell, Charles and Beverley McNamara, 'The sterotypical fallacy: a comparison of Anglo and Chinese Australians' thoughts about facing death' in *Mortality* Vol.2. No.2, July.

Walter, Tony, 1989, 'Gender and funerals', paper given at the British Association for the Study of Religion, Oxford.

---1990, *Funerals and How to Improve Them*, London, Hodder & Stoughton.

---1993, 'Death in the New Age', Religion, 23 (2): 127-45.

---1994, *The Revival of Death*, London, Routlege.

---1996, 'A new model of grief: bereavement and biography', in *Mortality* Vol.I, No. I, March.

---1997a, 'The ideology and organisation of spiritual care: three approaches', in *Palliative Medicine* (forthcoming)

---1997b, 'Developments in spiritual care of the dying', in *Religion*, forthcoming.

Watson, James (ed.), 1977, *Between Two Cultures: Migrants and Minorities in Britain*, Oxford, Basil Blackwell.

Weber, Max, 1958 (1922), *The Religion of India: The Sociology of Hinduism and Buddhism*, tr. by H.H Gerth and D. Martindale, New York, Free Press.

---1965, *Sociology of Religion*, tr. by Ephraim Fischoff, London, Methuen, 4th Ed.

Weightman, Simon, 1978, *Hinduism in the Village Setting*, Milton Keynes, Open University Press.

Whalley, Joachim (ed.), 1981, *Mirrors of Mortality: Studies in the Social History of Death*, London, Europa.

White Yajurveda, The Texts of the, 1927, tr. by Griffiths, Ralph, Banaras, Freeman and Co., Jagannath Prasad, 2nd Ed.

Williams, Raymond B., 1984, *A New Face of Hinduism: The Swaminarayan Religion*, Cambridge, Cambridge University Press.

Williams, R.G.A., 'Mourning Rituals: Their application in Western Culture', in Pegg, Patricia F. (ed.), pp. 1-10.

Winternitz, M., 1927-1933, *A History of Indian Literature*, tr. by S. Ketkar, Vols. I and II, Calcutta, University of Calcutta.

Worden, William J.,1993, *Grief Counselling and Grief Therapy: A Handbook for the Mental Health Practitioner*, London, Routledge, 2nd ed.

Wortman, C.B., and R.C. Silver, R.C., 1989, 'The myths of coping with loss', *Journal of Counselling and Clinical Psychology*, Vol. 57, pp. 349-357.

Zaehner, R.C., 1966, *Hinduism*, London, Oxford University Press.

---1988 (ed.), *Hutchinson Encyclopedia of Living Faiths*, London, Century Hutchinson Ltd.

Zimmer, Heinrich (ed.), 1969, *Philosophies of East and West*, Bollinger Series, New York, Princeton University Press.

Index

Authors referred to in the main text are cited below; references can be found in the Bibliography/

Ācāryas 17
Adaptation 12, 189-20
Adjustment 169, 181, and recovery 170
Adoption of son 72, f.n., of daughter 180
Ādvaita 42
Africa, East 20
Afsus 154
Akāla mṛtyu 53, 60
Akaṇḍ Pāṭh 138, 166
Akṣara, Akṣardhām 41, 59
Amāvās 110
Ambivalence, in relationships 167, towards body 131, of priests 105
Amils 138
Amṛta Varṣa 36, 111, 138, 142, 172
Ancestors 30, 34-5, 71, 93, 160, relationship with, 10, 158, 164, 170, 189, 194
Anger 127, 156-8, 163-4, metaphor for hell, 164, towards husband, parents 163, towards medical staff 163, 165
Animals, offerings to 46, 98, 111
Anniversaries 8, 95, 109, lunar and Gregorian calendar 107 (see *thithi*)
Anthropological perspectives 6, 12
Apertures for soul to leave 33, 36, 64, 67
Ārghya 97
Ariès 56
Arjuna's son 46
Ars Moriendi 56
Ārtī 22, 23, 25
Arya Samaj 16-17, 21-6, 138, 140, 151, 172, impurity 152, 'not Hindu' 140
Asceticism 32, 35, 147-8, 150, 153
Ashes 89ff., 90ff., 98-9, in Britain 91-2, 131-2, at Haridwar 91
Ashok 161, 167, 171
Asian patients 112ff., 198ff.
Āṣrama 14 f.n, 18, 56
Asthisañcayana 90 ff. (see ashes)
Ātma śānti ke līye 145
Ātman 29, 31, 32-4, 37, 39, 42, 67, 70, 72, 129-30, departure of 36 ff., from *brahmarandra* 64-5, 67, 70, identical with Brahman 32
Āśrama 14, 18, 35
Attachments 44, 51, 120
Aunts 48, 189
Auspicious 152, (see inauspicious)
Austerity (*tapas*) 32
Australian study 202
Autonomy 12, 33, 202, 205
Avatars 16
Baba Balak Nath 17
Bad death 60 ff., signs 61
Bali 10
Ballard 154, 189
Bangles broken, widows 80, 86, 150-51
Barmu 104, 145
Barot 16
Basham 14
Bayly 104, 119, 147
Beaulieu River 91
Bed, death on, 1, 65, f.n.
Beliefs 29ff., about death, afterlife 29ff.
Bereavement 9, 159, 167-71, 175, 181, 188-90, children 175ff., multiple 175, process 188, 190
Berger 4
Berger and Luckman 4-5
Bhagavad Gītā (BG) ix, 18, 19, 26, 30, 32ff., 35 37, 45-6, 52, 58, 67, 84, 87, 165,171-2, in mourning period 138, 142, 172, meaning 145, 165, 171, 187-8, 193, 196
Bhagavata Purāṇa, Rāhasya 138
Bhagvan 29
Bhajana 21, 22, 24
Bhakta 185-6
Bhakti 16, 18, 30, 32, 43, sects 29, *marga/ yoga* 43
Bhaktivedanta 17, 104
Bhūmi-dāna 62-4
Bhūta-pretas 38, 40, 65, 74-5
Birds, feeding 100, 104, 111, crows, 98
Blakemore and Boneham 192, 199-200, 202, 204
Bloch and Parry 6, 56, 111, 196
Boat, miniature, 62, 100
Body, creating 94 (see *daśgatra*), preparation of 72ff., in Britain 80ff., as Viṣṇu, Lakṣmi, Śiva etc. 74
Bonding, marital, mother-child 11, in arranged marriage 12
Bowlby 9,10

Bradbury 56
Brahmācarya 14
Brahma Kumaris 17, 186
Brāhmaṇas 31
Brahmarandhra 64-5, 67, 70
Brahman 29. 32. 34
Brahmins 14, 31, 34, 39-41, 43-4, 46, 51, 58, 62-5, 68, 87, 89, 91, 99, 141-2, 145, 187, ambivalent roles 105, food 139, Gujarati 149, invited 97, 100, 108, 145, *kāṭaliyā* 97 f.n., *kuśa* surrogates 94, 97, 100, lay, roles 26, *mahābrāhmaṇas* 26, 97, priest 2, 27, Punjabi 149, *sanātani* 152, widow 148, 153, women in priestly role 26, 39, 97, 108-9, 150
British Context of Hindu deaths 113 ff.
Brother 146, 164-7, 188, around coffin 173, as chief mourners, marriage to, 147, 149
Bull release and 'marriage' 96, 101
Burghart 19
Burial 54 f.n., water, 61, child's 179
Caitanya mṛtyu 57-58
Calendar, lunar, 94, 107, 110, 194, Gregorian 107
Care 113ff., 196ff., hospice/hospital 115ff., intensive 125, 128, medical 119, 122, palliative 113ff., terminal 118
Case Studies 121 ff., 172ff., 175ff., 197
Caste 14, 15 f.n., 16 f.n., Arya Samaj 17
Chandra 177-8, 185
Change 1-3, 5, 7,14, 17, 36, 53, 54, 71, 92, 96, 104, 111, 183, attitudes 50, karma 50, 52, psychological 133, 163, 171, soul changes bodies 45, 187, status 133, 152
Chants at point of death 43, 50, 58, 64, 67, 68, 69, 86
Chandod 76
Chief mourner 71-72, adopted son 71 f.n., daughter 82, 100, daughter-in-law or wife 72
Childbirth, death in, 61
Children, loss of 175ff., social beings 176
Chinese Australians 202
Circumambulations 73, 74 f.n., 76-7, 81, 85-86, at pyre 74, 76, 77, 92
Citragupta 38
Clarke, Peach and Vertovec 19
Clothes/ cloths for body 64, 73, 77, 85-6
Coconuts 73, 84-5, 105, as womb 15, widow returns marriage c., 152
Coffins 2, 81-2, 86, 130, bangles smashed 150-51, carried by relatives, friends 82-3, 86-7, open 83, 166
Cognitive satisfaction 190
Coin, gold to pay ferryman 66, 72, 81-2
Commonwealth Immigrants Act 1962, 20
Communication 2, 9, 69, 127, 199-202
Community support 140ff., 189
Concepts of after-life 35ff.
Condolence visits 141-4, 172, stress from 141, 172, value 144
Consolation 140, 142, 162, 169ff., 174ff., 186ff., from rebirth 187
Continuity 3, 195, 202, 204
Control, loss of, 2, 202
Corpse, ambiguous status 73
Cow, gift of, 62, 103, silver surrogate 62 (see Vaitaraṇī)
Cremation 2, 71, in India 76ff., in Britain 87ff., 194, 203
Crematoria 81-2, 89 f. N., 90, 92, Basingstoke and Bedford 76, 203
Cross-cultural perspectives 6, 160, 199, education 12, death and bereavement studies 6, variations 10
Cultural expectations 158, 160, 163, 170
Dakṣinā 64 f.n.
Dakṣināyaṇa 32-3, 59, 61, 96
Danañjay prāṇa 76
Darji 25-6, 39, 40-1, 43-4, 46, 51, 108, 110, 130, 145, 153
Darśana, 74, *antim* (last) 85
Daśgātra (10 organ) *vidhi* 94-95, 101
Daughter, as chief mourner, 82, death 180, loss of 176-181
Death 11, 53, 62, anticpated 58, averted 59, bad (*durgati*) 29, 30, (*ku-mṛtyu*) 53, 56, 192, conscious (*caitanya mṛtyu)* 58, 192, cross-cultural studies of, 6, foreknowledge of 53, good 1, 30, 53, 56, 162, 175, 192, 209, good enough 57, 192, head to north 60, home 1, 60, 197, hospital 1, 68, in Britain 68ff., in lavatory 62, legitimation 4, medicalised 56, 192, 198, models of, 7, 203, moment of 64ff.,67, natural 56, 119, of way of life, 159, on bed 65, f.n., on floor 58, 64-5, 68, 115, 128, outside 65, place and time 59, 57, pornography 8,

process 34, 192-3, professionalisation of, 92, prospects for the future 192ff., psychology of, 12, sacred 56, signs of 61, thoughts at point of, 34, transition 11, 29, 93, 192, threat to society 4, uncontrolled 61, universal 186, untimely 53, 61 (see suicide), violent 56, willed 58
Debts (see *ṛṇa*) 15, 34
Denial 9
Depression 156, 167
Deśacāra 85
Desires (*vāsanas*) 37
Detachment 187
Devas, devata 37, 42
Dhāmas 74 f.n.
Dharba, khuśa grass 65 f.n., 95, 102-3 substitute for priest 94
Dharma 11, 15-7, 57, 60, 146
Dharma Rājā (Yama) 33, 38, 45, 49, 96, personification of *karma* 49, 60
Dīkṣā 47
Disclosure 60, 119-20, 193, 198, 201-2
Display of body 131 (see coffin)
Dīvā 14, 72, 75, 80, 95, on hand 58, 141, 142, 190
Divine Society 90
Doctors 118, 120-23, 200-3, Asian 119-21, 123, Hindu 118, 123, 130, 132, Sikh 113ff.
Dogs 46, of Yama 38 (see animals)
Dreams 36, 39, appearance of d. in, 169, baby reborn 179, of death 173, 177, reminder 111
Duḥkha 142, 136, 186
Durga 16, 29
Dvija 14
Dwyer 17, 21
Dying, caring for, 113
East Africa 20
Effigies in *pañcaka* 61, 79, 85
Egypt 10
Eisenbruch 10, 158, 160, 167, 171, 183, 189, 190, 204
Elderly, caring for 114, social death 134
Emotion 129, abnormal/normal 129, collapse 120, delayed 161, for men/women 67, 143, hypocritical 144, outbursts 160, 162, 197, public displays 143, taboo 188 (see grief)
Employers 137, 203
Epics 17
Ethnicity 10, 19
Eulogy 82, 88
Euphemisms 43
Euro-centric bias 12
Euthenasia 118
Evil eye 51
Evison 54, 64-5, 73 104, stages f.n. 54
Explanations 176, 183
Facing reality of loss, Stage 2, 163
Family 2,3,12, 66, 171ff., 175-6, 180, 187, 192, dead children members of f. 158, dynamics 159, extended 2, 12, 179, 198, 202, nuclear 3, 12, presence 66, 69, saying goodbye 66, separation from 159, structure 2, ties 167-8, 170, 177, 179, traditions 27
Fatalism 119
Fate, luck (*nasīb*) 49, 165
Fasting 57, before funeral 139
Father, grandfather etc. 35, 97, 98
Fees 105-6
Fertility 105
Finding meaning 181ff.
Fire, Agni 76-8, 80, 82, at crematorium 92, incense as substitute 86
Floor, death on, 1, 58, 64-5 f.n., 68, 72, 115, 128, 198, Mother Earth 65, purified 65, in hospital 68
Food, 75, offering, 89, for *preta* 86, receiving 136, 140, restrictions 136-137, 139ff., thrown out 79
Frankl 56
Free will 50, 186
Freud 9, 157-8, 168
Funeral xiii, xiv 30, 81ff., for consolation 193-4
Funeral directors 2, 127, 130, 201
Future prosects 192, 197ff.
Gandhi, saying "Rām Rām" 174, on widows 148, 149
Ganga (Ganges) 1, 72, 90, 204, *-stotra* 84, water, 72, 84, 117, 132, 196, prevented from giving 69, 117
Gārhasthya 14
Garuḍa Purāṇa ix, 18, 31, 33-4, 36-7, 52, 72
Gāyatrī Mantra 67, 69, 83, 87, 120, 148, 188

Geertz 181
General practitioners 122-3, 119-121, 199
Ghī 58, 77, 84
Ghost (see *bhūta*) 7, 33, 38ff., 39, 40, 61, 65, 93, danger from, 7, attachment 39, thirst 38
Gifts, before death 62-4, 66, by priests 110, 117, carrying sin and inauspiciousness, 105-6, cow 62-3, for deceased 109, in memory 145, to Brahmins 104, 106-8, to charities 109, 111, 145 (see *dakṣiṇā*)
Gītā Pāṭh
Gold, or silver cutting wire 97, for mouth of corpse 72, 82, 84
Go-loka 41, 42
God 16-8, 25 f.n., 29ff., 29 f.n., 32, 35, 36, 40-3, 45-6, 48-50, 66, actively involved 185, and suffering 184, 198, fate 49, instruments of 50, name at death 68, personal 184, punitive 49, will, 49, 184-6, 191
Gonda 94
Goodbyes, importance of, 53, 56, 59, 65-6, 69, 122-3, 125, 127, 129
Gorer 8
Gotra 53
Gough 163-4
Grandfather, great-grandfather 31, 94, 97-8, 102ff.
Great and Little Traditions 27
Grief 9,10,12, 197, biological basis of, 10, complicated/ pathological 158, 167, 170, cultural variations 155-6, definition 9 f.n., denial 157, expressions of 140, 151-2, 163, meaning of, 9, f.n., process 9, socially constructed 155ff., 197, somatisation 156, stages 157ff., tasks 157, work 9, 157, universal 155
Grief and mourning 12
Gṛhastha 18, 35
Grof and Halifax 182
Guilt 11, 157, 164, 166, 189, ambivalence 167, Christian connotations 166
Gujarat 21, East African links 21
Gujaratis in Westmouth 24
Guru (*gurū*)23
Guṇas 37 f.n.
Guru Nanak 35
Hallucinations 168
Hanumān Chālīsā 171
Hare Kṛṣṇa (see ISCKON)
Haridwar 90-1
Havan 17, 23, 25, 33, 89, 111, 173
widows' 152
Heaven (*svarga*) 34, 36, 40ff., 41
Hell (*naraka*) 11, 29 f.n., 30ff., 38, 44ff.
Historical perspectives 30
Hertz 6-8, 132, 134, 154, 157, 165, 176
Hinduism 13ff., 18 ff.
Hindu Panjabi 140 f.n.
Hindus in Britain 13
Hockey 133
Holistic care 5, 115, 197
Home, religious activity 23 (see death)
Homily 82, 89, 142, 189
Hopelessness 156
Hospice 8, 12, 113, f.n., 198-9, f.n., 203, 205
Hospital 1, 2, 8, 113-115, Asian model 198, 202, helpful staff 129
House of Clay 30
Huntington and Metcalf 7, 196
Ichchā mṛtyu 57
Identity xii 4, 12-13, 20, 159, 171, 204
Ill-wishing 51
Immediate loss, Stage 1, 160
Immigrant, 2, law 2, 19ff., bereavement 159, 205
Immortality above/below belt 35
Impurity 7, 83, 140, body 77, 83 f.n., (See *sūtaka*)
Inauspiciousness 134 ff., 147-8, 150
infants 134, 158, 175ff., 191, burial 176, comparative studies 158, FSID, SANDS 178 f.n., explanations 184, Gods's gift 185, lack of support 177, no offerings 109, rebirth 47, 179, 187, social death 134
Informants ix, xiv
Interpersonal relationships 11
Interpreters 2, 116, 199-200
Instrumentality 49-50
ISCKON (International Society for Kṛṣṇa Consciousness) 17, 22, 25
Issues of care 197
Jains 25
Jalaram Bapa 17
Janam Sakhis 35, 187
Japanese study 10
Jaswant 123ff., dreams of 169, last words 125, goodbye 127, unprepared 129
Jāti 18, 53

Jewellery stripped 147, 150-1
Jīvātman 32, 37, 42
Jñāna, H. *gyān* (knowledge) 18, 29, 186
Journey, through hells 38, soul 85-6, to ancestors 66, 84, to God 57, to Ganga 90 92
Jung 181-182
Kabir 138
Kailāsa 41
Kakar, 12, 47, 159, 176, 177
Kāla 67 (see time)
Kali-yuga 45, f.n., 46
Kalpa 45 f.n.,
Kalsi 65
Kane 34 94
Kanitkar 74
Kanyā-dāna 149
Kapāla kriyā 36, 73, 78-79, 92, 193
Karma 1, 11, 29ff., 31-2, 34, 38, 45, 48ff., 60-1, 184-5, attitudes to *k.* and suffering 36, 48ff., bad 51, change 50, 51, children's 176, 185, transferable 48, 50-1
Karmakāṇḍa 84, 98
Karma Yoga 18, 29, 31
Kāśī 59-60, 90 (see Varanasi)
Kāṭaliyā (cutting) Brahmins 97, f.n.
Kaushik 66
Khare 119
Khattri 44, 47, 91, 99, 129, 145-6, princess 153
Killingley 15 f.n., 26, 33, 38, 45, 194-5
Kisagotami 186, f.n.
Kismat (fate) 11, 49
Klass 175
Klein 9, 10
Kleinman 156
Knipe 30, f.n.31, 34, 96, 98, 107
Knott 4, 18, 19, 21, 23, 25
Knowledge (also see *jñāna*) 32
Krause 156-7
Krishnamurti 26-7, 74
Kṛṣṇa 16, 18-9, 29, 32-3, 37, 41-3, 50, infant 43, 74, parrot story 46
Kṣatriya 31
Kübler-Ross 8-9
Ku-mṛtyu 53
Kumbha dāna 103
Kumhar 27, 149, 153, marriage, 153, widow 150
Kuśa/darbha grass 65, 95, 97
Last words 69, 125
Lalitā 99, 104
Language 2, 5, 11, 115, 198, of death 5
Laukika, 3
Last words 69, 125
Levirate 146
Liberation (see *mokṣa*) 29, 32, 34
Life cycle rites (see *saṃskāras*) 18, 26
Life support 118
Lila 172ff.
Liminality 7, 133-4, 157
Liṅga 22
Little Tradition 14
Living will 118 f.n.
Lohanas 21, 25, 99, 104-5, 139, 145, 149-51, *mandal* 25, remarriage 153, *śrāddha* 105
Loka 30, 33, 37 f.n., 38, 41-4, 47
Loss 159, multiple 159, of child 175-6, of country 159, social 159
Loss, grief and adjustment 155ff.
Luck 49, 165
Madan 35, 60, 61, 68, 183
Madhuben 165
Mahābharata 30, 32
Mahābrāhmaṇas xv, 26, 94, 97, 105
Mālā 74
Malice 177
Mandir 21, in home 135, 171 (see temples)
Maṅgala-sūtra 146, 151
Māta-ji 142
Marriage 12, arranged 12, bonds 168, mixed 170, rituals 27, rituals reversed 147, 150-1, second 147, 149, 153
Māsi so 145
Maya 69, 121ff., 161, 165-166, 170-171, 189, 192, 198
Mcnamara 57
Mcnamara and Waddell 199, 202
McNaught 116
Meaning, 181ff., 187, 197, Frankl 56, life hereafter 182
Medical intervention 9, 116-120, 126
Medical staff 132, 201
Meena 172ff.
Menski 4, 27, 166, 192, 195
Merit (see *puṇya*) 29, 38, 50-1
Metaphor 155, 199
Migration 20-21, loss of country 159

Misfortune 29, karma 48, malice 48, wrath of deity 48
Mistry 85
Misunderstanding 166
Mochis 21, 26
Mohan 188
Mokṣa 29, 32, 34, 40, 42-3, 45, 57, 59-60, 185, meaning of 43
Moment of death 64ff., in Britain 68ff.
Montagu of Beaulieu 91
Mother Earth 1, 65, 197
Mourning, 6ff., 9 f.n., 194, Ballard 153, before funeral 194, changed pattern 135, cross-cultural 6ff., incomplete 204, meaning 154, period in Britain 133ff., rituals 8, 9, 133, stages 140ff., WWI 8 (see grief, recovery, weeping)
Mukhāgni 85
Mukti (see *mokṣa*)
Mūrtis (images) 22, 25, 109
Muslim cultures 10
Nalini, anger 165, 168-9, disbelief 161, questioned God 184 (see Maya, Jaswant)
Naraka-loka (see hell) 30, 44
Narasingh Mehta 138
Nārāyaṇa 29
Nārāyaṇa bali 61, 65, 96, 98, 101, 104
Narratives 140, 192
National Council of Hindu Temples (NCHT) 28, 83, 88, 104, 193, Appendix 205ff.
Natural Death Society 56
Navarātri 24, f.n., 25, 107
NCSPCS report, Opening Doors, 199 f.n., 200
Nesbitt 13, 40, 47, 141
New body 34, 35
Niyoga 146, 147f.n.
North/south orientation 60, 66
Nursing homes 114
Nye 14
O'Dea 181, 196
O'Flaherty 35, 94
Oṃ 23, 67, 80, 83, 86-7
Omens 39, 179
Offerings 99, 103-104 (see gifts)
Order 4, 5
Oxfam 111, 145
Padma 178-180, 185
Padfield 67
Pagrī 89, 98, 138, 145
Pain 157
Palliative care 12, 199 (see hospice)
Pañca-dāna 62
Pañca devata 104
Pañca-gavya 63 f.n.
Pañcaka 59-61, 96, 104
Pañca-mahābhūta, pañca-tattva-ghāta 33, 36
Pandits 14, 16, 23, 24, 26ff., 27, 68, family 26, changing roles 193ff.
Paramātman 29, 32, 42
Parameśvar 29
Parents together in heaven 44
Parkes 157, 168, 171
Parry 26, 35, 36, 57, 60 f.n., 61, 73, 74, 78, 79, 83, 90, 96, 105, 148
Parsons 183
Patels 21,38, 50, 73, 99, 104, 136-7, 139, 142, 145, 149, 187, 200
Paths to liberation 18
Patidars 21, 25
Patient advocates 201
Pativratā 146
Peberdy 181
Penance 53, 63 (see *prāyaścitta*)
Phūl channa 87, 90
Pilgrimage 90, 92
Piṇḍa 26, 34, 74ff., 92, 94, 95, 97, 101, 103-4, 193, as body 105, as embryo 95, cutting, blending 102-3, six 75, 77, substitute for animal sacrifice 94, ten 94-5, 101 (see *daṣgatr*),
Pining 9, 157
Pitṛ 31, 35, 93, 95 symbiotic relationship 44, nourishing 31
Pitṛ-loka 30, 37, 41, 43, 127, 129-30
Pitṛ pakṣa 107ff., 194, 197
Pocock 3, 4
Pollution (see *sūtaka*)
Possession 39
Post-mortems 129, 203, Muslim 130, 203
Pot 36, 37, 76-7, 78-9, 85, water , light for ghost 95
Poulter 131
Purification 72, 77-8, 80, 83, 86, 89, 91
Pushtimarg 16, 25, 36, 48
Prādakṣiṇa 77
Pralaya 61
Pramukh Swami 17, 46, 59, 86
Prāṇas 36, 37, 76, *dhanañjay* 78
Prāṇaprathiṣtā 25 f.n.
Prasāda 23, 58, 110

Prāyaścitta 62-64 (see penance)
Prediction 57
Prema 162, 168, 176
Premonitions 59
Preparation, for death 54, 57, 58, 61, 62, 114, 125, 193, of body in Britain , 54, 63ff., of body in India 671ff., 80ff.
Presence 39, 168, 172, 189
Preta 31, 33, 93, 95-8, hunger and thirst 95 f.n., (see *ātman*, *bhūta-preta*)
Priests 26, changing roles 194-54, availability of, 2 (see pandits)
Prior 9
Procession in India 54, 71, 74ff., in Britain 71, 82ff., 193
Professionalisation 2, 130ff., 193, 204
Professional mourners 67
Protestant 8
Psychology 11
Puerto Rican immigrants 203
Pūjā 23, 101ff.
Pūjak (performer) 100 (see chief mourner)
Punishment 44
Punjabis 13, 21, 'not Hindu' 23, 140
Puṇya (merit) 29, 34, 38, 50-1
Purāṇas 17, 30, 35, 83, 107, 193 (see *Garuḍa Purāṇa*)
Purgatory 8
Purification 72, 77, 78, 80, 83-4, 86, 89, 91, 100-1, 105,
Purity/pollution (see *sūtaka*)
Pūrnimā 110
Purohita (see priests, pandits)
Puruṣottam 41, 43
Puruṣa sūkta 84
Pushtimarga 16, 17, 25, 36, 38, 41, 43, 149
Puśpaka vimāna 38
Pyre 71ff., 193
Racism 2, 117, 126, 199-200
Rādhā and Kṛṣṇa 22, 42
Radhasoamis 17
Rāma 16, 29, 38, 46, chanting name of, 67-8, 128, 142, 172, 174, Sītā, 42
Ramakrishna Mission 17
Ramanuja 42
Ramāyaṇa 46, 165
Ramesh, 120, 121ff.,121 f.n., 128, 129, 161, 168, 184, 189, 192, 198
Rāṇḍīrāṇḍa, 148
Readings 58, 68, 111, 137ff., 171, 197, *akhaṇḍ/ sādhāran pāṭh* 138, *Amṛta Varṣa* 138, 142, 172, at point of death 58, consolation from 175, 187
Reality, Ultimate, 32, 37, 182
Rebirth 11, 29, 31, 32, 34, 35, 36, 41ff., 45ff., 69, animals 46, Arjuna's son 46, babies, children, 46-7, consolation from 187, death as, 196, dreams, 47, 179, homosexuals as rats 49, in family 46-7, 111, 197, meaning from 187, signs 47, suicide 46
Recovery 9, 157, 169ff., 175, 189, 190, questioned 158 (see reorganisation)
Rees 115
Reincarnation (see rebirth)
Relocating the deceased 9, 158, 169, 197
Remarriage 147, 149, for men 149, in Britain 153, brothers 149, 153 (see marriage)
Reincorporation rites 7, 8, 133, 135, 138, 154
Regeneration 105
Relocating the deceased 158, 169, 196
Reorganisation 9, and recovery, stage 3, 169ff., and adaptation 169ff., 189
Repression 10
Reynolds and Waugh 5
Ṛg Veda 30
Rites of separation, reincorporation 135
Rituals, absence of, 160, action affecting death 31, 193, at point of death 195, combined 27, importance of 174, innovation 192ff., GP 33, renegotiated 192-196, sin carried in, 105, Vedic 33
Rivers 90-92, in Gujarat 76, 132, in Britain 131ff. (see Vaitarani)
Ṛṇa (see debt) 15, f.n., 74, 107
Rohini 140, 143-4, 151-2
Roop Kanwar 147-8
Rosenblatt 9, 133, 155-6, 158, 168, 170, 189
Rosenblatt et al. 8, 155
Sacred thread 73, f.n.. 74
Sadgati 27, 72, 53, 84
Sādhāraṇa dharma 15
Sādhāraṇ Pāṭh 138
Sahajanand Swami 16. 41
Salvation (also see Mokṣa) 43
Saṃkalpa 66, 84, 89

Sāṃkhya 37
Sampradāya (see sect) 16
Saṃsāra 29, 31, 34, 40, meaning from 182
Saṃskāras (see life cycle rites) 14, *antyeṣṭi* 15, 18, 26
Saṃkhya 37
Sanātana dharma 12, 14, 18, 140, 149, 152
SANDS 178
Sandhyā 26
Sangat 189
Sankara 42
Sannyāsa 14, 18, 123
Sanskritic tradition 2, 14, 17, 149
Śānti 186
Santoṣīmātā 17, 171
Sapiḍīkaraṇa 31, 93, 96-8, in Britain 11, 102ff., carries sin 105
Saptāha 118, f.n.,
Saraswati, Dayanand 17, 23, 58, 179
Sarvaprayāścitta 62-3 (see penance)
Śāstras 72
Śathapatha Brāhmaṇa 15 f.n.
Sathya Sai Baba 17, 22, 25, 28
Satī 146ff., 148, as goddess 146, satīhood 148, 154, *satī-strī* 146, 148
Satsaṅg 138, 145
Saunders 8-9
Schuchter and Zisook 158, 165, 170
Sect 16
Secularisation 53, 192
Separation 7, 133
Service, order of (see NCHT) 28, 194-5
Seva 16
Sharma 42, 48, 184-5
Shirdi Sai Baba 17, 22
Shock 9
Siddell 160
Sikh, as pandit 26, 82, funerals xiii, 7, 87, 165-166, readings 138
Signs, 61, 67, 173-4, blanket, flowers 125, in flour, 79-80/ shining face 50
Sin of deceased 26, 86, 90, 105-6
Sindhi 24, 138, 159
Sinking heart 156
Śiva, 16, Śiva-Śakti 17, shrine 88-89 (see chants)
Sivananda 36
Śmaśāna 75
Social and psychological dimensions of death 113
Social death of elderly, infants 134
Social group 6
Śoka 54 f.n., 135, 136ff., 143, 145, less for elderly 145, for young 145-6
Solmū, Solavah 145
Sonal 165-6
Songs 138
Soni 141, 149
Sons 35, adopted 72 f.n., chief mourner 71-2 f.n., to perform *śrāddha* 35, 71
Soul 29, newly released 33, ambiguity about where, 35, not released in Britain 193 (see Ātman)
Somatising grief 156, 200
Ṣmaśāna 75-7
Smith, Cantwell 13
Spiritual preparation 53, 57 (see preparation)
Śrāddha 2, 23, 26-7, 28, 31, 34-5, 51, 71, 93ff., annual 82, 106ff., as commemoration 104-5, at Gaya 107, combined 95, 99, 101-2, *ekoddiṣta*, 93, 95, 101, for infants 109, guilt 47, in Britain 82, 99ff., in India 90, 92, 94ff., Lalitā 99, *nava-miśra* 93, 101, preparation for, 100 purāṇa or uttāra 94, *pārvaṇa* 94, relocating deceased 196, *śrāvaṇī* 99, three groups 94ff.
Stages 9, 71, of grief 157ff., cultural differences 188, nine stages of rituals 54ff., van Gennep's 133-4
Stereotyping 116, 199-200
Stevenson 95, 96, 147-8
Still-births 51
Stone 80, 94
Stretcher/pole 73
Stroebe 9-10, 158, 189
Stutley and Stutley 25
Śūdras 14
Suffering and karma 50
Suicide 46, 56, 71, reborn seven times 46
Sukṣma deha, subtle body 37
Su-mṛtyu (good death) 53
Suresh 121 ff., life closing 122
Surrogate for rituals 28
Surya 168, 172ff., 185, 187, 191
Susheela 172
Sūtaka, 73, 135ff., 145, and *śoka* 54, f.n., danger from ghost 136, ending 135, 145, food in 136, for elderly 136, lifestyle in, 137, restrictions eased 194 *varṇas* 73
Suttee 148 (see *satī*)

Svarga 30, 38, 41-4
Śvāsas 36
Swaminarayan 16-17, 21, 22, 15, 36, 41-3, 86, 91
Swami Narayan 16-17, 41, 42
Syncretism 23, 28
Taittirīya Saṃhitā 15 f.n.
Tandon 91,
Tapas 32 (see austerity)
Tāra snān (star bath) 106
Tarpaṇa 31, 109, 110
Tears, river to cross 58
Temples 20, 22, 24
Terminology, English 11, 36, medical 115, psychological 11, 156, 166, 168, 201
Termu, terama (thirteenth day) 104 145
Texts 27, 30
Theodicy 184-185
Time, 67, astrological 33, cremation 2, 71, 81-82, 83 f.n., for adjustment 7, for mourning 93, 201, for rituals 100, 102, for śrāddha, 100, 102, from work 201, limit to mourning 8, 93, 201, *kāla* 67, 201, pilgrimage 9, *sūtaka* 73, 93, of death 67-69, right time 1, 53, 56, 57, 59-60 f.n., to depart 57-58, to recover 134, wrong 192
Tithi 40, 94, 107-10, 194
Three aims 35
Transendental Meditation 17
Transition 7
Transmigration 34 (see rebirth)
Tulasī 64, 66 f.n., 69, 72, 108-9, 132
Tulasīvivāh 66 f.n.
Tulsi Das 138
Turner 7
Twice Migrants 20,
Two ways 32
Undertakers 54, 71, 80-2, 87, 130-1, chapel 86, 188
Unfinished business 127, 167
Upanayana 71, 73 f.n.
Upaniṣads 31-2, 34, 52
Uttarayaṇa, northern path 32, 59
Vadodara 11, 76-7
Vadodara Group 11, 163-164
Vaikuṇṭhadhām 41-3, 59
Vaiśyas 14, 36
Vaitaraṇī Cow 33, 37, 38, 62, 65. 96
Vaitaraṇī Nadī (river) 33, 38, 96
Vallabhacarya 16, 58
Vānaprastha 14, 57, symbolic 192 (see *āśrama*)
Van Gennep 6, 7, 157, 160, 188, three stages of rites 133-4
Varanasi, Kaśī, xv, 148, place to die 59, 60 f.n., Brahmin informants 36
Varṇa 14, 18
Varṇāśramadharma 14, 18, 35
Varsī chhamāsi/ samān 106
Varuṇa 30
Vāyu (*prāṇa/svāsa*) 36
Vedas 17, 30 f.n.
Vedic, mantras at funerals 83 f.n., rituals 30, 52
Vedic Society 24
Victoria, Queen 158
Vimala 175-6, 180-1
Vimān (chariot) 38
Viśrāma 76
Viśvedevāh 98
Vishwa Hindu Parishad 25
Visions at point of death 69-70
Viśiṣṭādvaita 42
Visitors 140ff. (see condolence visits)
Viṣṇu 29, 37-8, 39, 41, *pūjā* 99, 102
Viśvedevā 98, 102
Vrindaban 42
Vrṣotsarga (bull release) 95-6, 101, 105
Wailing 67-8, 143, forbidden 143
Walter 5, 10, 157, 158 f.n.
Water authorities 132
Weber, 183-184
Weeping, 67, 129, 143, and wailing 143ff., controlled 142, forced 144 religious teaching 143
Weightman 15
Western concepts 11
Westmouth 9, 23ff., 72, 196, 200, temple committee 24,
Widows 104, 196, ascetics 148, 152, clothes 147-8, 151, elderly 136, family roles 152, Gandhi on, 148, historical perspectives 146 ff., havan, 152, inauspicious and impure 147, 150, in Britain 149ff., Kumhari 150, *niyoga* 147, restrictions 151ff., reversal of marriage 147, 150, 151, Roop Kanwar 148-149, *satī* 146-7 f.n., satīhood 148, *sūtaka* for 135-6, 140-2, virgin 153

Williams 41, 183
Women, 193, 205, ancestors 71, as Chief mourner 72, 82, 100, 193, bearers of tradition 27, exclusion 173, Gujarati 193, hopelessness 156, roles 202, 193, temple roles 24, 25
Worden 9, 10, 157, 158
World rejection 35
World view 13
Worship 22, 23, 24
Yajñopavitā 73 f.n.
Yama 30, 38, 49, as Dharma Rājā 44-5, kingdom (*loka*) 34, 41, judgement 31, mistakes 38
Yamdūts (messengers) 33, 38, 48-9, 50
Yamuna 72, 77
Year's Mind 8
Yoni 22
Young Hindus, 114, 130, 131, 135-8, 140, 143, 145, 149, 151-4, 163, 177, 184-5, 188, child as interpreter 116 (see also children, loss of)
Yugas 45 f.n., 46

PRINTED ON PERMANENT PAPER • IMPRIME SUR PAPIER PERMANENT • GEDRUKT OP DUURZAAM PAPIER - ISO 9706
ORIENTALISTE, KLEIN DALENSTRAAT 42, B-3020 HERENT